Vico
Selected Writings

Vico

Selected Writings

edited and translated by
Leon Pompa
PROFESSOR OF PHILOSOPHY
IN THE UNIVERSITY OF BIRMINGHAM

CAMBRIDGE UNIVERSITY PRESS

CAMBRIDGE
LONDON NEW YORK NEW ROCHELLE
MELBOURNE SYDNEY

Published by the Press Syndicate of the University of Cambridge
The Pitt Building, Trumpington Street, Cambridge CB2 1RP
32 East 57th Street, New York, NY 10022, USA
296 Beaconsfield Parade, Middle Park, Melbourne 3206, Australia

First published 1982

Printed in The United States of America
by Vail-Ballou Press, Inc., Binghamton, N.Y.

Library of Congress catalogue card number: 81-12215

British Library Cataloguing in Publication Data
Vico, Giambattista
Vico: selected writings.
1. Philosophers, Italian—18th century
I. Pompa, Leon
195   B3580.E5

ISBN 0 521 23514 6
ISBN 0 521 28014 1 pbk

To Giorgio Tagliacozzo

Contents

Contents

[The First New Science]
The principles of a new science of the nature of nations leading to the discovery of the principles of a new system of the natural law of the gentes

Book IV The ground of the proofs which establish this Science

[*The Third New Science*]
*Principles of a new science concerning the common
    nature of nations*

Preface

For a good part of the last hundred years Giambattista Vico has been in the anomalous position of being widely regarded by philosophers within Italy as their greatest national philosopher, but of being less well known beyond Italy than many of his less highly regarded compatriots. This position began to change after the Second World War with the appearance of the first English translations of some of his works. Most notable were the translations by T. G. Bergin and M. H. Fisch of Vico's *Autobiografia* and the final version of the *Scienza Nuova* in 1944 and 1948 respectively. These were subsequently revised as interest in Vico grew and to them was added the translation in 1965 by E. Gianturco of Vico's *De nostri temporis studiorum ratione* of 1709. The publication of these translations made some of Vico's most important work accessible for the first time to English-speaking scholars, resulting both in an upsurge of interest in it, as many fascinating facets began to come to light, and a bewildering profusion of books and articles, offering a variety of often incompatible interpretations and evaluations of various aspects of his thought. It is true, nevertheless, that some of Vico's most important works have never been translated into English nor has any anthology of translations yet appeared. The present volume has been prepared to meet this latter need and, at the same time, to fill in some gaps from the works not yet currently available in translation.

The paramount aim has been to offer a representative selection from Vico's works, but here a reservation must be expressed. Vico was a many-sided thinker, whose interests and investigations extended into epistemology, social and political philosophy, jurisprudence, rhetoric, mythology, philology, anthropology, history and many other disciplines. In making a representative selection from works touching on so many areas of research, some principle of choice had to be exercised. One way in which this might have been done would have been to have followed the pattern of many anthologies by subdividing the collection into a number of sections, each devoted to excerpts on a single topic drawn from a variety of different works. Unfortunately, for a number of reasons, Vico does not lend himself easily to such treatment. Both in thought and expression he can be extremely obscure, with the main sense of his claims only to be picked up by considering long extracts from his writings. Again, no matter how detailed his treatment of particular points, he is always alive to the wider issues with which these are concerned, although he lacked any great facility for clarifying the connection between the detailed application of certain theories and the theories themselves. Consequently, to reach any reasonable conviction that one has grasped the significance of his general position, it is often necessary to work through long passages in which it is given detailed application. Finally, for a long period his thought was in a continuous state of development, leading to considerable differences between theories expressed in his earlier and later works. These considerations suggest that it would not have been helpful to structure the selection according to topics and that an anthology incorporating some reasonably substantial part of certain works, presented in their chronological sequence, would be more appropriate both for understanding the development of Vico's thought and for grasping the integral nature of his doctrines. Even here, however, it would not be possible in any manageable anthology to include more than a small portion of Vico's writings. Much has had to be sacrificed and, in the end, the principle upon which I have drawn has been to include as much as possible of those works which are relevant to understanding the development and nature of the doctrines contained in what is widely accepted as Vico's masterpiece, the *Scienza Nuova* in the editions of 1730 and 1744. This has meant the inclusion of parts of works currently available in translation, at the expense of others not available, but no volume could claim to offer a characteristic selection were it to contain nothing from *De nostri temporis studiorium ratione* and the *Scienza Nuova* of 1744. Most regretfully, the *Autobiografia* has had to be sacrificed, but it is elsewhere available. Again, the whole of the two long volumes on jurisprudence, *De universi juris uno principio et fine uno, liber unus* and *De constantia jurisprudentis, liber alter*, of 1720 and 1721, and the *Notae* of 1722, have had to be omitted. But, indispensable as these are for an understanding of Vico's theories of jurisprudence, for an understanding of the science of humanity to which he later aspired their claims must give way to those of the *Scienza Nuova* of 1725, from which I have accordingly included long extracts. An anthology is bound to be a series of compromises of a debatable nature, and in the case of a thinker of such rich and varied interests as Vico this is even less avoidable than usual. I shall be satisfied, however, if the present volume offers scholars and students without Italian the opportunity to come to a wider acquaintance with the thought of this difficult but rewarding philosopher.

It is appropriate here to say a word about the translations themselves and to acknowledge my many debts. For the selection of materials, the Introduction and the notes, I am wholly responsible. The translations from Latin works, which constitute the first two sections, are the result of a collaboration between Mrs Christine Shepherd and myself, during which the manuscript changed hands several times. I am here, however, in very considerable debt to my wife, Carol, who assisted me greatly with the Latin on my side of this collaboration, although the responsibility for the philosophical sense of the final product is wholly mine.

The translations from Italian, which constitute the rest of the volume, are entirely my own work. My main debt here, as must be that of any translator of the final *Scienza Nuova,* is to Professors Bergin and Fisch, whose complete translation of this work is now a classic in its own right. Vico's Italian is undeniably very difficult indeed. His works were invariably written at great speed; he used sentences of great length, which are often tortuous, chaotic and incorrect in construction; he expressed himself frequently with a grim irony, which can sometimes confuse the sense of what he says; his works are illuminated by brilliant aphorisms together with a deliberate play upon words, while interlaced to the point of incomprehensibility by obscure and condensed intellectual allusions; he used ordinary language in an idiosyncratic and technical way without offering the help of many definitions. In the face of all this, the difficulties besetting any translator are obvious. Accordingly, although the present translation of the final *Scienza Nuova* differs considerably from that of Bergin and Fisch, I have availed myself of every help which their translation could give me and have not gone out of my way to provide totally new forms of translations from those which they provide in those places where, in my view, rather than provide the reader with an option between two reasonable alternatives, this would result only in a poorer translation or tend to confuse issues which need not otherwise be confused. Having acknowledged the great assistance I have received from Bergin and Fisch's translation, it remains to be emphasised that I am solely responsible for the present translations from the Italian.

The translations themselves have been made from the editions by Fausto Nicolini in the *Scrittori d'Italia* series, published by Laterza, Bari. I have retained the system of numbered paragraphs which Nicolini provided for the *First* and *Third New Science,* which is widely used by Vico scholars for ease of reference. Given Vico's contorted and highly idiosyncratic style, plus the different conventions governing punctuation, I have found it necessary, in trying to achieve a balance between the demands of accuracy, readability and preservation of the style and tone of the original, to make considerable alterations to the length and structure of some of Vico's sentences, a task which Nicolini himself had found necessary in his editions of the original Latin and Italian writings. Since it would have been altogether too lengthy to record each of these alterations individually, I can only express the hope that a satisfactory balance has been achieved and that any reader who consults the originals will find that the changes I have made do not distort the sense of Vico's claims.

Perhaps the greatest difficulties in translating Vico arise, however, from his vocabulary. On the one hand, there is the problem presented by his use of words, such as *socii, famuli* and *gentes,* which had a technical meaning in Latin for which there exist no non-Latin equivalents. In most cases, however, since it is clear from their context in Vico's writings what he takes them to mean, I have simply retained the Latin words themselves. On the other hand a potentially more misleading circumstance arises from Vico's habit of exhibiting in his writings his (later) thesis that the development of words in a nation's history is an expression of the development of its conceptual scheme. Accordingly many Italian words are used in an unusual way which derives from Vico's (often faulty) view of their historical relation to the meaning of their Latin roots. To preserve this relation I have had to employ English words which share these Latin roots, even though the most common meaning of these words would not be that which Vico gave to the Italian words of which they are a translation. Discussion of the more important of these words is offered in the Glossary, which the reader is recommended to consult as much as possible. With regard to the titles of the many books to which Vico refers, I have generally left the title in its original form, except where a translation of the title helps make intelligible the passage in which it occurs or where there exists a commonly accepted title in translation.

I would like to express my gratitude to the University of Edinburgh, which granted me a sabbatical term in 1976, of which a part was spent working on this volume, to the British Academy, which awarded me a European Exchange Fellowship to enable me to spend my sabbatical in Italy doing further research on Vico, and to the University of Rome, which gave me every conceivable library facility while I was there. In addition I am most grateful to Dr Jeremy Mynott, of Cambridge University Press, for the encouragement he has given me throughout this project and for the patience with which he has put up with an almost endless series of delays in completing it, and to Mrs Shirley Shakespeare and Mrs Katharine Spencer, of the Department of Philosophy of the University of Birmingham, without whose skilled decipherment and typing of my handwritten copy it would never have reached a presentable state.

Glossary

To ascertain.
Vico uses the Italian verb *accertare*. Ordinarily this means to assure or verify, but Vico's meaning is derived from the root of the verb, *certo* or the certain (*q.v.*), by which he means the particular or individual. Thus when the true is ascertained it is particularised by being provided with a content such as to allow it to apply to, and be seen as, a universal feature or aspect of a particular historical fact or state of affairs.

The certain.
Vico uses the Latin *certum* and the Italian *il certo,* giving them the meaning of 'what is particular or individuated or determinate'. See n. 18, p. 77.

Common sense.
The set of beliefs shared by the members of a group or community in virtue of which they are members of the group or community. These include those beliefs which are necessary for any form of stable and enduring social life whatsoever, i.e., the beliefs involved in Vico's first three principles of religion, marriage and burial of the dead, as well as others which develop only at certain stages in the course traced by the ideal eternal history, which constitute further principles of cohesion and diversity in societies which are at once both highly organised and highly diversified.

Ingenuity
A capacity, peculiar to man, for perceptive or insightful creation or construction. Although it requires imagination, it is not identical with it, since imagination can work blindly whereas ingenuity has a cognitive element in it. See n. 15, p. 69.

Mind
This is used in a broader and a narrower sense. In its broader sense it is the cognitive capacity of which perception, imagination, ingenuity, reason and so on can be thought of as modifications or modes (*q.v.*). In its narrower sense it is a synonym for 'understanding', i.e., it is itself a specific mode of cognition.

Mode
Vico uses the Latin *modus* or *forma* or *genus,* and the Italian *guisa,* giving the latter, which normally means manner, fashion or way, a technical sense. As such it means either some or other important mental capacity, such as a form of understanding or of imagination, or the way in which something comes to have a

certain character in virtue of the mode by which it is produced, or, occasionally, the character itself. See n. 14, p. 88.

Modification

Primarily used in the same sense as mode (*q.v.*). It is sometimes, however, used in a more general way to apply not to different mental capacities but to anything which is such that it can be regarded as a variant expression of some central subject. Thus, different proverbs are described as modifications of the same truth. See n. 14, p. 88.

Natural law of the gentes

Vico uses the expression *il diritto naturale delle genti*. This is that system of beliefs about what is right, just or reasonable about what is due to them, shared by the individuals who compose a given society, which is common to all societies at the same stage of mental development. It is conditioned by beliefs about what is necessary for them in their institutional roles, beliefs which are, in turn, conditioned by more fundamental metaphysical beliefs. It is not, therefore, the same as positive law and the fact that it is normally out of line with positive law for some section of the community is one of the sources of the conflict which Vico finds between classes. I have followed Bergin and Fisch in translating it as the natural law 'of the gentes' rather than 'of the nations' to avoid any suggestion that it has to do with international law or with the law governing the relations between the citizens of different nations.

Senses

Vico uses the Italian *sensi* variously for the senses of perception, the meanings of words and beliefs and judgements. See n. 2, p. 81.

Sects (of times and of philosophers)

A sect of time is a period of time in which the beliefs involved in the practices of a society have one of the sets of characteristics traced in the 'ideal eternal history'. A sect of philosophers is a school of philosophers whose doctrines reflect these beliefs in a more intellectualised form. See n. 12, p. 87.

The true, truth

Vico uses the Latin *verum* and the Italian *il vero*. In the singular I have preferred 'the true' to 'the truth' but in the plural, for purely stylistic reasons, 'truths' to 'trues'. Both mean 'that which is true' or 'that which would be stated by a fully demonstrable proposition', but not the proposition itself. They could therefore be translated by 'the thing which is true', provided that this was understood in such a way as to allow what is established by a geometrical proof to be such a thing.

In his article 'Vico and Pragmatism', Professor Max Fisch has argued that Vico's use of *verum* was derived from the scholastic doctrine of the transcendentals and that, as such, it means 'intelligible'. This may be correct but it would be too much of an interpretation to be incorporated into the text as a translation of *verum* and, in particular, of *il vero*.

To verify

Vico uses the verb *verificare*. Verifying is the reciprocal process to ascertaining which Vico's science requires, i.e., it is the application of the true to the certain or the universal to the particular. Which universal should be applied, i.e., whether it should be the imaginative or the rational universal, depends upon an ultimate and over-arching claim about the pattern which makes human history intelligible. Hence the ultimate *verum* is not that which is applied to the *certum* at any one stage of historical investigation but that which is presupposed in interpreting history *as a whole*.

Introduction

The life and works of Giambattista Vico

Giambattista Vico was born in Naples, the son of a bookseller, in 1668, and died there in 1744. From an early age he revealed a quick, inventive but impatient mind. His early education was accordingly relatively unsystematic as he underwent tuition with a number of tutors and schools, from all of which he dismissed himself sooner or later. In 1686, he became tutor to the Rocca family at the castle of Vatolla, situated well to the south of Salerno, where he was employed for nine years. In this period he undertook an extensive course of reading which provided him with the basis of a prodigious, if erratic, knowledge of classical philosophy, literature and law, as well as of the work of his great Renaissance predecessors, Boccaccio, Dante, Petrarch and Machiavelli.

The nine years at Vatolla represent the only period of his life which Vico spent outside Naples. In his *Autobiography* he remembered it as a period of intellectual isolation and hence of self-education. This is certainly incorrect. Vico travelled often to Naples, where he remained in contact with the lively intellectual life of the city which, reacting against the conservative influence of the Church and the University, had given birth to a number of private intellectual societies or academies. Here the prevailing atmosphere in philosophy was one of general eclecticism, stemming largely from a rejection of Aristotelianism and inspired by a search for alternatives. Among the authors who were eagerly discussed were Plato and the neoplatonists, the classical atomists, such as Lucretius and Democritus, physicists such as Galileo, Torricelli and Gassendi, the English thinkers, Francis Bacon, Hobbes, Locke and Boyle, the rationalists, Descartes, Malebranche, Spinoza and Leibniz, and, later, Bayle. Many of Vico's friends were suspected of being atheists and that Vico may himself have had a period of atheism is suggested by the sombre Lucretian tone of a poem, *Gli affetti di un disperato,* which he wrote in 1692.

Vico was appointed to the Chair of Rhetoric at the University of Naples in 1699, the year of his marriage. The Chair carried a poor stipend and, as Vico subsequently had eight children, he was from then on beset by financial and material worries, finding it necessary to augment his income by accepting commissions to compose ceremonial orations, official histories and biographies.

Among Vico's official duties was the requirement that he deliver an annual inaugural oration, of which six were given between 1699 and 1706. These show that at this period his philosophical leanings were towards a blend of neoplatonism and Cartesianism. The latter is perhaps best shown in the first oration, in which he took over, almost verbatim, Descartes' ontological and causal proofs of God's existence, as well as the *Cogito* in a form which is much closer to Descartes' than to those of St Augustine and Ficino. At the same time, however, the orations show an interest in the nature and conditions of virtue, and its promotion in a less than perfect world, which could hardly leave him content with Cartesianism for long.

The seventh oration was an altogether more ambitious work and it contains the seeds of many of the theories developed in Vico's mature thought. Entitled *On method in contemporary fields of study,* it is cast in the form of an investigation into the merits of different educational methods, to be achieved by assessing the advantages and disadvantages of those of the classical and modern worlds. Historically, then, its context is the seventeenth- and eighteenth-century debate over the humanist values of the ancient world versus the scientific values of the modern world.[1] In effect, however, since Vico has primarily the Cartesians in mind as representatives of the modern approach, much of the work is concerned with an investigation of the fields of study to which the Cartesian methodology of doubt, analysis and demonstration can or cannot profitably be applied. Taking the natural sciences first, Vico argues that geometry is a wholly conventional science and that this explains why the method of demonstration can be applied in it and lead to the truth.[2] This is so, Vico claims, because in geometry there is no appeal to anything beyond what is laid down by convention, so that when a geometrical proposition is demonstrated by the application of these conventions, it is made true in virtue of them rather than by revealing an essence which obtains independently of them. In physics, however, this is not so. The forms which physics aims to grasp are not created by a conventional demonstration, since they exist – and here Vico's neoplatonism is evident – as entities in God's mind.[3] Accordingly, although they are objective they are external to the human mind, so that the propositions which are the product of the geometrical method can at best stand in a relation of verisimilitude or probability to the forms which govern the physical world. It is notewor-

[1] See the introduction by E. Gianturco to his *On the Study Methods of Our Time,* for an excellent account of the controversy and of the place of Vico's work in it.
[2] See below, pp. 40–1.   [3] *Ibid.*

thy that in advancing these claims Vico is in no way concerned to deny the value of modern developments in the pure sciences. On the contrary, he emphasises the degree to which these advances have been the bases of equally great advances in mechanics, physics, chemistry, pharmacology and various applied sciences. His criticism is directed against an incorrect assimilation of the nature and grounds of physical truth with those of mathematical truth which, in his view, carries with it the danger of failing to attend to the natural world experimentally.

Given this view of the nature of demonstration, Vico proceeds to ask how far it might help us to form reliable judgements in human affairs, and here he comes down decisively against any possibility of applying the geometrical method. Human affairs are too varied and complex, too dependent upon the vacillations and vagaries of human will and intelligence, for such an inflexible method to be appropriate. This does not mean that prudence, the art of practical judgment as it would now be called, cannot be taught. On the contrary, such an art already exists in topics, which is exemplified in the art of the lawyer. This is the art, synthetic and not analytic, of knowing where to look for evidence for, and how to construct arguments to show, what is probably the case in everyday life. Vico's critical remarks about the neglect of this art are directed initially to its comparative decline in legal training[4] but they are part of a wider complaint about its neglect in relation to the whole question of the acquisition of rules of conduct suitable to practical civil life and to politics.[5]

Vico's discussion of the acquisition of skill in practical reasoning leads him to consider certain capacities which such skill presupposes, in which he attaches special weight to imagination or the ability to see connections, similarities and analogies where they are not immediately evident. Imagination never ceased to occupy a place of central importance in Vico's thought, in his discussions both of the nature, and of the genetic development, of human capacities; and in the latter case it is invariably conceived as occupying a certain place in a natural sequence through which these abilities develop. In this work, where Vico's intention is to establish how education should be structured in the light of the different requirements of knowledge and practice, the notion of a natural genetic sequence of capacities is advanced in connection with the allegation that the premature inculcation of the critical method stifles the growth of the imagination which practical wisdom requires, at an age when it is still capable of development.[6] The concept of a natural development of human capacities, which throughout his life Vico applied to individuals

[4]See below, p. 39.   [5]See below, pp. 41–4.   [6]See below, pp. 37–8.

as such, was later to be applied to the concept of the development of a nation as a whole, and thus to become a cardinal feature of his notion of historical development.[7]

Finally, in this seminal work, one should note Vico's concern over the neglect of ethics and the study of its relation to social life. Vico does not envisage the possibility that even in a healthy state the mass of people will act from a rational discernment of their duty. What is required, therefore, is that those who, through philosophy, can discern the virtues, should possess also the oratorical skill to persuade the masses to act in accordance with them.[8] The low evaluation of democracy which this implies, which was almost certainly derived from Plato, remains characteristic of Vico's whole mode of thought and is a permanent feature of the way in which he sees the problems of political philosophy.

Within a year of *On method in contemporary fields of study* Vico had produced the most important of his early works, *On the ancient wisdom of the Italians taken from the origins of the Latin language.* This was, in fact, only the first part of a projected three-part treatise, the other books of which were to deal with physics and ethics. Despite the fact that Vico never completed the whole treatise, the first book remains the most important source for his early theory of knowledge, containing a reasonably full and systematic statement of the theory, although the precise relationship of this theory to that advanced in his later work is, as we shall see, problematic.[9]

On the ancient wisdom of the Italians reveals Vico's increasing preoccupation with many of the themes of its predecessor. Before discussing these, however, it is necessary to mention a difficulty with which the reader will immediately be confronted. This concerns the form of the work, which, as its full title indicates, arises from Vico's claim that the philosophical theses he advances in it are all to be found in classical Latin, in which, he argues, a sophisticated philosophical theory was embedded.[10] Given this thesis, Vico is forced to embark on a twofold enquiry: a philosophical explication of the theories themselves and a philological account of the meanings which certain words would have in Latin if it were true that they owed their meanings to this theory. This approach, which involves Vico in a considerable amount of fanciful and implausible philology, is at once both characteristic of Vico's whole approach to philosophy and yet violently at odds with his later theories. It is characteristic in the sense that it reflects his belief that philosophy

---

[7] See below, pp. 16ff., the *First New Science* (hereafter *N.S.*[1]) 48ff. and the *Third New Science* (hereafter *N.S.*[3]) 211–19. References to the two versions of the *New Science* are given in paragraph numbers.
[8] See below, pp. 44–5. [9] See below, pp. 24–9. [10] See below, pp. 49–50.

cannot dispense with a content derived from the artifacts which men make in the course of their history.[11] The manner in which Vico himself proceeds to respect this requirement is, however, completely at variance with the further requirement, upon which he laid great stress in his later work, that scholars should not interpret past evidence as expressions of theories to which they themselves subscribe.[12] This is the vice which Vico was later to brand as the vanity (*boria*) of scholars[13] and for which he was to castigate many eminent thinkers. It is ironic that his procedure in *On the ancient wisdom of the Italians* should be as gross an example of this vanity as any of which he was later to accuse other scholars.

The central epistemological thesis of this work, usually known in its abbreviated form as the *verum–factum* theory, is the identity of the true with what is made or done,[14] that is, with that which owes its very being to having been made. Such things are made, however, from certain elements which can be either real or fictive, so that something can be true in virtue of having been made and yet not be real (as in the case of geometry, which arises from fictions) or both true and real (as in the case of the things which God makes, the things of the physical world).[15] The theory which Vico is advocating here may be thought of as a relativised theory of truth: that which is true is relative to a certain kind of making. Since making is, however, an activity and, as such, requires a subject, Vico advances to the connected claim that the rule and criterion of the true is to have made it.[16] It is doubtful whether, in stating his position thus, Vico intends to add to the original claim anything other than the point just mentioned: that creating is an activity and that it thus logically requires a creator. Nevertheless it now enables him to connect truth and knowledge, for knowledge is 'cognition of the genus or mode [i.e. form] by which a thing is made'. The mind does not know this mode explicitly or antecedently to producing a given construction: rather it comes to know it because in arranging or combining the elements in question, it creates the resultant form. Vico's statement of this theory is far from clear but his own favourite case of geometry may be taken to provide an example of what he has in mind. In geometry we have certain elements, the rules, definitions and axioms of the system. By applying the rules to the axioms and definitions, theorems are produced which have no truth other than that belonging to the form given to them by their derivation from the elements. Their truth is thus relativised to the world of geometry but not to the physical world. They can, in a sense, be said to exist but only insofar as they can be, or have been, constructed. But since their

---

[11] See *N.S.*³ 134–40.   [12] See *N.S.*³ 314, 329.   [13] See *N.S.*³ 127–8, 318, 329.
[14] See below, pp. 50–2, 59–60.   [15] See below, pp. 53–4.   [16] See below, p. 55.

construction is wholly dependent upon a synthesis from elements which are themselves human fictions or abstractions, they exist as ideal constructions. It is possible, however, either for such constructions to be produced in the understanding that the truth of what is constructed is a property of a form which owes its being to its relation to the elements from which it is constructed, or to be mistaken about this in some or other way. Knowledge arises when the whole process is understood for what it is, i.e., when the elements are understood for what they are and the form or mode of the construction for what it is. Knowledge involves, therefore, not merely knowing *that* something is true, but understanding also why it is true and whether or not it is real. Hence Vico's claim that knowledge is of the cause of the true, where the 'cause' is the form which is generated by the construction from the elements of the system. Since, however, everything which is involved in this is of human creation, we cannot gain such knowledge antecedently to working out the form which follows from the elements, so that for knowledge of the cause we need to construct the true.[17]

It would be impossible here even to begin to discuss this position, raising, as it does, the whole issue of conventionalism and intuitionism in mathematics.[18] Vico's position has, however, as has often been noted, a considerable resemblance to theories of Hobbes and of Gassendi,[19] but the consequences which he proceeds to draw are in many respects different. The first consequence, which follows directly from the theory itself, is that the truths which we know in virtue of creating them cannot have the ontological status of the simple natures or clear and distinct ideas of Cartesian philosophy. Nor, again, can it be thought, as had many physicists, that the structure of mathematics is identical with that of physical reality. The latter proposition could be true only if the elements from which the physical world itself was constructed were identical with those from which mathematical theories about it were constructed. To see why this is impossible, however, it is necessary to mention a second strain of thought present in this work – Vico's neoplatonic metaphysics. According to this, God creates the physical world *ex nihilo* because he has modelled it upon certain metaphysical forms, the elements of which lie wholly in his mind. Man, however, is not in contact with these meta-

---

[17] See below, pp. 64–5.

[18] See *Vico and Herder,* by Isaiah Berlin pp. 12–21, for an illuminating discussion of Vico's theory. See also 'Vico and Mathematics' by A. Corsano, in *Giambattista Vico: An International Symposium,* pp. 425–37, and *Vico,* by R. Flint, pp. 86–111.

[19] See, for example, Professor Max H. Fisch's introduction to *The Autobiography of Giambattista Vico,* E. Gianturco's introduction to *On the Study Methods of Our Rime,* and Sir Isaiah Berlin (*op. cit.*) for the influence of Hobbes, and Tullio Gregory's *Scetticismo ed Empirismo* (Bari, 1961) for that of Gassendi.

physical forms but only with the physical form of the things which are modelled on them. The ultimate elements of the physical world are therefore external to the human mind and hence beyond the scope of human knowledge. Unable to achieve the ideal of divine knowledge, man can, however, approximate to it in varying degrees in his own branches of knowledge, the degree of approximation being directly proportionate to the extent to which the objects of knowledge in these fields are wholly or partially of human construction. Thus mathematics is the most certain branch of human knowledge, followed by mechanics and physics, in which the mathematical basis comprises respectively less of the whole science, while morality, the study of the human mind, comes at the bottom of the list. Thus, although Vico rejects the Cartesian account of the basis of the certainty of mathematics, his constructivist theory of knowledge gives mathematics an important role to play in determining the certainty of the different fields of knowledge. Things which are knowable to God, but which would otherwise be totally problematic for man, become knowable to the extent that the one wholly knowable field of knowledge, mathematics, allows man to construct models and perform experiments producing results which are analogous to what occurs in the problematic world in question. Thus, although refusing to identify mathematics with reality, Vico can offer an explanation why mechanics, in which mathematics find its most direct field of application, is more certain than physics. Physics, however, is more certain than human behaviour because, since human action is governed by free will and caprice, mathematical theories are inapplicable to it.

It should be noted that Vico's overall position here is not wholly consistent. If the *verum–factum* principle, as explained above, is accepted as applying both to divine knowledge and to a certain kind of human knowledge – the purely conventional knowledge, that is, of mathematics – Vico's appeal to the kind of making involved in successful physical experiment will not suffice to bridge, or even to begin to bridge, the gap between divine and human knowledge of the physical world, for the former will of necessity be wholly different in kind from the latter. Vico does, indeed, assert a difference between divine and human knowledge,[20] but he fails to draw the correct conclusions from this when he comes to give his account of knowledge in the natural sciences. For in an experiment in physics results do not 'follow' logically solely from the application of certain procedures themselves, nor can an experiment lay claim to being successful by being said to 'imitate' works of nature, since this will be equally true of unsuccessful experiments. What makes an experi-

[20] See below, pp. 52–5.

ment 'successful' is just its results conforming to certain lawful predictive expectations. The success of experiments carried out in accordance with theories will therefore lend support to those theories but not in such a way as to justify the claim that the theories thus supported are known to the degree to which they are an account of some unknown process whereby things are created metaphysically, or of some unknown mode in which they exist metaphysically. The conclusions which Vico draws about the epistemological status of that part of the world of human knowledge which is not constructed by human convention are therefore not properly grounded in the *verum–factum* principle.

On the other hand, this alteration of the conclusions which Vico should have drawn from the *verum–factum* principle does nothing to weaken – indeed it strengthens – the claims he makes about the inapplicability of the geometrical method to the world of human affairs, if the elements of the latter are, as at this stage he believed, unknown to us. Hence Vico can quite properly go on to develop points relevant to the necessity for the art of judgement, of which he spoke in *On method in contemporary fields of study*. Thus he can quite justifiably claim here that, since the clearness and directness of an idea or proposition cannot be guaranteed by a cognition which derives from the nature of the idea itself, it can best be reached by assessing the idea or proposition in the light of every appropriate consideration, which is precisely what topics is meant to teach us to do. Clearness and distinctness are not therefore based upon the cognition of some asocial, ahistorical essence, but upon the conclusions to which we come after the assessment of relevant evidence.

All this, of course, is evidence of the degree to which Vico had moved further from his earlier Cartesianism. This comes out markedly in other parts of *On the ancient wisdom of the Italians*. Any *a priori* proof of the existence of God, such as the Cartesian proof, which Vico had himself been prepared to accept in the Inaugural Oration of 1699, is declared invalid, for since we can know or prove only what we have made, we can prove God's existence only if we have ourselves made Him.[21] For the same reason metaphysics cannot be established *a priori*, though we can come to some knowledge of it *a posteriori*, by reflection upon the presuppositions of things, a claim which reveals an interesting anticipation of the doctrines of the *First* and *Third New Science*.[22] Even the *Cogito*, the answer to methodical scepticism, is now rejected on the ground that, although there can be no better evidence for one's own existence than one's consciousness of thinking, simple consciousness is not, as such,

[21]See below, p. 65.   [22]See below, pp. 28–9; 65; *N.S.*[1] 40; *N.S.*[3] 331–2.

knowledge in the required sense. Thought is a sign, but not a cause, of existence; therefore certainty about our thought does not provide knowledge, in the relevant sense, of one's existence.

On the ancient wisdom of the Italians reveals Vico in a state of intellectual transition. Profoundly dissatisfied with the *a priori* and arid nature of Cartesianism, distressed by its failure to appreciate the value, and to contribute to the development, of the humanist disciplines, he has rejected the theory of knowledge from which these consequences followed and replaced it by another which attacked the epistemological and metaphysical underpinnings of Descartes' taxonomy of knowledge – the *Cogito,* the *a priori* proofs for God's existence, the priority of analysis – yet which, when taken in conjunction with Vico's own neoplatonism, left that taxonomy largely where it was. Mathematics remains the most certain field of knowledge, to be followed by mechanics, physics and human affairs, because they involve a lesser degree of human constructiveness, just as, for Descartes, the same order obtained because it traced a declining degree of clearness and distinctness.

Vico's realisation that the *verum–factum* principle could lead to the abandonment of this taxonomy of knowledge and its replacement by that to be found in the *New Science* represents the crucial turning point in his philosophical development. It is not the case, of course, that the map of knowledge to be found in the *New Science* is the straightforward converse of that outlined above, for Vico was never to abandon his view that mathematics was one of the most certain, indeed paradigmatic,[23] areas of human knowledge. The status ascribed to it in *On the ancient wisdom of the Italians* remains therefore unaltered. The decisive shift in the *New Science* follows from the change in Vico's views about our knowledge of human affairs and of the natural world. Formerly the least certain area of knowledge, human affairs, as embodied in the civil world, are conceived in such a way that the difference between them and the natural world becomes one of principle and not of degree, and the history of the civil world becomes the most certain knowledge accessible to man. The philosophical ground for this shift is, nominally at least, unproblematic. It lies in Vico's discovery that, at a certain level, changes in human affairs are governed by causes within human nature which are not simply a matter of arbitrary choice and caprice but which are so conditioned by their historical and social context that there can be a science of them. To avoid possible misunderstanding at this point, it should be added that, concurrently with this, Vico claims without reservation that providence is the cause of such change in human affairs,[24] thereby raising a standard

[23] See *N.S.*[3] 349 for the classical statement of this point.
[24] See *N.S.*[1] 45; *N.S.*[3] 133, 341, 1108.

difficulty, discussed below, about the interpretation of his notion of prov-idence.[25]

The historical influences which led Vico to this radical development are generally obscure, although that of Grotius is not in doubt. Vico studied *The Law of War and Peace* while preparing a commissioned his-tory of Antonio Caraffa, which was published in 1716, and, indeed, went as far as to prepare notes for a new edition of Grotius' great work. According to his *Autobiography,* however, he abandoned work on this on the grounds that it was inappropriate that a Catholic should contrib-ute to the works of a heretic author. This may have been largely a matter of religious prudence, although in the *New Science* Vico tempers his admiration for Grotius with a constant criticism of the Dutch thinker's failure to admit the necessity of religious faith as a humanising force, for which he offers genuine philosophical grounds.[26] At any rate, by reading Grotius, he saw for the first time how philosophy and philology, the one concerned with the universal and eternal, the other with the particular and contingent, could be combined to produce a science of human affairs. After reading Grotius, moreover, Vico went on to read the works of his opponents, in particular the theories of Selden and Pufendorf on the state of nature and the concept of natural law, and, in this connec-tion, Hobbes. But although these influences, in particular that of Grotius, enabled Vico to see how there could be a science of the civil world, the continued influence of his humanist predecessors, already evident in the concern shown in his earlier works that human customs and beliefs be viewed in the context of particular cities and societies at particular times and places, led him to reject the classical doctrine of a natural law, uni-versally accessible to human reason, on which these writers had founded their theories of society. Here what seemed clear to Vico was the inability of the natural law theorists to deal plausibly with evidence which pointed towards the fabulous or mythical nature of early human thought and hence with the 'crude and rough' nature of the men from whom such thought was born. These misgivings coincided with others which had arisen from Vico's wide, if erratic, reading of the philologists (and par-ticularly Le Clerc),[27] who were now interested in the historical interpre-tation of myth, and from his knowledge of the tradition of philological

---

[25] See below, pp. 21 ff.   [26] See *N.S.*[1] 16, 23; *N.S.*[3] 318, 395.

[27] Although Vico mentions Le Clerc in the *First New Science,* he makes no direct reference to any of Le Clerc's specific theories. He admired Le Clerc sufficiently, however, to send him copies of his two-part treatise on law (see below, p. 11) and the *First New Science,* the first of which was favourably reviewed. In his *Vico e Bayle: Premesse Per un Con-fronto* (Naples, 1971) G. Cantelli has shown such a coincidence of views between Vico and Le Clerc upon various problems arising from the treatment of myth that it is certain that Vico was well acquainted with Le Clerc's work.

scholarship which had built upon the Renaissance concept of the close relationship between man and his social and historical setting, and which was prominent in the works of the juridical writers, Budé, Cujas, Hotman and others, with which Vico was well acquainted.[28]

Another influence in this shift was that of Hobbes. This is undeniable in connection with Vico's theories about the origins of humanity. In the *New Science* Vico accepts, with some modifications, Hobbes' account of the state of nature. Nevertheless, he wholly rejects the accompanying explanation of the way in which this state is transcended, as expressed in Hobbes' atomistic theory of historical change, because of its failure to recognise the decisive role of providence. The possible influence upon Vico of Hobbes' claim that we can demonstrate only what we can make, including the civil world, has already been mentioned.[29] It remains here to note only that this doctrine cannot be identified with the epistemological theory of the *New Science* because of the modification which the latter requires to allow for the role which Vico ascribes to providence in the making of society,[30] a role which is not, of course, admitted by Hobbes.

The transition to the doctrines of Vico's later philosophy occurred via the publication of a large work in two volumes, entitled *On the single beginning and single end of universal law* and *On the coherence of jurisprudence,* followed by a third volume of *Notes,* between 1720 and 1722. (The whole work will hereafter be referred to by its usual abbreviation, *On universal law.*) The occasion for the work was Vico's candidature for the prestigious Chair of Civil Law, which, had he secured it, would have relieved him of his financial worries. In the event, however, almost certainly as a result of internal university politics, he was never in serious contention for the Chair and, when this became evident to him, he withdrew his candidature. This failure was a serious blow to Vico's academic ambitions, and indeed he thereafter abandoned all attempts to improve his official position. His intellectual efforts now turned almost exclusively to the development of the philosophical approach to history and to human society to which his thinking had been leading him. In *On universal law* this had already received partial expression but in such a way (naturally, given its subject matter) as to centre round a philosophy of the historical development of law. It is evident, however, that in this work Vico was already finding this framework restrictive, and in one of its chapters, entitled 'Attempt at a new science', he contemplated the possibility of an extension of the principle he was applying to the philos-

---

[28] Berlin, *op. cit.,* pp. 125–42, has recently produced the strongest evidence for the importance of these writers as an influence upon Vico.
[29] See n. 19, p. 6.   [30] See below, pp. 24–9.

ophy of law to that of the historical development of the whole range of human social products. Within a year of his failure to secure the Chair of Civil Law Vico had produced a vast new work, usually known as *The new science in negative form*, because the first half of it constituted a critique of the incoherence and implausibility of the views of other scholars. This work, subsequently lost, was never published, through the withdrawal of Vico's patron. Determined to publish it in some form, however, albeit at his own expense, Vico recast it in a positive form which was, he asserts in his *Autobiography*, at once shorter and more effective, and it was published, in a humble edition in 1725, under the title, *The principles of a new science of the nature of nations leading to the discovery of the principles of a new system of the natural law of the gentes.* This is the work now known as the *First New Science.*

In 1730 a second edition, so heavily modified as almost to constitute a different work, was published under the title *Five books by G. B. Vico on the principles of a new science of the common nature of nations,* now known as the *Second New Science.* In his *Autobiography* Vico gave as his reason for the very different form of this work that he realised that it had been a mistake in the *First New Science* to deal with the origin of ideas separately from that of language,[31] since the two were, in fact, 'united by nature'. In Vico's view the new version was so superior to its predecessors that he claimed that, apart from one or two passages they contained, it entirely superseded them. It is typical of the difficulties under which Vico constantly laboured that the whole of this long work was written in great haste within a period of three months, a haste which may have something to do with the fact that in the period 1730–3 Vico was occupied with three further sets of 'Corrections, Improvements and Additions', some of which were incorporated in the third edition of the *New Science* (hereafter the *Third New Science*) upon which Vico was working at the time of his death in 1744 and which was published posthumously in that year.

Between 1725 and 1728, and again in 1731, Vico also wrote the first two parts of his *Autobiography,* going up to the publication of the *Second New Science.* Undertaken as a commission, the *Autobiography* was not published until it had passed from the hands of Vico's son, Gennaro, to the Marquis of Villarosa, who published it in 1818 with the addition of a short third part of his own, taking it up to Vico's death. Villarosa suggests in this that the ill-health from which Vico latterly suffered brought with it a serious decline in his intellectual powers, but this is undoubtedly an exaggeration. Although it is true that after the publica-

---

[31] See below, pp. 103–38, for Vico's account of the origin of ideas, and pp. 139–53, for his account of that of languages.

tion of the *Second New Science* Vico stated that he had completed his life's work, he continued to produce a number of lesser writings and was actively engaged in supervising the proof-reading of the *Third New Science* when he died. There is no reason to believe that he did not consider this to be the definitive edition of The *New Science*.[32]

The New Science

I

The first, and often the last question which besets any reader of The *New Science* is: what is the subject of this science? This is a contentious question and in what follows I can do little more than indicate some reasons for my own view.[33] If we accept, as is normal, that The *New Science* is an outcome of the *verum–factum* thesis,[34] then in one sense, at least, the answer is clear: it is the science or knowledge of the causes of what man has made. Obviously, however, this answer is not specific enough, for it indicates neither who 'men' are, nor what kinds of things they make, nor how they make them.

Let us begin by considering what it is that is made. One answer which Vico offers is that it is 'the world of nations or civil world',[35] an answer which is implied in the titles of all the versions of The *New Science*. Vico does not explicitly say, however, why his science should be of this class of things which man makes rather than of some other class, but the reason is not difficult to discern: it is that this class of things is identical with the class of things which providence makes. And the reason why this should constitute the proper object of Vico's science is that providence, in making these things, operates via causes which work in favour of, rather than against, man's continued existence.[36] These causes are the

---

[32] In his excellent monograph (*op. cit.*, pp. 35–6) Flint disagrees with this assessment and thinks that the differences between the *Second* and *Third New Science* do more 'to disfigure than to enrich it'. Since Vico invariably wrote in great haste, none of his works has the clarity one might like. I can find no internal grounds, however, to support Flint's claim.

[33] It is only proper to warn the reader that the view I propound below is itself contentious, being based upon the supposition that Vico meant something fairly rigorous by the term 'science'. For a fuller development of this view, see my book *Vico: A Study of the 'New Science'* (Cambridge, 1975). For the most fully worked out alternatives, see *The Philosophy of Giambattista Vico*, by Benedetto Croce, translated by R. G. Collingwood, and *Vico and Herder* by Isaiah Berlin.

[34] This has, however, been denied by Hayden V. White, in his review essay of *Vico: A Study of the 'New Science'* in *History and Theory*, 15(2), 1976, pp. 196ff.

[35] N.S.[3] 331, 1108.   [36] N.S.[1] 45; N.S.[3] 342, 1108.

institutions (understood as involving a context of human understanding, desires and needs) which shape and direct men's actions towards an ultimate good – the preservation of man.[37]

What has been made, then, is a world of human institutional artifacts, which provides for man's continued existence. The suggestion that such a context is necessary for human survival implies, of course, that were such a context to fail to obtain, man would fail to survive. This is an implication which Vico explicitly accepts, grounding the necessity upon his view of individual man who, in accordance with Christian doctrine, he looks upon as being in a fallen condition.[38] This is revealed not only in the way in which Vico tries to make his account of human history compatible with an interpretation of the Bible as literal history, but also in the way in which the notion of fallen man is involved, in a series of counter-factual conditionals which Vico explicitly asserts, in his account of the *nature* of the human world. Were it to be the case, which it is not, that the only factors which operated in that world were individual man's basic psychological capacities, then man would certainly cease to exist. This is not the place to enter into the vexed question of the sincerity of Vico's religious beliefs, nor whether, given the ever-present influence of the Inquisition in Naples, his attempt to square his account of human history with a literal historical reading of the Bible was largely a matter of prudence.[39] What is clear, however, is that Vico's view of the basically vicious nature of man is compatible with the Christian doctrine of the Fall. Like the theory of a state of nature, however, the doctrine of the Fall can be read either as an historical fact or as a constituent limiting case in a theory of society, and there is no doubt that in The *New Science* Vico reads it in both ways.[40]

Man makes his world, then, but clearly it is not man *quâ* individual who does so, but man involved in the world in his various social capacities. Only by dint of this distinction can Vico claim that the psychological propensities which, in any state of nature, would destroy man, can and do, in a social state, contribute to the overall end of preserving his existence.

Vico's position is, however, more complex than this suggests. For from these elements, i.e., the hypothetical self-destructive nature of fallen man and the equally hypothetical nature of social man, he wants to explain

---

[37] N.S.[1] 46; N.S.[3] 132–3, 332–7, 386–90.   [38] N.S.[1] 47; N.S.[3] 129–33, 310.

[39] On this question, see F. Vaughan, '*La Scienza Nuova:* orthodoxy and the art of writing' in *Forum Italicum,* 1968, and The *Political Philosophy of Giambattista Vico* (The Hague, 1972).

[40] See 'Natural science and social theory: Hobbes, Spinoza and Vico' by Amos Funkenstein, in *Giambattista Vico's Science of Humanity.*

not only why society endures but also why its forms change. The answer lies in a subtle dialectical relationship between the two kinds of element. If both fallen man and socialised man are idealised limiting cases, neither can be eliminated from the concept of a real social situation. Even in society, then, individual man acts for his own particular ends, but his activities can never escape from the network of relationships in which, *quâ* socialised, he is enmeshed. In a celebrated passage Vico can therefore claim that individual man acts for what he takes to be his own self-interest, but what he takes to be his self-interest is also a socialised interest, necessarily related to his social role, so that his action will have social consequences he neither foresaw nor desired. Thus, in a given context, man will act for what he takes to be his own particular ends, but the socialised nature of these ends will bring about changes in the social system itself. In the new system what man takes to be his individual ends will differ from those which he had formerly, but the actions which he undertakes on behalf of these new ends will again bring about unexpected social change.[41] If there look to be affinities here with Hegel, one must be careful not to take them too far. For in Hegel, spirit develops in what from a long-term point of view is a necessarily progressive direction, by means of a series of changes which are dialectical opposites. In Vico's scheme, on the contrary, not only is the series not necessarily progressive in the long term, since social progress is followed by social decline, but the stages involved in it are not genuine dialectical opposites but reveal, rather, a steady improvement in human rationality, justice and civil virtue, at least up to the state of perfection.[42] This involves an increasingly rich notion of the self as, under the influence of increasingly complex social structures, the self changes by coming to grips with the identity of its interests with those of other social units. Thus, at one stage, the individual *quâ* father identifies his interest with those of his family, at another, *quâ* citizen, with those both of his family and of his city and so on. Similarly the decline towards decadence and the barbarism of reflection involves a diminution in social complexity and a corresponding loss of the possibility of this sense of a complex identity of interests.[43]

It is clear that Vico is here grappling with what, following Wundt, has come to be known as the problem of the heterogeneity of ends.[44] It might, indeed, seem that he has said enough to resolve the problem. Vico does not, however, seem to think that he has, for, in addition to the above schema, he suggests that, in seeing this transformation of individ-

[41]*N.S.*[1] 41; *N.S.*[3] 341.   [42]See *N.S.*[1] 11; *N.S.*[3] 241–5, 349.
[43]See *N.S.*[3] 1102–6, especially 1106.
[44]See Maria Goretti's 'The heterogenesis of ends in Vico's thought: premises for a comparison of ideas', in *Giambattista Vico's Science of Humanity*.

ual aims in socially conditioned and socially useful ways, what we are witnessing is the way in which providence secures its own end – the preservation of man on earth. This is true even where, in the last throes of human corruption, providence applies the most drastic remedy, by bringing about the conditions for the recurrence of the whole sequence.[45] The possible affinity between Vico's account of the way in which providence works and Hegel's insistence upon the *cunning* of reason has not gone unremarked, but it is, again, necessary to treat this with some caution. For in Hegel's case, in which we are told that there is a progressive trend which is not open to total explanation by the series of transformations of the subjective and objective components of the state, there is at least something left to be explained.[46] In Vico's case, however, it is not at all clear what there is to be explained over and above the fact that man's short-term decisions turn out to have a certain consequence in the long run. But since this consequence is simply that mankind should not perish, it is not clear that it could not be fully explained by the elements mentioned above, without recourse to the further influence allegedly exercised by providence. In short, it is not clear what work there is for providence to do and, therefore, what is to be achieved by an appeal to providence in this connection.[47]

II

The foregoing theory, which might appear to offer an arguable conceptual framework for understanding historical change, is presupposed by Vico's substantial theory of history, which is a theory about a determinate sequence of stages of development to be followed by every nation whose development is conditioned solely or primarily by internal factors. This constitutes one of the most interesting aspects of his science. It is based upon a discovery which, he tells us, cost him many years of hard work: the discovery of the poetic nature of the founders of nations.[48] Before looking at some salient features of the theory, it is worth noting briefly the context in which Vico discovered it. The foregoing formal theory of historical change presupposes man as already socialised, since it is at least a necessary condition of the direction of the change produced by self-interest that a certain institutional system should exist. That Vico

[45] See *N.S.*[3] 1103–6.
[46] See my 'Vico and Hegel: a critical assessment of their accounts of the role of ideas in history', in *Vico: Past and Present,* vol. 2, pp. 35–46.
[47] Vico does, however, appeal to providence in other connections. See below, pp. 21ff.
[48] See *N.S.*[3] 338.

was aware of this is indicated by his claim to have resolved the age-long question whether man is sociable by nature or by convention – a question which, he tells us, previously not even Grotius had been able to resolve.[49] Despite this, however, Vico engages in another inquiry which, had he fully accepted his own claim, he should never have undertaken: that of explaining how early man emerged from a state of nature into a social state.[50] The source of his confusion seems clear enough. It is to be found in the possibility of treating the notions of a state of nature and of the fall of man either as historical truths or as ideal limiting cases and, like most of his protagonists, Vico responded by treating them as both. Yet if the question of the historical truth of the state of nature, understood strictly as a state without institutions, rests upon an error, that of the nature of the institutions and life of early man is a genuine question and it is to this that Vico's discovery is to be related.

This is one of the contexts in which Vico's complaints about the philosophers and the philologists are to be understood.[51] The philosophers, Vico accepts, have approached the question systematically, as they ought, but he rejects their claims, including those of his beloved Plato,[52] on the grounds that they involve the anachronistic ascription to former ages of modes of thought and, indeed, theories, proper to philosophy and hence proper only to the sophisticated times which gave birth to philosophy itself.[53] This is an example of the intellectual vice which Vico calls the 'vanity of scholars',[54] which has guided their interpretations of the great evidential remnants, both literary and non-literary, of the past, and caused them to locate versions of their own philosophical doctrines in the works of Zoroaster, Hermes Trismegistus and so on. The 'philologists', by which term Vico means historians in general, have, on the other hand, not approached the task systematically enough, hence their accounts lack both certainty and continuity[55] and they have, as a result, failed to reduce philology to a science. This, indeed, is one of the declared tasks of Vico's work, and in this context it means simply that philology, the study of historical evidence, will be conducted in accordance with the criteria appropriate to a science.

The conflation of the notion that the state of nature could be historically true with that of it as an ideal limiting case, and of the notion of a transition from a non-social to a social state with that of early social

---

[49] See *N.S.*³ 134–5, 309.
[50] I am indebted to Dr Duncan Forbes, in his review of my *Vico: A Study of the 'New Science'*, for noting my earlier failure to appreciate the importance of this point. See *The Historical Journal*, 1975, pp. 895–6.
[51] See *N.S.*¹ 27–31; *N.S.*³ 138–40, 326–9, 394–7.   [52] See *N.S.*¹ 13.
[53] See *N.S.*¹ 20, 23; *N.S.*³ 394–7.   [54] *N.S.*³ 128.   [55] See *N.S.*¹ 32.

development, bear upon Vico's treatment of the key to the substantial theory of the new science. For, in effect, they mean that Vico's theory of the poetic nature of early man is offered not merely to show how poetic factors affected the development, and hence the nature, of early institutions, but also how they could be responsible for the creation of institutions in a non-institutional context.

In the account which Vico offers, three points are particularly noteworthy. First, in the genetic process, institutions arose through the operation of certain psychological capacities natural to early man – specifically an all-embracing imagination which, working on principles of self-projection, turned the as yet unintelligible physical world into a huge, animate being.[56] In the context of this anthropomorphic metaphysics, men's natural fear of one another was dominated by their fear of this god, and of his children who, on the appropriate occasions, were subsequently created by poetic man.[57] Hence certain practices – augury, sacrifice and marriage – became necessary, in order to discover this god's wishes, and to forestall his anger. Understood in one way the sequence which Vico offers here can be taken to recount an historical transition from a state of nature to a social state, but understood in another it recounts the nature and ground of man's early institutions. Vico, in fact, took it both ways, so that he spends a considerable amount of effort trying to reconcile his account historically with the Biblical account of early history, while also trying to show how, independently of this relation, it makes sense, in the light of the available evidence, as a description of the way of life of early man. The thesis of poetic man carries with it, however, a new conception of what counts as evidence and how to interpret it. Hence Vico finds himself drawn into the eighteenth-century debate about the nature of myths,[58] the nature of their creators, the question of the historicity of the Bible, and of the nature of primitive law, primitive society, and early language and thought. In these and many other areas Vico advanced theses of great originality, all of which, however, presuppose his account of poetic man. In these theories are to be found the grounds for many of the claims which have been made for Vico as a seminal, if neglected, figure in the history of the human sciences.

The second point of note here is the account which Vico gives of the imagination. When he talks of the imagination of poetic man, he is not using the notion in the sense in which it might be said of some mathematician or physicist that he displayed great imagination in his work.

[56] See *N.S.*³ 120, 374–6.   [57] See *N.S.*¹ 267; *N.S.*³ 401–3.
[58] See *The Eighteenth Century Confronts the Gods*, by Frank Manuel (Cambridge, Mass., 1959).

The imagination which Vico ascribes to poetic man is a creative capacity which both works in accordance with certain principles, i.e., by imitation and non-rational association, and produces, as a result, particular images. This is important, for it explains why Vico believes that man cannot be both imaginative and rational at once. For Vico takes reason to be a form of understanding which is abstract in the sense that it utilises abstract concepts, whereas the imagination utilises particular images. Accordingly the perceptive processes and thought of early man are not the same as those of later men. Poetic man sees the world as a specific and particular whole, with parts which stand to the whole in a way which is, at best, only functionally analogous to, though it is the historical precursor of, the later distinctions between universals and the particulars which can be subsumed under them. Vico himself refers to these 'thoughts' as a 'credible impossibility'[59] and it may reasonably be wondered whether this process can seriously be considered a form of thought, as Vico insists that it be. The difficulty can, however, be resolved in the following way. Whatever else thought does, it must connect with our actions by helping to direct our motives. Hence, if it can be shown that later we can explain the actions of poetic man by showing them as responses to feelings and motives aroused by such images, then, no matter how different in form this may be from propositional thought, it would make sense to take it to be a form of thought.

The ideographic nature of the poetic imagination is important for Vico, for it provides him with a natural non-rational principle by which he can account for the products of this imagination, e.g., for the forms which the fables, law, and written language took, and the ways in which, via principles of ideographic association, these images themselves could be transformed under the influence of new events and happenings in the world. It provides him, in effect, with a natural mechanism by which a world of inter-related human artifacts could come into being, without having to credit the creators of these artifacts with an implausible transcendent rationality.

The third point to note is the importance of custom. Vico's insistence upon the non-rational nature of the birth of civilisation represents the positive side of his complaints about the vanity of scholars. Not surprisingly, given Vico's knowledge of jurisprudence, it comes out most strongly in his attack on the natural law theorists, with their ahistorical notion that law was based upon a non-temporal concept of equity which was accessible to rational beings throughout all history. It is a straightforward mistake, Vico claims, to think, as Grotius had, that the law of

[59]N.S.[1] 258; N.S.[3] 383.

his own time could have operated in the time of poetic man. For in primitive times not only was law not informed by a grasp of the rationality of equity, as Grotius had suggested, but it was not enacted. The place of enacted law was occupied by custom[60] and custom depends upon imitation, which is one of the principal natural capacities which Vico ascribes to early man.[61] The importance of custom in the life of poetic man can scarcely be exaggerated.[62] What is to be noted in the context of the present discussion, however, is that it is by means of the notion of custom that Vico tries to explain the emergence of the law of social man from a state of nature in which there is no law. For, as Hobbes and the other social contract theorists failed to perceive, contracts presuppose much institutional machinery and cannot, therefore, be the basis of an institutionalised state. Nor, again, can Grotius' appeal to reason supply such a basis, since it ignores early man's incapacity to grasp the rational. Custom, however, arises from the innate and primitive capacity to imitate. Thus it is such that it could operate in a state of nature, and from the patterns of behaviour which it engenders, something like law could develop. Vico's insistence upon the customary nature of the law of poetic man is, therefore, apart from any intrinsic merits it may have as a theory, an example of his attempt to explain the historical emergence of society from a state of nature.

Vico's theory of law is useful here as an example of the sequence involved in his substantial theory of historical development, i.e., from a society governed by imagination, superstition and custom to one governed by rational understanding. The fundamental principle in this sequence is that of social man's historically developing insight into the essence of things. Vico distinguishes three kinds of law: poetic, heroic and human. Poetic law is customary law, adopted through fear of a god of imaginary origins. Heroic law is a law of formulae in which the formulae themselves, which are codifications of custom, are mistaken for the spirit of the law (equity, according to Vico) which informs them. It is applied, accordingly, strictly and inflexibly because there is nothing but the formulae for men to fall back upon. Human law is law informed by an understanding of the nature of equity itself. Hence it is benevolent because, although it is stated in formulae, its application is governed by an understanding of the supreme principle of law.[63] The suggestion is therefore of a developmental sequence in which a truth of law is contained implicitly in its rudimentary origins and in which the historical

---

[60] See *N.S.*[3] 308–13, 919–21.   [61] See *N.S.*[3] 215–17.

[62] For a helpful discussion, see 'The theoretical and practical relevance of Vico's sociology for today' by Werner Stark in *Social Research*, 43 (4), winter 1976.

[63] See, for example, the triadic scheme described in *N.S.*[3] 915–27.

development of law is governed by man's developing insight into the nature of this truth.[64]

Precisely the same principle operates in the case of religion. Man – or at least gentile man – starts with 'some' idea of divinity,[65] i.e., of divinity as a material divinity. This idea is, in fact, false,[66] since it is a product of the poetic imagination working in accordance with non-rational principles. Yet it has some elements of truth in it, insofar as this divinity is thought of as omnipotent and as one.[67] This idea then fragments into that of a plurality of gods, as man's powers of discrimination develop and he comes to distinguish more aspects of the (largely social) world for which he needs gods. Thus a theogony of gods arises,[68] leading to the household gods of, for example, the Romans. Finally, however, as the individual comes to grasp his self-identity with mankind and thus comes into possession of his fully human, and hence rational, nature, so he comes to believe in one god who is wholly spiritual.[69] This picture is complicated, it is true, by Vico's belief that this one god is the Christian god. Nor, moreover, can it be said that it is worked out in any great detail. But it is clear enough in outline. Poetic man's imagination enables him to create an image of God which functions as an idea. Though false in many respects this idea nevertheless contains certain elements which are indispensable to man's grasp of the truth in religion, elements which are preserved in the series of conceptual changes by which he comes to grasp this truth.

These examples raise two points of importance. First, they serve to bring out the function which Vico ascribes to providence in his theory. To see this it is necessary to note that in each case Vico is faced with the difficulty of explaining how it can be that, in the absence of a rational capacity for discerning the truth – e.g., that there is one god or that one ought to act in accordance with equity – the poetic imagination should produce beliefs which, though false, nevertheless contain the elements of later true beliefs rather than of later false beliefs. To resolve this difficulty Vico appeals to providence, which, he asserts, gives man precisely those non-rational creative capacities, operating on those associative principles, which will produce false beliefs from which true beliefs will follow

---

[64] Vico's interest in such a phenomenology of understanding, particularly in relation to law, goes back to his earliest writings. See, for example, *On method in contemporary fields of study*, chapter 7, pp. 41–5 below.

[65] See *N.S.*[1] 45; *N.S.*[3] 338.   [66] See *N.S.*[3] 338.   [67] See *N.S.*[1] 60.

[68] See *N.S.*[1] 57–59; *N.S.*[3] 392.

[69] The general principle behind this sequence, the notion, that is, that human understanding develops from a phase in which everything is seen as particular and material to one in which it is seen as universal and spiritual, is given in a number of passages. See, for example, *N.S.*[3] 236, 331, 916–18.

rather than false beliefs from which false beliefs will follow. Taken at its face value this claim seems to commit Vico to a causal theory of providence and it may well be that, given his personal religious beliefs, this is how he thought of it. But if it is taken wholly in this way, it must be said that it offers a highly inadequate solution to the difficulty. For not only does it require that providence be endowed with the very features – rational insight into the truth, foreknowledge of the end of history and so on – with which Vico was rightly reluctant to endow primitive man, but, even were this done, it would offer no acceptable explanation how one such set of imaginative beliefs should lead to later beliefs which were epistemologically preferable to those which would follow from any others. A miraculous, and to that extent unintelligible, factor is thus left at work in the very heart of the process of historical development.

Vico's remarks on this subject are, however, obscure and ambiguous, and much of what he says points to a somewhat different theory. The main features of this can be seen by noting that Vico ascribes to religious belief and to law the function of serving as a social bond or constraining force, which holds men within social ways when their vicious instincts would drive them to destroy society. The importance of religion in this respect is shown both by the fact that Vico explains the breakdown of society by a decline in religious belief and by his denial of Bayle's claim that a society of atheists is a possibility.[70] If religion is a necessary social bond it follows that only societies with religious beliefs can endure and that any society which has endured must have had religious beliefs. On this view, Vico's account of the way in which providence achieves its end – the preservation of the human race – is not a description of the achievement of an 'end' at all, but of a necessary causal condition of social survival and development.

If this is Vico's 'implicit' view then the question changes, of course, from 'how can it come about that man has those imaginary false beliefs which have elements of truth in them?', to 'in what sense can poetic man's imaginary religious beliefs, which have a social function, also have elements of truth in them?'.

This serves simply, however, to raise the second point which arises in connection with Vico's account of the implicit ideality of religion and law: in what sense is it the case that poetic man's imaginary beliefs are the antecedents of later true beliefs?[71] The second view advanced above suggests that they are so in a purely causal sense. But if this is so, and if only those societies endure in which men possess religious beliefs which are the causal outcome of earlier religious beliefs, what grounds does this

---

[70] See *N.S.*[1] 8; *N.S.*[3] 334, 1109–10.   [71] See *N.S.*[1] 49.

provide for claiming that these beliefs increasingly approximate to the truth? The answer, I suggest, is that unless we hold that the social efficacy of beliefs depends upon their being in some sense true, which is a highly disputable claim, the mere fact of the causal nature of their connection gives us no reason to believe that they increasingly approximate, or ever did approximate, to some truth embodied in their causal outcome. It thus seems that, if we confine ourselves to their ontological implications, the success or failure of certain beliefs in functioning as social bonds has no bearing upon their truth. This is not, of course, to deny that they will be accepted as true; but Vico plainly means more than this when he asserts that in the fully human age men grasp the essence of the things themselves. The grounds of this latter claim accordingly are not to be found in Vico's ontology itself. If this is so, it serves to provide a further respect in which Vico's theory is to be distinguished from Hegel's, to which it is so often assimilated. For Hegel's ontology is genuinely and explicitly teleological, whereas Vico is presenting a causal ontology in teleological robes.

This leads to the concluding question which I wish to mention in connection with Vico's ontology: that of his determinism. If the process of history, as Vico conceives it, is a causal process, is he thereby committed to determinism? And if he is, what is to be made of his claim that man has the power to make free choices?[72] It is certainly true that Vico offers a theory which implies that there are laws of historical development,[73] while at the same time insisting that men act with intelligence, that they have the power of free choice and that they often act in ways which run counter to the prevailing tendencies of the institutional context.[74] These remarks have, indeed, inspired commentators to see Vico either as an arch-determinist or as an apostle of the doctrine of free will. But it is necessary to adopt one of these positions only if there is thought to be a contradiction between them. Such a possibility can be removed in Vico's case, however, by recognising that it is history as a whole, taken as the development of systems of institutions, which he holds to be determined, and that it is to the men who act within these frameworks that he ascribes the power of free choice. That the constraining influence of institutions must *in general* be successful is certainly true and, given that it is and that human choice is *in general* influenced by these constraints, the outcome of the actions which men perform by choice must be determined. But this is an innocuous form of determinism. It amounts only to saying that the historical development of institutions is the outcome of a causal process, but not that everything in that process is similarly determined.

[72] See N.S.[1] 47; N.S.[3] 141, 340–1, 1108–9.
[73] See N.S.[1] 90; N.S.[3] 145, 245, 349, 393.   [74] See N.S.[1] 45; N.S.[3] 341, 1108.

It might still be thought, however, that if the development of human reason is, as suggested above, dependent upon natural causal factors, the reasons which determine human choice will themselves be determined. But this is to assume that Vico holds that the development of reason is wholly determined by natural causal factors – in this case, psychological factors. In fact, however, although Vico claims that human reason develops from the heroic mind and the latter, in turn, from the poetic mind, it is clear that he never maintained that any one of these wholly *determines* any of the others. The process which Vico is here describing is a genuine developmental process, a process, that is, which allows for the growth of new capacities which could not arise in the absence of older capacities, but which is not, nevertheless, causally determined by them. Vico is certainly committed to the view that wherever the poetic mind arises it must be succeeded by the heroic mind, but only *in general*. His claim is compatible, therefore, with allowing that some individual persons might fail to make the transition, and commits him only to the view that such individuals as do make the transition, which is necessary in general but not for the individual as such, could not have made it except in the context of a previous mode of experience. This means, of course, that imagination is both historically and ontologically prior to reason, or, to put it in Vico's language, that reason is a modification of imagination; but it does not mean that, in the case of any given individual, imagination necessarily issues in reason. There is still room, on this model, for the free development of individual potentialities within the constraints of the general needs of the situation.

III

In the foregoing section I have given a short outline of the formal and substantive claims involved in the notion that Vico's science is a science of what men have made. In this section I shall briefly consider the question of the sources of, and methods required by, this science. This is a difficult issue and I can do no more than mention some of the various views of it which have been offered and indicate the reasons which incline me towards the view which I favour.

Before doing so, however, it is pertinent to note an interesting difference which arises in this connection between the *First New Science* of 1725 and the *Second* and *Third New Sciences* of 1730 and 1744. In the latter Vico makes a number of explicit references to his epistemological theories and links them to his metaphysical views, rather as he had in *On the ancient wisdom of the Italians*. In the *First New Science*, however, although Vico there advances the same metaphysical views and the same kinds of historical accounts as in the later works, there is no systematic attempt to link epistemology and metaphysics.[75] It would be wrong, however, to draw from this the conclusion that the *verum–factum* doctrine is not, in some sense, the basis of all the versions of the new science. The explanation is probably just that, in the haste in which Vico developed the doctrines of the *First New Science,* he simply had not the time to work out a satisfactory way of presenting how he saw the relationship between the *verum–factum* thesis and the doctrines of his new work.[76]

Be that as it may, the unarguable basis of the new science is that human history is knowable to men because men have made it, but that the natural world is known to God because He has made it.[77] In asserting the connection between knowledge and making Vico is, of course, reiterating the claim of *On the ancient wisdom of the Italians.* But in asserting that human affairs or human history are the only things knowable to man, and that the physical world is not, he is almost completely reversing the hierarchical scheme of the earlier work. There is one respect, however, in which this is not so. Vico is still prepared to accept that geometry constitutes a branch of knowledge proper, since it is wholly of human construction. But he distinguishes it from historical knowledge on the ground that it deals with fictions whereas history deals with reality.[78] Having said this, however, a very obvious difficulty arises. What God makes are things which constitute the matter of the physical world. There is an analogous sense in which, if we are prepared to accept the constructivist account which Vico offers, the geometer can be said to create the matter of the geometrical world, i.e., the content with which he is concerned. In history, however, there are two possible makers: historical agents and historians. Each can be thought of as a maker but what they make does not coincide. For the historical agent is the maker of events and institutions, i.e., of *res gestae* themselves, whereas the historian is the maker of the *history* of those events and institutions. The things which historical agents and historians make are thus quite different and at first sight it would look as though the only legitimate analogy could be between God's making of the physical world and the historical agent's making of the historical world. Yet Vico seems to require the analogy to

[75] This is not, however, to imply that there is no suggestion of such a link in the *First New Science,* for *N.S.*[1] 40 parallels the famous general claim of *N.S.*[3] 331.

[76] In his article 'Law and the historical origin of the New Science', in *Giambattista Vico's Science of Humanity,* the late Guido Fassò argues that, since Vico fails to mention the *verum–factum* principle in any works between *On the ancient wisdom of the Italians* and the *Second New Science,* he did not arrive at the epistemological principle which is at the basis of the latter work by a conscious development of the *verum–factum* principle. However, this overlooks the fact that the principle is stated at *N.S.*[1] 40 as clearly as at *N.S.*[3] 331. So Fassò's account is at best only a part of the truth.

[77] See *N.S.*[3] 331.   [78] See *N.S.*[3] 349.

hold both between God and the historical agent and God and the historian. For his fundamental principle asserts that since the world of civil society has been made by men, its principles are to be found in the modifications of our own human mind,[79] where, as he makes clear, by our 'own human mind' he means 'the mind of him who meditates this science', i.e., the historian.[80] The claim thus seems to be that since the world of *res gestae* has been made by historical agents, the principles of that world can be recovered from the mind of the historian who is writing the history of that world, but not from the minds of the agents who made it. Vico's fundamental principle thus looks to involve a *non sequitur* based upon an equivocation in which the term 'man' is used to refer at times to the historical agent and at others to the historian.

It might, of course, be held, as it was, for example, by some of the late nineteenth-century Italian positivists, that Vico is not making any reference to the mind of the historian and that his suggestion is only that the principles of human history are to be found in the minds of the historical agents involved in it.[81] But this is highly implausible since, as noted above, Vico explicitly states that the principles to which he refers are to be found in the mind of him who meditates this science. Moreover, were the claim about the relation between the historical agent and his products, it would cease to be an epistemological claim and become solely a general statement of the ontological theories mentioned above. It would thus be of no value in telling us how we are to come to *know* these theories, as Vico intended that it should.

To resolve this difficulty one must attend first to the important distinction which Vico draws between *coscienza* and *scienza*[82] i.e., between consciousness of, or belief in, the particular, and knowledge of the universal, which is the cause of the particular. Historical agents act in the light of their beliefs about particular things and to that extent they possess *coscienza*. They lack, however, understanding of the causes of those beliefs, hence Vico will not ascribe *scienza* to them. It follows that the principles which Vico requires for historical knowledge, although they may inform historical activities, are not known to historical agents. Vico's claim that these principles must be found within the mind of the historian is therefore perfectly consistent with his refusal to grant the historical agent *scienza* of what he is doing. Vico is thus asserting that the historian's world is a construction which, though it includes the agent's world, nevertheless goes beyond the latter. And it is in virtue of so doing that it provides us with *scienza* of reality.

---

[79] See N.S.³ 331.   [80] See N.S.³ 349, 374.
[81] See *Sul Rinnovamento della Filosofia Positivista in Italia,* by P. Siciliani (Florence, 1871).
[82] See N.S.³ 137–8.

The question now becomes that of the nature of the principles to which Vico here appeals and of the source of the historian's knowledge of them. These are highly disputed issues, and various suggestions have been made, none of which are entirely satisfactory. One suggestion, already mentioned, derives from the late nineteenth-century Italian positivists, for whom the principles were largely sociological and their derivation inductive. But in this case Vico's position would be untenable, since the inductive inferences would presuppose the very knowledge of the causes of historical events which they are supposed to make possible. A second suggestion, which has been more influential historically, is the quasi-Hegelian interpretation offered by Croce, in which the principles in question are treated as a set of *a priori* categories, to be used by the historian in interpreting the evidence.[83] Support for this suggestion is provided by the fact that Vico talks of a reflection upon these principles and, in consequence of this, of meditating first 'in idea' what will subsequently be shown to be true as a matter of fact.[84] But there are difficulties also for this interpretation. It is noticeable, for example, that, despite his references to 'meditating in idea' what he will later establish in fact, Vico at no point offers anything like an *a priori* deduction or justification of any set of categories. Nor, indeed, does he appear to believe that they have the logical force which one might expect of *a priori* categories. On the contrary, indeed, he offers certain 'proofs' of his science,[85] of which two appeal to criteria – consistency, economy and fruitfulness[86] – which would certainly be acceptable in an empirical science. A third possibility is that Vico is thinking of some set of truths about ourselves accessible to us by introspection. This, however, would hardly suffice, since such a set of truths could hardly, without begging the question, be extended from the *coscienza* which we have of ourselves to provide the causes which are required for *scienza*. A fourth possibility, proposed by Sir Isaiah Berlin, is that Vico is referring to a special form of knowledge, achieved by empathetic understanding of what it is to be a human being, engaging in characteristically human pursuits: a capacity, in other words, for grasping what human beings of the past, in their historically and culturally conditioned states, could and could not have done.[87] The difficulty here, however, is that possession of such a capacity would seem, at best, to help us to interpret the evidence of the past in terms of the historical agent's own point of view. It would, in other words, help us to distin-

[83] *The Philosophy of Giambattista Vico.*   [84] See *N.S.*[1] 390; *N.S.*[3] 138–40, 163, 359.
[85] See *N.S.*[3] 343–9.   [86] *N.S.*[3] 344–5.
[87] *Op. cit.* pp. 26–37. See also 'Vico's philosophy of imagination' by D. P. Verene, *Social Research*, 43 (3), autumn 1976, in which imagination or '*recollective fantasia*', to use Verene's expression, is said to be the basis of Vico's epistemological theory. For a detailed criticism of both views, see my 'Imagination in Vico' in *Vico: Past and Present*, vol. 1, pp. 162–70.

guish credible from incredible interpretations of the way in which historical agents, collectively or individually, saw their world. But it would not
enable us to know the causes which Vico holds to be necessary for a
science.

It would seem, then, that the principles which Vico requires must
enable the historian to understand not only how historical agents saw
their world but the causes of their so doing. From what was said in the
preceding section, it is evident that they must therefore include the principles of the development of human nature, taken as a process which is
necessarily both social and historical in character. It comes as no surprise, then, to find Vico including religion, marriage and burial of the
dead as the first of his three principles. For these are, on his account,
institutions which perform functions necessary for any form of social and
historical development.[88] These, however, cannot exhaust the principles
which Vico requires, for his substantial account involves the notion of
the history of a nation as a structured process, passing through certain
necessary phases, the conditions for the occurrence of which are law-
determined: a structure informed, that is, by the sequence of birth, matu-
rity and death.[89]

But if these are the principles to which Vico's fundamental formula
refers, is it plausible to suggest that the historian can rediscover them in
his own mind? The answer plainly depends upon how we interpret the
notion of 'mind' involved here. If we take it to be the historian's mind,
quâ the individual he is, the suggestion would seem to be hopeless. There
is nothing in the concept of the consciousness of an individual *quâ* individual which could serve as a ground for knowledge of the laws which
determine the structure of a characteristically historical process. But if
we remember that for Vico an individual is primarily, though not exclusively, a function of his historical and social context, then it becomes
more plausible. If we take the individual not as a Cartesian ego, standing
over against the world, but as an historical and social construction which
is, in one sense, an expression of the world's historical and social nature,
then there is no reason why, by reflection upon, or self-conscious thought
about, *himself in his world,* the historian should not be able to discern
these principles. For if, as Vico claims, these principles are universal and
necessary,[90] then they will operate as much in his own case as in that of
anything else which can have a history. Certainly, that Vico accepted
some such view is shown by the frequency with which he alludes to the
analogy between the life of a human being, from childhood to old age,
and that of a nation from infancy to final dissolution. The notion that

[88] See *N.S.*[3] 332–7.   [89] See *N.S.*[1] 11; *N.S.*[3] 245, 393.   [90] See *N.S.*[3] 163, 332.

there are certain fundamental capacities which operate at a certain period of life in both cases and which make possible the development of the next set of capacities which are potential in the nature of the structure, is very strong in the *New Science*. Vico is not therefore appealing to introspection as our warrant for the most fundamental presuppositions in his epistemology. Rather the appeal is to a form of self-understanding which is available to the historian precisely because the world in which *he* exists is structured by the same features which have structured previous phases of its history. The historian's own world, and hence the historian himself, is the product of an historical process, the principles of which leave their trace in his world and therefore in him.[91] By understanding these principles at work, the historian can begin to understand history.

The past, therefore, becomes recoverable. What is recovered is not, however, merely the past as it was for historical agents, for that would be mere *coscienza*. It is the past as it was for those agents, understood in the light of its causes. The family fathers created a sense of self-identity, which included an identity of their interests with those of their family, but they did not know why those interests came to be identified nor why it was in the nature of the case that this identification must have consequences which would conflict with their original motives for creating it. The historian, on the other hand, with his understanding of human nature in its historical and social dimensions, does know this, and it is in virtue of this fact that historical knowledge can transcend mere *coscienza* and become *scienza*.

[91] See *N.S.*[1] 80.

On method in
contemporary fields of study *

1 The order of our enquiry

In his invaluable little book *On the Dignity and Advancement of Learning* [1] Francis Bacon indicates how far we ought to pursue new arts and sciences, additional to those we already have, and how far we ought to pursue those we now have, in order that human wisdom may be brought to perfection. But in discovering a new world of sciences he shows himself worthy of a new earth rather than of our own. For his vast aspirations so exceed the extent of human industry, that he seems to have shown what, of necessity, we lack for reaching absolute wisdom, rather than what we can accomplish. I think that this has come about because, as is often the case, the desires of people of high achievement are vast and infinite. Thus Bacon has acted in the field of learning like the political leaders of the greatest empires, who, when they have attained supreme power in the human sphere, pit their great resources against nature itself, trying in vain to pave seas with rocks, cross mountains by sail, and perform other feats forbidden by nature. For, in truth, everything that man is permitted to know is finite and imperfect, like man himself. But if we compare our own with ancient times, and weigh the advantages against the disadvantages of learning in each case, perhaps our score will be the same as that of the ancients. For we have discovered many things which were completely unknown in former times, while the ancients knew many things of which we are completely ignorant. We have many abili-

---

* Delivered in 1708 to mark the opening of the academic year at the University of Naples, the lecture was enlarged and published in 1709. See above, pp. 2–4.

[1] Published in 1623, this was meant to be the first part of *The Great Instauration,* of which *The New Organon,* published in 1620, was to have been the second part. In it Bacon offers a critique of contemporary branches of science, and at the end, he adds a list of *desiderata,* to which Vico here refers. Vico's criticism of Bacon's ambition was justified in that Bacon was unable to complete the third part, in which the sciences were to be reconstructed in accordance with the method advocated in *The New Organon.* Despite his criticism of Bacon, Vico was, however, much influenced by him, and in his *Autobiography* extolled him as one of the four authors by whom he had been most influenced, the others being Plato, Tacitus and Grotius. For a discussion of these influences, see Enrico de Mas' 'Vico's four authors' in *Giambattista Vico: An International Symposium.* Bacon was a continuous influence upon Vico and it is important to note that in the *Third New Science* Vico took himself to be applying Bacon's method. See *N.S.* [3] 163, 359.

ties which enable us to succeed in one branch of learning; they had many which applied to another. They were wholly occupied in cultivating certain arts which we virtually neglect; we engage in some which they plainly despised. They linked to their advantage many disciplines which we have separated; we have linked others which they treated separately to their disadvantage. And finally, a considerable number of disciplines have changed both in appearance and name.

All this provides me with a topic to debate before you, noble youths: 'Which is the more correct and superior method of study, ours or that of the ancients?' In discussing this, we shall compare the advantages and disadvantages of both, considering which of our disadvantages can be avoided and by what method this can be done. As for those disadvantages which are unavoidable, we shall consider what there are in the system of the ancients by which they can be counterbalanced.

If I am not mistaken this is a new subject, though so necessary is it for knowledge that it is surprising that this should be so. I shall avoid censure if you understand that my aim is not so much to find fault either with the disadvantages of our method or with those of the ancients as to compare the advantages of the methods of both ages. This should be your aim: that if you know more than the ancients in some fields you should not know less in others; that you should have a method whereby you can know more than the ancients in total; and that you should be content to put up with the unavoidable disadvantages of our method of study when you remember the disadvantages of that of antiquity.

So that you may comprehend the whole matter more easily, you must understand that I am not here comparing our sciences with ancient sciences, nor our arts with ancient arts. Rather, I am discussing the respects in which our method of study is superior to that of the ancients and those in which it is inferior, and what is the cause of the latter in order that it should be rectified. The new arts, sciences and discoveries must, therefore, at least be distinguished, if not separated, from the new instruments of, and aids to, knowledge, for the former constitute the material of study, the latter [its] way and method, the proper subject of our discussion.

The method of study seems, indeed, to be entirely comprised of three things: instruments, aids and goal. Instruments are concerned with the methodical arrangement of things, for anyone who is truly well equipped when he sets out to learn any art or science, approaches it properly and methodically. But instruments precede the study of things, while aids accompany it. As for the goal, although it comes at the end, the student must have it in view from the beginning and throughout the whole method of study. We shall arrange our discourse in accordance with this order, i.e., we shall deal first with the instruments, then with the aids, of our method of study. The goal, however, permeates the whole, just as blood circulates through the entire body. And in the same way as the movement of blood is observed where the arteries are more perceptible, we shall discuss the goal of our method of study where it is most in evidence.

Among the new instruments of the sciences some are themselves sciences, others arts, others mere works of art or nature. [But] the instrument common to all the sciences and arts is the new critical method:[2] analysis is the instrument of geometry; geometry itself, together with its method and perhaps the new mechanics, is the instrument of physics; chemistry, with its offshoot pharmacology, is the instrument of medicine; the microscope is the instrument of anatomy, the telescope that of astronomy, and, finally, the mariner's compass that of geography. As for the new aids, I include among them the creation of arts for a number of subjects which the ancients entrusted to common sense, the abundance of excellent examples, the types used in printing, and the universities set up for learning. But as for the goal, today there is only one, namely the truth, which is sought, celebrated and honoured by everybody in all study. Whether it be the ease, usefulness or value of all these things that is under consideration, our method of study will, beyond doubt, seem more correct than, and superior to, that of the ancients.

2   The advantages which our methods of study derive from the instruments of science

The critical method gives us that first truth, about which one can be certain even when one doubts;[3] and it is by this first truth that the critical method is judged entirely to have defeated the New Academy.[4] Moreover, with astonishing ease of method, analysis provides solutions to geo-

---

[2] The Cartesian method. In 'Vico and anti-Cartesianism', in *Giambattista Vico: An International Symposium,* Yvon Belaval suggests that Vico shows little detailed knowledge of Descartes' works themselves and that his attacks are largely mounted against later Cartesians such as Pascal, Malebranche and Spinoza.

[3] The *Cogito.*

[4] The Third or New Platonic Academy, founded by the sceptic, Carneades. It is not clear whether Vico endorses this claim here, but by the time of *On the ancient wisdom of the Italians* he was ready to reject the *Cogito* as a bulwark against a well-thought-out scepticism. See below, pp. 57–8.

metric problems which were unsolved by the ancients. The ancients used geometry and mechanics as instruments of physics, without, however, doing so all the time. We both use the same instruments constantly, and also employ others which are superior. It is no part of our brief to decide whether geometry is made clearer by analysis or whether mechanics is made anew by it, but it is beyond doubt that leaders in the field employ a geometry which has been enhanced by a number of new and very clever discoveries. And in order that they may never be abandoned by these in their journey along nature's dark path, they have introduced the geometric method into physics. Bound to it, as to Ariadne's thread, they complete their fixed course and, like the architects of some mighty work rather than physicists feeling their way, they describe the causes whereby this wonderful world machine was constructed by almighty God. Consider, moreover, the great help which chemistry, which was entirely unknown to the ancients, has given to medicine! For, aided by the similarity with chemical phenomena, medicine does not just guess at but sees clearly very many functions and diseases of the human body. Pharmacology, its offshoot, was something for which the ancients certainly cherished a desire, but we are now possessed of what they [merely] desired. Some have applied chemistry to physics and others applied mechanics to medicine, so that the combination of chemistry and physics has created, virtually by hand, meteors and other natural phenomena, while the combination of mechanics and medicine utilises the movements of a machine to diagnose and cure diseases of the human body. Anatomy has already surpassed ancient medicine by illustrating the circulation of the blood, the origin of nerves and countless humours, and the vessels and canals of the human body. In addition, with the help of the microscope, it has thrown great light upon the delineation of numerous glands, tiny organs, plants, worms and insects and, in particular, to provide a clear insight into generation, upon the incubation of the egg. The ancients were denied sight of all these discoveries . . .

. . . And consider the many great and wonderful discoveries by which mechanics, enhanced by geometry and physics as they are taught today, seems to have enriched human society! One may assert, without fear of contradiction, that the warfare of our time derives from these three sciences. So far is it in advance of that of former times that, faced with our method of fortifying and storming cities, Minerva would hold her own Athenian fortress in contempt, while Jupiter would curse his three-forked thunderbolt for being blunt and clumsy.

Having noted the power of our instruments of the sciences, let us turn to that of our aids to study. For appropriate arts have been created for many things which were formerly left to practical wisdom alone. For example, deterred by its difficulty, the ancients despaired of completing the task of jurisprudence. Moreover, in poetry, oratory, painting, sculpture, and the other imitative arts, we have an abundance of excellent examples. With these to remind them, men can now imitate more properly and easily the very best of nature herself. Moreover, the invention of type has blessed us with an abundance of books, so that we have many scholars versed not just in one or two writers, but well informed by much varied, and almost infinite, reading.

Let us now examine the advantages of our method of studies, and see whether it lacks any good features which the ancients had, or involves any drawbacks which the ancients lacked. Let us see [moreover] whether we can avoid the drawbacks of our own method while still reaping the benefits of their method, and how this may be done. And as for those disadvantages which we cannot avoid, let us see by what weaknesses of their method they may be counterbalanced.

3 The disadvantages of the new critical method

First of all, with regard to the instruments of the sciences, our studies begin today from the critical standpoint. In order that its own first truth may be divested not merely of all falsehood, but of the slightest suspicion of falsehood, this critical method requires that, in addition to falsehoods, all secondary truths and all probabilities be banished from the mind. Such an approach is certainly inappropriate, since common sense must be developed in young people as soon as possible. Otherwise, when they are older, their everyday behaviour will be strange and intemperate. For, as knowledge derives from truths and error from falsehoods, so common sense arises from probabilities. For probabilities stand halfway, so to speak, between truth and falsehood, since they are almost always true and very rarely false.

Thus, since common sense, above all else, should be inculcated in the young, one must be wary lest it be stifled in them by our critical method.[5]

---

[5] Descartes' method required that anything that might be false be assumed to be false. This meant that philosophy could not take the contingent, and therefore the probable, as its starting point (see, for example, *Meditation II*). This was, however, a theoretical requirement, and at the practical level Descartes accepted that, until such times as the truth had been fully revealed by the application of his method, we had no alternative but to act in accordance with judgements of probability (see, for example, *Discourse on the Method*, Part III, and *The Principles of Philosophy*, Part I, Principle III). Nevertheless, this assertion

Moreover, just as common sense is the rule of all practical wisdom, so it is of eloquence. For orators in a law court often work harder over something which is true but which lacks any degree of probability than over something which is false but carries some measure of credibility. Thus there is a danger that our critical method may make young people less competent in eloquence.

Finally, our exponents of the [critical] method allocate their own first truth a place before, beyond and above all bodily images. But they teach it to young people prematurely and before they are old enough for it. For the young are strong in imagination as the old are strong in reason, and boys should in no way be deprived of this faculty, since it has always been considered the happiest indication of future genius. As for memory, which is, if not the same, certainly almost the same as imagination, it is vital that it should also be zealously cultivated in boys who have no other outstanding faculty of the mind. We should in no way blunt talents for those arts in which imagination, memory, or both, play a big part, e.g., painting, poetry, oratory or jurisprudence, nor should the critical method, our common tool for all arts and sciences, be a stumbling block to anyone. The ancients avoided these disadvantages, since almost all of them held geometry to be the [appropriate] logic of boys. For, taking as their model doctors, who follow where nature leads, they taught boys a science which could not be properly understood without an acute ability to form images, so that gradually and gently, and without any violation of nature, they became accustomed to reason according to the ability of their years.[6]

Next, [we must note that] the critical method alone is honoured today. Topics has not merely been superseded, but it has suffered complete neglect.[7] This is again inappropriate. For just as the invention of argu-

---

of the epistemological superiority of the true over the probable led, in the hands of the Cartesians of the later seventeenth century, to the requirement that education should begin with a study of logic, understood in, of course, the Cartesian sense of the discovery of first truths.

[6] Many of the sentiments expressed in this passage remained fundamental to Vico's thought (see, for example, N.S.[3] 211–15). By the time of the new science, however, they had been expanded into a substantial theory about the nature of historical development, as stated in N.S.[3] 216–19. See above, pp. 18–19.

[7] Topics was that part of Rhetoric which had to do with the invention of arguments which marshal probabilities in support of conclusions (see p. 3 above). The development of this art had, however, resulted in a series of categories, the commonplaces, for classifying the kinds of evidence relevant to the conclusion under discussion. Vico saw the appeal to these categories as a way of bringing out that inventiveness of the mind which he considered essential at a certain stage in education. The Cartesians, on the other hand, denied their utility, since they were irrelevant to the establishment of the truths with which they were concerned.

ments is prior by nature to the critical assessment of their truth, so the teaching of topics should precede that of the critical method. But men have now abandoned this skill and consider it useless. Provided that one is a critic, they say, it is enough that one be taught something for one to discover its truth.[8] Moreover they perceive the attendant probabilities by the same rule of truth, without the employment of topics. But can anyone be certain that he has perceived everything? This is the reason for that supreme and rare virtue of oratory, in virtue of which it is called 'complete', i.e., that it leaves nothing untouched, nothing unrevealed, nothing to be desired by the listeners. For nature is uncertain, and the chief, indeed the sole, end of the arts is to assure us that we have acted correctly. The critical method may be the art of true oratory, but topics is the art of eloquent oratory. Topics is the art of finding the connecting term (which the Scholastics call *medium* and the Latins *argumentum*). Since they already know all the *loci* of argument[9] in debate, its practitioners have the ability to see instantly what can be argued in a given case, as if they were skimming through the elements of writing. Whoever has not acquired this ability scarcely deserves the name of orator. In urgent matters, which brook neither delay nor postponement, such as arise most often in our courts in criminal cases, which are the true province of oratory, the orator's chief task is to bring immediate help to defendants who are allowed only a few hours for the statement of their case. But when any doubt is presented to them, proponents of the critical method reply: 'Allow me time to think about it . . .'

Yet Arnauld, in every way the most knowledgeable of men, despises topics, thinking it of no account. Who is to be believed – Arnauld, who repudiates it,[10] or Cicero, who professes and declares that topics gave him most assistance in the development of eloquence? Let others be the judges of this. We, however, lest in giving to the one we should detract from the other, assert that the critical method makes us truthful, while topics makes us eloquent . . .[11]

---

[8] The Cartesians did not, of course, make any appeal to authority. Rather, since truth was a property of certain propositions in themselves, once one had been taught how to understand those propositions one grasped them as true.

[9] The relevant lines of argument.

[10] The *Port-Royal Logic,* Part III, chapter 17, where topics is rejected on the grounds that it is not used in practice and that, were it to be used, it could not satisfy the requirements of proof.

[11] Vico maintained this requirement for the development of skill both in the construction and in the evaluation of arguments throughout his works. He did not, as is sometimes suggested, hold that one should be abandoned for the other, but considered that neither should be disregarded in favour of the other.

4   *The disadvantages of introducing geometrical methods into physics*

We must now consider whether the geometric method, which has been introduced into physics,[12] may not have the disadvantage that, since one cannot deny any part of it without attacking its very basis, one of the following procedures must be adopted: either one must unlearn this type of physics altogether and turn to observation of the universe; or if one wishes to adhere to it, it must be restructured in accordance with some new method; or any new phenomenon must be set out as a corollary of this type of physics. For this reason recent physicists are like people whose parents have left them property lacking nothing in the way of splendour and usefulness, so that all that remains for them to do is to rearrange [their] plentiful furniture, or adorn it with some slight embellishment to suit current taste.

Experts say that the physics they teach, based on the geometric method, is identical with nature itself, and that wherever one turns in contemplation of the universe, it is this physics which one observes. They hold, therefore, that we are indebted to those authors who have freed us from the great trouble of contemplating nature further, and who have bequeathed us such splendid and well-furnished buildings. When we cannot avoid the conclusion that nature is as they say it is, they must be offered the greatest thanks. But if nature should be constituted otherwise, if even one law of motion is false (and I need not say that it is not just one that has now been found false), they must pay continuous attention, lest in a dangerous manner they should take the laws of nature for granted and busy themselves with the roofs of their buildings whilst, to their peril, neglecting their foundations.

Let us not deceive ourselves or others, gentlemen: these methods, or sorites, which are the most accurate ways and means of demonstrating in geometry, but which represent a defective and fallacious kind of reasoning where the subject matter does not permit of demonstration, were rejected by the ancient philosophical schools when the Stoics used them as a weapon in debate. And the tradition that the ancients shunned Chrysippus' logic as extremely deceptive has endured to this very day.

Therefore, those things in physics which are alleged to be true by virtue

---

[12] The reference is to Descartes' analytical geometry and its extension into physics. For a good account of what this involved, see *The Metaphysical Foundations of Modern Science,* by E. A. Burtt (revised edition, New York, 1954), chapter 4.

of the geometric method are mere probabilities: geometry provides them with a method but not with a demonstration. We demonstrate geometrical things because we make them; if we could demonstrate physical things we would make them.[13] The true forms of things, by which their [physical] nature is shaped, exist in almighty God alone.[14] Let us therefore work at physics as philosophers, so that the soul be set in order. And in this let us do better than the ancients. For they pursued these studies in order to contend impiously with the gods for happiness, but we in order to humble our human pride. Let us indeed seek after the truth for which we are so eager, but where we do not find it, let this very desire for it lead us to almighty God, who alone is the way and the truth . . .[15]

7 The disadvantages which the end of our methods of study impart to eloquence and to our moral and civil doctrine

But the greatest disadvantage of our method of study is that, in expending so much effort on the natural sciences, we neglect ethics, and in particular that part which deals with the nature of the human mind, its passions, and how they are related to civil life and eloquence. We neglect also the parts of ethics which deal with the distinguishing features of virtues and vices, with good and evil arts, with the characteristics of customs as determined by age, sex, condition, fortune, race and state, and with correct behaviour, the most difficult of all arts. As a result, a noble and distinguished subject, i.e., the teaching of politics, lies virtually abandoned and neglected by us.

Since the sole aim of study today is truth, we investigate the nature of things, because this seems certain, but not the nature of men, because free will makes this extremely uncertain. This method of study gives rise to the following disadvantages for young men: that later they neither engage in public life with enough wisdom, nor know sufficiently well

---

[13] This is the first statement of the *verum–factum* principle, which was to be the foundation of Vico's later epistemology (see p. 5 above). For characteristic statements of the theory in its various stages of development, see p. 55 below, *N.S.*[1] 40, and *N.S.*[3] 331.

[14] For a fuller account of Vico's neoplatonism, see pp. 53–4 below.

[15] The thought in this obscure conclusion appears to be that where, as in the case of physics, we find that we are unable to produce demonstrations because we have not made all the elements involved, we realise that some other being, i.e., God, must have made them. The inference is, of course, invalid, but the two propositions involved in it are formally very similar to those put forward in *N.S.*[3] 331.

how to imbue oratory with morality and inflame it with feeling. With regard to prudence in public life, we should remember that the mistresses of human affairs are opportunity and choice, which are extremely uncertain, being governed for the most part by simulation and dissimulation, which are both extremely deceptive. Thus those whose only concern is for the truth find it difficult to attain the means, and even more the ends, of public life. More often than not they give up, frustrated in their own plans and deceived by those of others.[16] We assess what to do in life in accordance with those passing moments and details of things which we call 'circumstances'. But many of these may be extraneous and inappropriate, others often not conducive, and sometimes even opposed, to their own goal. Men's deeds cannot therefore be judged in accordance with an abstract and inflexible rule of moral conduct. Rather should they be assessed in accordance with that flexible rule of the Lesbians, which does not force bodies to conform to it, but bends itself to conform to them.

Knowledge differs from practical wisdom in this respect: those who excel in knowledge seek a single cause to explain many natural effects,[17] but those who excel in practical wisdom seek as many causes as possible for a single deed, in order to reach the truth by induction. This difference arises because knowledge is directed towards the highest truths, practical wisdom towards the lowest. The fool, the astute illiterate, the imprudent academic and the wise man each has his distinguishing characteristic and mark. In his daily life the fool pays heed neither to the highest nor to the lowest truths; the astute illiterate is aware of the lowest truths, but fails to see the higher ones; the imprudent academic derives the lowest truths from the highest; while the wise man derives the highest from the lowest. We must note also that universal truths are eternal, whereas particular truths become false with the passing of time. Eternal truths are therefore above nature, for nature contains nothing which is not unstable and changeable. In addition, the good coincides with the true, and has the same power, and the same properties.[18] Accordingly the fool, who is ignorant both of universal and of particular truths, pays a continuous penalty for his own thoughtlessness. As for the astute illiterate, who grasps particular truths, but cannot comprehend a general truth, the craft which stands him in good stead today will harm him tomorrow. The

---

[16] The reference, which is very vague, may be to Plato's lack of success in his direct political ventures.

[17] In the *Third New Science*, Vico maintains that economy of explanation is a requirement of knowledge (see *N.S.*³ 345).

[18] The reference is to the Scholastic doctrine of the transcendentals, according to which the one, the true (i.e., that which is true) and the good are identical and, hence, convertible. For an interpretation of Vico which stresses the importance of this doctrine, see Max Fisch's essay, 'Vico and Pragmatism' in *Giambattista Vico: An International Symposium*.

imprudent academic, who moves from a universal truth straight to particular truths, uses force to make his way through the maze of life. But the wise man, keeping his eyes on eternal truth amid the turnings and uncertainities of life, follows an indirect route because straight ones are impossible, and prepares plans which will be successful in the long term, as far as the nature of things allows.

According to what we have just said, therefore, it is wrong to transfer to the sphere of practical wisdom the method of judgement which is proper to knowledge. For the latter judges things according to correct reason, whereas men are for the most part fools, governed not by reason, but by caprice or fortune. Moreover, it judges things according to how they ought to be, whereas, in fact, they happen for the most part at random. Since those who transfer this method to the sphere of practical wisdom have not cultivated common sense and, content with a single truth, have never sought after probabilities, they fail altogether to consider what men feel in common about this one truth or whether the probabilities appear true to them. This mistake was held to be a great fault not just in the case of private citizens, but also in the case of princes and rulers, and has sometimes been the cause of great damage and evil. For example, while the French assemblies were in session, Henry III, King of France, condemmed to death Henry, Duke of Guise, an extremely popular prince, who was under a warrant of safe conduct. Although his reasons for doing this were in fact just, the case was referred to Rome because they did not seem so. There Cardinal Ludovico Mandruzzi, a man of great wisdom in public affairs, commented on the incident in these words: 'Princes should ensure not only that things be true and just, but that they seem to be so.' The truth of this wise saying was amply borne out by the evils which resulted from that incident in the kingdom of France. The Romans, who were particularly skilful in matters of practical wisdom, were quite right to be concerned with how things seemed. Both their judges and their senators used the phrase 'it seems' when giving their opinions.

Let us now sum up all these points. Because of their excellent knowledge of the most important affairs, philosophers were formerly called 'politicians', from the word for state affairs as a whole. Later, taking their name either from a small part of the city of Athens or from the place where they taught, they were called Peripatetics or Academics. As was appropriate, they made rational, natural and moral teaching parts of civil wisdom. Today these subjects have again reverted to the physicists.

At one time the three branches of philosophy were handed down by the Peripatetics and Academics in a manner suitable to eloquence. As a result, great orators with magnificent verbal ability emerged – Demosthenes from the Lyceum and Cicero from the Academy. Today it is taught

in such a way as to dry up all of the springs which make oratory con-
vincing, eloquent, pointed, ornate, well-ordered, full, expressive and
impassioned. The minds of listeners are moulded like:

> . . . virginum nostrarum, quas matres student
> demissis humeris esse, et vincto pectore, ut graciles sient:
> si qua est habitior paulo, pugilem esse aiunt, deducunt cibum
> tametsi bona est natura, reddunt curatura iunceas.

[. . . our maidens, whose mothers compel them to bend their shoulders and bind
their breasts, for the sake of being slim; if one of the girls is a little too plump
they call her a boxer and put her on a diet, and although nature be bountiful, they
reduce her, by their care, to the slenderness of a reed.]

Scholars may well contend here, in reply to the point about civil wisdom, that I would have courtiers, not philosophers, that I neglect truth
in favour of appearance, and that I reject virtue in favour of the semblance of virtue. This is far from being the case. Rather would I have
philosophers who are also courtiers, who care for truth, [but] of the kind
that is seen, and who follow an honest course, [but] of a kind which is
approved by all.

As for eloquence, the same men declare that their own method of
study, far from causing them inconvenience, provides the greatest of benefits. 'How much better it is', they claim, 'for true arguments to make
that impression on the mind which unites with reason and can never be
separated from it, than to sway the passions by those charms of oratory
and fires of eloquence which, when they are extinguished, allow the mind
to return to its natural inclinations.' But what is one to do if eloquence is
wholly concerned not with the mind, but with the passions? The mind
may indeed be held captive by these tenuous nets of truth, but the passions
cannot be swayed and overwelmed except by grosser devices. For eloquence is the power of persuading people to duty, and the persuasive
orator is he who produces in his listener the degree of passion that he
desires. Wise men arouse this passion in themselves by the will, which is
a most compliant attendant of the mind. Thus it is enough that one teach
them a duty for them to perform it. The mass of the common people,
however, is carried away and swayed by appetite, and appetite is both
tumultuous and turbulent. And since it is a blemish of the soul, acquired
by contact with the body, and conforming to the nature of the body, it is
affected only through bodies. Consequently the soul should be drawn to
love by means of bodily images; for once it loves it is easily taught to
believe; and when it believes and loves it should be inflamed so that it
wills things by means of its normal intemperance. Unless the orator

achieves these three things, his work of persuasion will have been fruitless.

Two things alone can convert to good use the perturbations of the
soul, those evils of inner man which spring from appetite, as from a single
source: philosophy, which regulates them in wise men, so that virtues
may emerge; and eloquence, which fires them in the common people so
that they perform the duties of virtue.

On the ancient wisdom of the Italians taken from the origins of the Latin language *

Book I
Metaphysics

Introduction

Reason for writing – The relation of the learned languages of nations to their philosophers – The origins of the learned Latin tongue to be derived from the Ionians and Etruscans – The wisest Italic school – The excellence of the Etruscans in metaphysics – Their precedence over the Greeks in geometry – This work is modelled on Plato's *Cratylus*. It is contrary to [the doctrines of] Varro, Scaliger, Sanchez and Schoppe

When I was studying the origins of the Latin language, I observed that the origins of a great number of words were so scholarly that they seem to have arisen not from common popular usage, but from some inner learning. And clearly there is no reason why a language should not be rich in philosophical terms if philosophy is much cultivated by the race in question. Indeed, I recall that when Aristotelian philosophy and Galenic medicine flourished, illiterate men were frequently heard using the phrases 'abhorrence of a vacuum', 'the repulsions and attractions of nature', 'the four humours', 'qualities', and many others of a similar kind. But now that the new physics and medicine have prevailed, one hears the common man everywhere talk of the 'circulation' and 'coagulation of the blood', of 'useful and harmful ferments', and of the 'pressure of air', etc. Prior to the Emperor Hadrian, the words 'being', 'essence', 'substance', and 'accident' did not exist in Latin, because Aristotle's *Metaphysics* was unknown, [but] after that era scholars made the work widely known, and the words became common currency. Since I had noted, then, that the Latin language was full of relatively learned phrases, yet history records that until the time of Pyrrhus the ancient Romans had no pursuits other than agriculture and war, I surmised that the phrases had been taken over from some other learned race, and that they were being used without knowledge of their meaning.

I find that there are two learned races from whom they could have received these words – the Ionians and the Etruscans. There is no need for me to expatiate on the learning of the Ionians, since amongst them

---

* Published in 1710 (see pp. 4–9 above). The work was dedicated to Vico's friend, the philosopher and mathematician, Paolo Mattia Doria, who is the 'Paulus' occasionally addressed in the text.

the Italic school of philosophy flourished and was at its most learned and brilliant. The fact that the Etruscans were a very erudite race is proved, however, by the pre-eminent learning revealed in their sublime religious rites, for civil theology has improved wherever natural theology is cultivated, and religions are more worthy of veneration where more elevated ideas about the supreme Deity exist. Consequently our Christian religious ceremonies are the purest of all, for our beliefs about God are the holiest of all. [To revert, however,] the greater simplicity of Etruscan architecture, as compared with the rest, also provides a strong argument that they preceded the Greeks in geometry. In addition, on the one hand, etymological evidence shows that a considerable portion of the language was imported to the Latins from the Ionians, while, on the other, it is well known that the Romans derived their religious cults, together with their sacred phrases and pontifical words, from the Etruscans. I conclude with certainty, therefore, that the learned origins of Latin words stemmed from both these races and for that reason I intend to discover the ancient wisdom of the Italians from the origins of the Latin language itself – a task hitherto unattempted, as far as I know, but one worthy perhaps to be included among the *desiderata* of Francis Bacon.

This is the way, indeed, in which Plato tried to pursue the ancient wisdom of the Greeks in his *Cratylus*. It is, accordingly, far from my intention to follow the path trodden by Varro in his *On origins,* by Julius Scaliger in his *On the sources of the Latin language,* by Francesco Sanchez in his *Minerva* and by Karl Schoppe in his notes on that book. For they tried to discover the causes, and understand the system, of the language from the philosophy which they themselves had learnt and were practising, whereas we, who adhere to no particular school, will strive to investigate the wisdom of the ancient Italians from the very origins of the words.

1

I On *verum* and *factum*

In Latin *verum* and *factum* are the same – The meaning of *intelligere* – The meaning of *cogitare* – The meaning of *ratio* – Man is described as *rationis particeps* – The true is what is made – Why the first truth is in God – Why it is infinite – Why it is complete – What knowing is – Thought is proper to man, understanding to God – Divine truth is a solid representation of things, human truth is a two-dimensional representation of them – Science is cognition of the mode[1] by which a thing is made – Why the true and what is made were the same for the ancient philosophers of Italy – In our religion a distinction must be drawn – Why divine wisdom is called *Verbum*

In Latin, *verum* [the true] and *factum* [what is made] are interchangeable or, in the language of the Schools, convertible terms, and the same holds for *intelligere* [to understand], *perfecte legere* [to read completely] and *aperte cognoscere* [to know clearly]. Moreover, the word *cogitare* [to think] was used where we, in the vernacular, use *pensare* [to think] and *andar raccogliendo* [to collect]. Furthermore, in Latin, *ratio* was used to mean both a collection of the elements of arithmetic [a calculation] and the property peculiar to man by which he differs from and surpasses animals. Man was also commonly described as an animate being, *rationis participem* [partaking in *ratio*], rather than as having complete mastery over it. Moreover, as words are symbols of ideas, ideas are symbols and tokens of things. Hence, as reading is the action of one who collects the elements of writing from which words are formed, understanding is collecting all the elements of a thing, whereby the most complete idea possible is expressed.

One can thus infer that the ancient philosophers of Italy held the following beliefs about the true: that the true is what is made; that the first truth is therefore in God, because God is the first Maker; that the first truth is infinite, because God is the Maker of all things; and that it is complete, because it makes manifest to God since He contains them, the elements of things, extrinsic and intrinsic alike. Furthermore, to know is to arrange these elements. Thought is therefore proper to the human mind, but understanding proper to the divine mind. For God surveys all the elements of things, extrinsic and intrinsic, because He both contains and arranges them, whereas the human mind, because it is finite and external to everything other than itself, collects only the outermost elements of things, rather than all of them. Consequently, while it can, indeed, think about things, it cannot understand them. It therefore participates in reason, but lacks mastery of it.

Let me illustrate my point by a simile: divine truth is a solid representation of things, like something moulded; human truth is a line drawing or two-dimensional representation, like a picture. And just as divine truth is what God orders and produces as He comes to know it, so human truth is what man arranges and makes as he knows it. In this way

[1] Throughout this work Vico uses the terms 'mode' 'form' and 'genus' interchangeably. See, for example, p. 52, where knowledge is said to be 'cognition of the genus or mode by which a thing is made', and p. 58, where 'to know is to grasp the genus or form by which a thing is made'.

knowledge is cognition of the genus or mode by which a thing is made, and by means of which, as the mind comes to know the mode, because it arranges the elements, it makes the thing. Divine truth is solid because God grasps all things; human truth is two-dimensional because man grasps the externals of things.

So that what I have just been saying may the more readily be reconciled with our [own] religious beliefs, we must realise that the ancient philosophers of Italy thought that the true was convertible with what is made, because they thought that the world was eternal. Accordingly, pagan philosophers worshipped a god such that, contrary to the dictates of our theology, he was occupied always with things external to himself. In our religious beliefs, therefore, in which we acknowledge that the world was created from nothing in time, the following distinction must be drawn: that created truth is convertible with what is made while uncreated truth is convertible with what is begotten. Thus, with truly divine elegance, the scriptures have called God's wisdom, which contains within itself the ideas of all things and accordingly the elements of all ideas, *Verbum* [the Word]. For in the Word the true is identical with the understanding of all elements, and this understanding constructs this universe of things and could, if it wished, establish innumerable worlds. And from the things which God, in His divine omnipotence, knows, there arises the most complete and real Word which, since it has been known by the Father from eternity, has also been begotten by Him from eternity.

II On the origin and truth of the branches of knowledge

Why revealed theology is the most certain knowledge of all – Human knowledge is a kind of dissection of nature – The objects of knowledge are one thing in God, another in man – God is being; created things partake of being – That is truly one which cannot be multiplied – The infinite is beyond body, and is not contained in any place – Things which are theories in man are works in God – Man's will is free, God's will is inexorable – In Latin *dividere* and *minuere* have the same meaning – The *via resolutiva*: empty, [when it proceeds] by syllogisms; conjectural [when it proceeds] by numbers; tentative [when it proceeds] by [the chemical methods of] heating and dissolving – Abstraction results from a defect of the human mind – Abstraction is the mother of human knowledge – Man fashions for himself a world of shapes and numbers – Mathematics is operational knowledge – God defines things in accordance with the true – Man defines names – *Quaestio definitionis* and *nominis* are identical in Latin – In human knowledge the same thing occurs as in chemistry – Knowledge is most useful to the human race when it is most certain – That knowledge resembles divine knowledge in which the true and what is made are convertible – The criterion of the true is to have made it – Why knowledge is less certain the more it is concerned with matter – Physical theories are proven when there is something similar which we can operate – When human truth is convertible with the good

Given these opinions of the ancient philosophers of Italy about the true, and the distinction between what is begotten and what is made which obtains in our religion, we maintain first that, since the true is in the one God completely, we must acknowledge absolutely that which He has revealed to us. Nor, since we are absolutely unable to understand it, should we try to discover the genus or mode by which it is true. From this we can return to the origin of the branches of human knowledge and, finally, can obtain a criterion for recognising the true. God knows all things because He contains within Himself the elements from which He synthesises them, whereas man strives to know them by analysis. Thus human knowledge is a kind of dissection of the works of nature.

To give a well-known example, human knowledge has dissected man into body and mind, and mind into intellect and will. Moreover, from body it has cut out or, as they say, abstracted, shape and movement; and from these, as from everything else, it has produced [the concepts of] being and unity. Hence metaphysics is concerned with being, arithmetic with the unit and its multiplication, geometry with shape and its measurement, mechanics with peripheral movement and physics with internal movement, medicine with the body, logic with reason, and ethics with the will.

The same considerations apply to this dissection of things as to routine dissections of the human body. The more able doctors betray considerable doubt as to the position, structure and function of its parts and as to whether, for example, upon death, the position and structure of the living body may not have altered, as a result of the solidification of fluids, the cessation of movement and the dissection itself. Consequently the function of the parts can no longer be explored.

For the things which we are discussing – being, unity, shape, movement, body, intellect and will – are one thing in God, in whom they are a whole, and another in man, in whom they are divided. In God they live, in man they die. And since God is all things *eminenter* [eminently], as the Christian theologians say, and the perpetual generation and corruption of beings do not in any way change Him, since they neither increase nor diminish Him, finite and created beings are dispositions of infinite and eternal being. Thus Plato means the Supreme Deity when he talks of absolute *ens* [being]. But what need have we of Plato's testimony, when God Himself defines Himself to us as 'what I am' and 'what is', as though, relative to Him, individual things have no being? Our ascetics, or Christian metaphysicians, put it this way: we are as nothing before

God, however great we may be, or for whatever reason we are great. And since God alone is one because He is infinite (for there cannot be a plurality of infinites), relative to Him created unity dies. So does body, for the infinite has no dimensions. So, too, movement, which is defined by place, for body dies and place is filled with body. So, too, human reason, because, since God contains within Himself what He understands and since all things are present to Him, what are mere theories in us are works in God. Finally, our will is pliable, whereas God's will is inexorable, since He has no end open to Him other than Himself and since He is the best.

We can see traces of what we have been discussing in [certain] Latin words: for the one word *minuere* means both diminution and division, as though the things we divide lose their original composition and are diminished, changed and marred. May not this be the reason why the so-called *via resolutiva* [the method of resolution] is found to be empty when it utilises the classes and syllogisms of the Aristotelians, to be conjectural when it utilises numbers, as in algebra, and to be tentative when it utilises the processes of heating and dissolving, as in chemistry?

When, therefore, man sets out to investigate the nature of things, he eventually realises both that it is impossible to achieve his goal, because he does not contain within himself the elements by virtue of which composite things exist, and that this is a consequence of limitations of his own mind, since everything exists outside himself. Turning this defect of his mind to useful ends, he then invents for himself two things by abstraction, as they call it: the point, which can be drawn, and the unit, which can be multiplied. But both are fictions: for if a point is drawn it ceases to be a point, and if a unit is multiplied it is no longer one. Moreover, man has taken it as his right to proceed from these to infinity, so that he can draw lines without end, and multiply the unit indefinitely. In this way he fashions for himself a world of shapes and numbers,[2] such as can be contained entirely within himself, and by the extension, shortening and connection of lines, and the addition, subtraction and calculation of numbers, he produces an infinite number of works, because the truths he perceives within himself are infinite.

For operations are needed not only in problems, but in theorems as well, where contemplation alone is commonly thought to suffice. For when the mind collects the elements of that truth which is under consideration, it cannot but produce truths which it knows. Hence the physicist cannot define things from the true, i.e., assign to everything its proper nature and make it from the true, for that is permissible to God, but

---

[2] Reading *numerorum* for *numerum*.

forbidden to man. He therefore defines the names themselves and, like God, without underlying matter and as though from nothing, creates things, as it were – a point, a line, a surface. Thus, by the name *punctum* [point] he understands that which is without parts; by *linea* [line] the projection of the point, i.e., length, devoid of breadth and depth; and by *superficies* [surface] the union of two different lines at the one point, or the combination of breadth and length without depth. In this way, because he is denied possession of the elements of things from which the existence of things themselves certainly arises, he fashions for himself those elements of words by which ideas are incontrovertibly excited.[3] The wise authors of the Latin language saw this clearly enough, for we know that the Romans used the expressions *quaestionem nominis* [investigation of the name] and *quaestionem definitionis* [investigation of the definition] interchangeably, and that they took themselves to be investigating a definition when they investigated that which was occasioned by a given word in the common mind of man.

From all this it is evident that the same thing happened in human knowledge as in chemistry. For while the latter was directed towards something quite useless, it exceeded the end it had set itself and produced pharmacology, a working art of great use to the human race. Similarly, while human curiosity was searching for truths denied it by nature, it produced two sciences of great use to human society, arithmetic and geometry, from which it evolved mechanics, the parent of all the arts necessary to mankind. Human knowledge arises, therefore, from a defect of our mind, i.e., from its extremely limited character, as a result of which, being external to everything and not containing what it strives to know, it does not produce the truths which are its aim. The most certain things are those which, redressing the defects of their origin, resemble divine knowledge in their operation, inasmuch as in them the true is convertible with what is made.

From what has been said so far, it is possible to conclude with certainty that the criterion and rule of the true is to have made it. Accordingly, our clear and distinct idea of the mind cannot be a criterion of the mind itself, still less of other truths. For while the mind perceives itself it does not make itself, and because it does not make itself it does not know the genus or mode by which it perceives itself. And since human knowledge arises from abstraction, knowledge is less certain according to whether some branches of it are more concerned than others with bodily matter. Thus, mechanics is less certain than geometry and arithmetic, because it examines movement, though with the help of machines. Physics is less

---

[3] *Cf. N.S.* [3] 349, where the constructive and fictive nature of mathematics is still maintained.

certain than mechanics, for where mechanics is concerned with the external movement of surfaces, physics investigates the internal movement of centres. Ethics is less certain than physics, for physics is concerned with the internal movements of bodies, which derive from nature, which is certain, whereas ethics investigates the movements of minds, which are deep-seated, and derive, for the most part, from desire, which is infinite. Accordingly, in physics we prove those theories to which we may effect something similar, while ideas of natural things are considered clearest and are most widely received where, in their support, we can set up experiments in which we create something similar to nature.

To conclude in a word, the true converts with the good if what is perceived as true derives its being also from the mind by which it is perceived. Thus human knowledge imitates divine knowledge in which, when God perceives the truth, He begets it internally from eternity, and makes it externally in time. Just as for God the criterion of the true is, in the act of creating, to have communicated goodness to his thoughts – 'and God saw that it was good' – so among men the criterion is to have made the truths which we perceive. But in order that these matters may be put on a firmer footing, they must be defended against the dogmatists and the sceptics.

III On the first truth meditated by René Descartes

Metaphysics establishes the proper subject for each of the other branches of knowledge – The boundary between dogmatists and sceptics – Descartes' 'deceitful demon' is the same as the divinely inspired dream of the Stoics – Also Mercury's imitation of Sosia in Plautus' *Amphitryo* – Consciousness is different from knowledge – What knowledge is – What consciousness is – The hidden causes of thought – The view of our religion – Our metaphysicians liken the human mind to a spider – Whether knowledge of being arises from consciousness of thought – What knowledge is according to the sceptics

The dogmatists of our age hold that prior to metaphysics all truths are doubtful, not merely those which are concerned with practical living, e.g., moral and mechanical truths, but also physical and hence mathematical truths. For they teach that there is one metaphysic, which gives us undoubted truth, from which, as from a fountain, flow secondary truths in other branches of knowledge. Since none of the other branches of knowledge prove the being of things, or that mind is one thing and body another, they cannot provide any certainty concerning the subjects with which they deal. Consequently the dogmatists think that metaphysics establishes the proper foundation for each of the other branches of knowledge. Hence their distinguished thinker[4] bids anyone who wishes to be initiated into its sacred rites to free himself not only from the persuasions or prejudices, as they say, which from infancy have been acquired through those deceptive messengers, the senses, but also from all truths which have been learned from other branches of knowledge. The acolyte should devote himself to listening to metaphysicians with a mind which, if not like a clean slate, since it is not in our nature to forget, is at least like an unopened book, which he may later open in a better light. Thus the boundary which divides the dogmatists from the sceptics will be the first truth which this metaphysics discloses to us. What that truth is, this most distinguished philosopher explains as follows.

Man can entertain doubt about whether he feels or is alive or is extended or even about whether he exists. To show this Descartes calls upon the help of a demon who can deceive us, just as in Cicero's *The Academics* the Stoic has recourse to a device to prove the same thing, and makes use of a dream inspired by the gods. But it is impossible for anyone not to be conscious that he is thinking, and from this consciousness not to deduce with certainty that he exists. According to Descartes the first truth is therefore 'I think, therefore I am.' And, indeed, by adopting the shape of Plautus' Sosia, Mercury led him to doubt his own existence in just the same way as Descartes' deceitful demon or the Stoic's divinely inspired dream. Contemplating his double, Sosia acquiesced in this first truth:

> Certe, edepol, quom illum contemplo, et formam cognosco meam,
> quemadmodum ego saepe in speculum inspexi, nimis similis est mei.
> Itidem habet petasum ac vestitum: tam consimile'st atque ego,
> sura, pes, statura, tonsus, oculi, nasum, dens, labra,
> malae, mentum, barba, collum; totus, quid verbis opus'st?
> Si tergum cicatricosum, nihil hoc simili est similius.
> Sed quom cogito, equidem certo sum ac semper fui.

[Indeed, when I look at him and recognise my shape, exactly as I have often seen it in the mirror, he resembles me overmuch. He is wearing the same hat and clothes; entirely alike are the calves of his legs, his feet, his stature, the style of his hair, his eyes, nose, teeth, lips, cheeks, chin, beard, neck – in short, everything. If his back is covered in scars, that absolutely completes the resemblance. But, since I think, upon my word, I am and have always been.][5]

But the sceptic does not doubt that he thinks. On the contrary he maintains with such tenacity that what he seems to see is certain that he defends it with ridicule and calumny. Nor does he doubt his being.

[4] Descartes.   [5] *Amphitryo.*

Rather does he look to his well-being by a suspension of assent, lest to the difficulties of the actual world he should add those of belief. But, he claims, the certainty that he thinks is neither knowledge (*scientia*), nor a rare and fully considered truth, the discovery of which requires such a lengthy meditation by the greatest of philosophers; rather is it [merely] the everyday consciousness and perception which belongs to any ignorant fellow such as Sosia. For to know is to grasp the genus or form by which a thing is made, whereas consciousness is of those things whose genus or form we cannot demonstrate.[6] Thus, in everyday life consciousness is taken as testimony for things of which we lack any clear sign or proof. So, although the sceptic may be conscious that he thinks, he is ignorant of the causes of thought, or of the way in which thought is made. Indeed, all the more does he now profess his own ignorance, since in our religion we profess a completely incorporeal human soul.

This [belief in an incorporeal soul] is the source of those thorns and prickles among which the keenest metaphysicians of our time stumble and by which they are stung, when they enquire how the human mind acts on the body and the body on the mind, since bodies cannot touch or be touched except by other bodies. Prompted by these difficulties they have recourse to a hidden law of God as to a [hidden] mechanism. They believe that nerves excite the mind when they are activated by external objects, and that the mind incites the nerves when it wants to act. Thus, they imagine that the human mind lies dormant in the pineal gland, like a spider at the centre of its web. Whenever there is any movement of a strand of the web, the spider feels it. But when, without any movements of its web, the spider senses the approach of a storm, it [itself] sets the strands of its web trembling. The metaphysicians invoke this hidden law because they lack knowledge of the genus by which thought is made. And for this reason the sceptic will remain steadfast in denying knowledge of thought.

The dogmatist will reply, however, that the sceptic acquires knowledge of being from consciousness of thought, since the latter supplies incontrovertible certainty of being. For nobody can be absolutely certain that he exists unless he deduce his existence from something of which there can be no doubt. Thus the reason the sceptic is not certain that he exists is that he does not deduce this from something quite incontrovertible. In answer to these arguments the sceptic will deny that knowledge of being is acquired from consciousness of thought, maintaining that to know is to be acquainted with the causes from which something arises. But I who

---

[6] The distinction between knowledge and consciousness is maintained in the rest of Vico's writings, *cf. N.S.*[3] 137–40.

think am mind and body, and if thought were the cause of my being, it would be the cause of body. However, there are bodies which do not think. Thus I think, rather, because I consist of body and mind. Body and mind united are therefore the cause of thought, for were I solely body I would not think, but were I solely mind I would understand. Thinking is not, indeed, the cause of my being a mind, but a sign of it, and a sign is not a cause. Thus the wise sceptic will not deny the certainty of signs, but he will deny that of causes.

IV Against the sceptics

God is the comprehension of all causes – Divine knowledge is the rule of human knowledge

Clearly the only way in which scepticism can be refuted is if the criterion of the true is to have made the thing itself. For the sceptics accept the appearances of things, but deny knowledge of their real natures. They admit effects, and accordingly concede that effects have their own causes, but they deny knowledge of the causes, because they are ignorant of the genera or forms by which each thing is made. But these admissions can be turned against them in the following manner.

This comprehension of causes, which contains all the genera or forms by which all effects are given – effects whose images the sceptics admit are presented to their consciousness but of whose true nature they profess themselves to be ignorant – this comprehension, because it extends to all [causes], including even the most remote, is the first [thing which is] true. For the same reason, since nothing is excluded, it is infinite. Similarly, it is prior to body, of which it is the cause, and accordingly it is spiritual. This is God and, indeed, the God whom we Christians profess, by whose norm of the true we must measure human truths.[7] Those truths are,

[7] I interpret this obscure argument in the following way. Insofar as the sceptic's case is that we do not know the explanation of what we experience, i.e., of the 'effects', he is committed to the existence of causes. But if we accept the *verum–factum* theory, it follows that wherever there are effects there must be a creative knower of those effects. Hence, for all those things which we know that we do not ourselves create, there must be another creator, viz., God.

If this interpretation is correct, the argument appears to be a development of that put forward at p. 41 and n. 15. As a general proof of God's existence it involves a *petitio principii*, since in assuming that the *verum–factum* principle applies to God, it simply assumes the point at issue. On the other hand, it might be used as an *ad hominem* argument against any sceptic who was prepared to accept both the *verum–factum* principle and that we know that there are effects, but who wanted to deny that we can know that there is a God. It is difficult to see how Vico could use it as such, however, in view of the fact that all the premises involved in such an argument would be *a priori*, and, as he argues at p. 65 below, he wants to put a general prohibition on all *a priori* proofs of God's existence.

indeed, human whose elements we fashion for ourselves, contain within ourselves and, by means of postulates, extend indefinitely: when we arrange these elements we make the truths which we come to know through this arranging; and because of all this, we grasp the genus or form by which we do the making.

2   *On genera or ideas*

Genus and *forma* mean the same in Latin – *Species* means both *individuum* and *simulacrum* – In what way genera are infinite – The metaphysical form resembles the form used by a modeller, the physical form resembles that of a seed – Physical forms are formed from metaphysical forms – The usefulness of forms – Why geometry, when pursued by means of forms, is most certain, both in its result and in its procedure – Why the same discipline, when pursued by means of particulars, is certain in its result but uncertain in its procedure – Why arts based on ideas achieve their aim with certainty – Why arts based on conjecture do not – The futility of Aristotelian genera – Why sciences are less useful the more generic they are – The advantages of an experimental physics – Lawyers are judged by their treatment not of general rules but of exceptions – The best orators are those who stick to the particulars of a case – Who are the most useful historians? – The best imitative artists are those who improve details – The origin of the Platonic ladders of ideas – Practical wisdom is not about those things which are contained in the genus – In what way genera are metaphysical matter – The outstanding difference between physical and metaphysical matter – The disadvantages of universals: in law, medicine and daily life – All mistakes from homonyms are to be put down to genera – Men naturally avoid homonyms – Whether genera lead philosophers into error more than the senses lead the vulgar into prejudice – The meaning of *certum* in Latin – *Verum* and *aequum* mean the same in Latin – Because man is neither nothing nor everything, he perceives neither nothing nor the infinite – Universals are a certain kind of archetype

In Latin, when they say *genus* they mean form; when they say *species* they mean two things – what the schools call *individuum* [the individual] and *simulacrum* or *apparenza* [appearance]. Philosophers of every persuasion believe that genera are infinite. It follows, therefore, that the ancient philosophers of Italy believed the genera to be forms which were infinite, not in extension but in perfection, and, because they were infinite, to exist in one God. On the other hand, they held that species, or particular things, were representations modelled on these forms. And, indeed, if the ancient philosophers of Italy believed that the true was identical with what is made, it follows that the genera of things were not the universals of the Schools, but were forms.

Here, however, I am referring to metaphysical forms, which are as different from physical forms as is the form used by a modeller from that of a seed. For the form which the modeller uses remains identical while it is being employed as a model, and is always more perfect than the thing formed from it. But the form of a seed changes and becomes more complete as the seed develops each day. Consequently, physical forms are formed from metaphysical forms. It should be easy, moreover, to determine that genera are infinite in perfection rather than in extension by a comparison of the relative usefulness of both. Geometry, which is taught by the synthetic method, i.e., by forms, is completely certain both in result and in procedure. For by proceeding from the smallest to the infinite by means of its own postulates, it shows how to synthesise the elements from which the truths which it demonstrates are formed. And it can do this because man contains within himself the elements which it employs. It follows from these same considerations, however, that the procedure of analysis is uncertain, although its results may be certain. For it starts [instead] from the infinite and descends to the smallest. And although it is possible to discover everything in the infinite, the method by which that discovery can be made is not given to us.[8]

Those arts which reveal the genera or modes by which things are made, e.g., painting, sculpture, modelling and architecture, proceed with greater certainty towards the goal they have set themselves than those which do not reveal them, i.e., the conjectural arts such as oratory, politics and medicine. The former arts reveal them because they are concerned with the prototypes which the human mind contains within itself, whereas the latter do not because man does not have within himself the form of the things which are conjectured. Now forms are individual, in the sense that any increase or decrease in the length, width or depth of a single line changes an appearance so as to render it unrecognisable. The result is that the more that sciences or arts rest upon Aristotelian rather than Platonic genera, the more they confuse the forms, and the more magnificent the sciences or arts become, the less useful they are. For this reason Aristotelian physics stands in bad repute today, because it is too universal. In contrast to this, by the use of heat and machinery – these being the instruments of modern physics, which produces things which

---

[8] Vico is arguing for the merits of synthetic as against analytic geometry. The argument, which is very obscure, appears to be that in synthetic geometry we know the theorems which we produce because we see how their formal properties are nothing but the consequences of properties of the elements from which they are produced. In analytic geometry, on the other hand, we have to have a starting point, but since there are an infinite number of possible starting points, corresponding to the infinite number of true and false theorems, and since we do not know, antecedently to the construction of the relevant theorems, which are true and which are false, analysis does not, of itself, provide us with knowledge of these starting points.

resemble particular works of nature – the human race has been enriched with numerous new truths.[9] In the same way, in jurisprudence a man is not highly admired [merely] if a good memory enables him to remember positive law or the general or supreme rules. Rather does one esteem the man who probes with keen judgement into the most detailed, factual circumstances of a case, which merit justice, or the exceptions which remove it from universal law. The best orators are not those who range about in the common places,[10] but those who *haerent in propriis* [stick to particulars], to adopt Cicero's verdict and terminology. [Similarly], useful historians are not those who offer imprecise accounts of facts and generic causes, but those who search for the ultimate circumstances of facts, and discover particular causes. And in the imitative arts, e.g., painting, sculpture, modelling and poetry, excellence belongs to those who embellish an archetype from the realm of common nature not with common but with new and wonderful details, or who decorate an archetype which has been represented by another artist with their own superior details and make it their own. [But] because originals are always superior to copies, some archetypes can be conceived which are better than others. As a result, the Platonists construct ladders of ideas, through the more perfect of which they ascend by degrees, as it were, to Almighty God, who contains within Himself the best of all things.

Practical wisdom, on the other hand, is itself nothing other than an insight into what is suitable, whereby the wise man speaks and acts in each new situation in such a way as to apply the most appropriate considerations. Thus the wise man, from his long and wide experience of what is noble and useful, cultivates a sharpened mind. In this process he acquires clear and accurate conceptions of new things, which alone prepare him to speak and act spontaneously but with dignity in everything, and he bravely holds his mind in readiness for any unexpected terrors.

Universal genera do not, however, provide for what is new, wonderful and unexpected. The Schools are right enough when they say that genera are metaphysical matter, provided that this is taken to mean that genera render the mind formless, so that it is better able to take on the forms of individual things. This is clearly true; for it is easier for a man to perceive facts and matters as they ought to be perceived if he has genera or simple ideas about things, than if he has furnished his mind with particular forms, and regards other particular forms from them, since it is difficult to adjust one formed thing to another formed thing. It is dangerous, therefore, to judge and to deliberate on the basis of examples, because circumstances never, or very rarely, agree in every respect. Indeed, this is the difference between physical and metaphysical matter. No matter

[9] *Cf.* p. 36 above.   [10] See p. 38, n. 7, above.

what the particular form physical matter produces, it is always the best, because the way in which it is produced was the only one [possible]. But, since all particular forms are imperfect, metaphysical matter contains [the form which is] the best by its very genus or idea.

Having seen the advantages of forms, let us now describe the disadvantages of universals. To speak in universal words is the practice of children and of barbarians. In jurisprudence mistakes occur most often through working according to positive law itself or under the authority of rules. In medicine those who proceed by the inflexible application of theories are more concerned that their systems should remain intact than that the sick should be healed. And in daily life how often do people who attempt to live by means of theories go astray? The Greek term for such people has passed over into our vernacular and we call them 'theorists'.

In philosophy all errors derive from homonyms, commonly called ambiguities, which are nothing other than words common to several things, for without genera ambiguities would not exist, since men are naturally averse to homonyms. This is shown by the case of the boy who is ordered to summon Titius. Should there be two people with that name, and he has not been told which one to summon, he will immediately ask, since nature directs itself to the particular, 'Which Titius do you wish me to call?' Consequently I do not know whether genera lead philosophers into error more than the senses lead the vulgar into false beliefs and prejudice. For genera, as we have said, confuse forms or, in common parlance, make ideas confused, just as prejudices make them obscure. Indeed all sects in philosophy, medicine and jurisprudence, and all controversies and disputes in daily life, derive from genera, because genera are the source of the homonyms, or ambiguities, which are [usually] said to derive from error. Mistakes occur in physics because the names for matter and form are generic, in jurisprudence because the term 'justice' is used very widely, in medicine because the words 'healthy' and 'infected' are too general, and in daily life because the word 'useful' lacks precision.

The following traces, extant in the Latin language, indicate that the ancient philosophers of Italy thought in this way. *Certum* means two things: on the one hand, what is ascertained and beyond doubt, and on the other, what is particular as opposed to what is common, as if what is particular were certain, but what is common were doubtful.[11] Similarly *verum* and *aequum* were the same.[12] For *aequum* [what is right] refers to the ultimate circumstances of things, whereas *iustum* [what is in accor-

---

[11] Cf. *N.S.*³ 321–2. The development of the doctrine of the implicit ideality of the notions involved in common sense, by the time of the new science (see pp. 21–3 above), meant that in the *Third New Science* Vico no longer accepted the claim that the common was doubtful.

[12] Cf. *N.S.*³ 324.

dance with law] refers to the genus itself, as if whatever depended upon a genus were false, but the ultimate particulars of things were true. The genera are infinite in name only, for man is neither nothing, nor everything. Therefore he neither thinks about nothing, except through some negative, nor about infinity, except by the negation of the finite. The angles of a triangle are equal to two right angles. This is surely so. But it is not an infinite truth for me. Rather [is it true] because the form of a triangle, whose above-mentioned property I recognise, is impressed on my mind, and that form is for me the archetype of all other triangles. If people maintain that the genus is infinite, because numerous triangles can be fitted to that archetype of a triangle, I shall not dispute with them. For I am willing to concede the terminology, provided that they agree with me about the thing itself. Nevertheless, it is incorrect to call a ten-foot measuring rod infinite, on the ground that it is possible to measure every extended object by it.

3   *On causes*

In Latin *caussa* and *negotium* mean the same – Why *effectus* is the name given to what arises from a cause – To prove [something] by means of causes is to effect [it] – The effect is the true which is converted with what is made – The genera of causes – *Probare a caussis* is to gather together the elements of a thing – Arithmetic and geometry genuinely prove by causes – Physics cannot be proved by causes – Anything finite is born of infinite power – Wise Christians recognise God's infinite power in even the smallest thing – It is impious piety to desire to prove God's existence by means of causes – True metaphysics shares the clarity of light – The most appropriate simile

In Latin the words *caussa* [cause] and *negotium,* which means operation, are interchangeable, while what arises from the cause they call *effectus* [the effect]. This seems to agree with our claims about the true and what is made. For if the true is what is made, to prove [the true] by means of causes is the same as to effect [it]. Thus *caussa* and *negotium* will be the same, i.e., the operation, while the true and what is made will be the same, namely, the effect.

Matter and form are thought to be the chief causes in natural objects, as is the end in ethics and the author [creator] in metaphysics. Thus it is probable that the ancient philosophers of Italy thought that one proves by causes by setting matter, or the unformed elements of things, in order, and also by synthesising that which was formerly separate into one. This arrangement and synthesis of elements gives rise to the definite form of a thing, which bestows its particular nature on matter.

If all this is true, arithmetic and geometry genuinely demonstrate by causes, although it is not generally thought that they prove [things] in this way. And the reason why they demonstrate by causes is that the human mind contains [within itself] the elements of the true which it can set in order and arrange, and from the things set in order and arranged emerges the true which they demonstrate. Thus the demonstration is the same as the operation, and the true is the same as what is made. And for this very reason we cannot prove physics by causes, because the elements of natural things are outside us. For although they may be finite, to set them in order, arrange them and produce an effect from them is a task of infinite power. If we have regard to the first cause, it takes no less power to produce an ant than it took to create this whole universe, for the formation of an ant requires no less movement than does the creation of this world. This world was created from nothing and an ant is produced from underlying matter by virtue of the same movement.

Certainly in their devotional discussions our theologians, i.e., those who are pre-eminent both in their knowledge of the Supreme Deity and in their holiness, often arrive at knowledge of God through contemplation of a tiny flower, because they recognise infinite power in its creation. And that is what we said in our dissertation *On method in contemporary fields of study*: 'we demonstrate geometrical things because we make them; if we could demonstrate physical things we would make them'. Consequently, whoever tries to prove Infinite God *a priori* is to be censured for impious curiosity.[13] For this would be tantamount to making himself the God of God, and denying the God whom he seeks. The clarity of metaphysical truth is like that of light, which we recognise only by means of darkness. If, after looking long and hard at a latticed window through which light enters a building, one directs one's gaze to an object which is completely dark, one will seem to see not light, but illuminated lattices. Clear metaphysical truth is like this: it is confined by no boundary and distinguished by no form, because it is the infinite beginning of all forms. Physical things are dark, i.e., formed and finite, and in them we see the light of metaphysical truth.

6 *On mind*

Mens in Latin is the same as our *pensiero* – 'Mind is bestowed by the Gods' – Ideas are created by God in men's spirits – 'The mind of the spirit' – The Aristotelians' active intellect – The Stoics' ethereal sense – The Socratics' 'demon' –

[13] See p. 59, no. 7, above.

Clarification of Malebranche's teaching – God is the first author of all movement – The origin of evil – Man's free will – God's light shines in the very shadows of error – Why metaphysics is concerned with indubitable truth

The Latin word *mens* means the same as our *pensiero* [mind]. *Mens* was also said 'to be given to' or 'placed in' human beings 'by the gods'. It is fitting therefore that the authors of these phrases should have thought that ideas are created and awakened in men's spirits by God. They therefore talked of the *animi mens* [the mind of the spirit], ascribing to God unrestricted right and control over the movements of the spirit, so that *libido,* the faculty of desire, 'is for each his own God'. This God, which is peculiar to each, seems to be the Aristotelians' active intellect, the Stoics' ethereal sense and the Socratics' 'demon'. The most acute metaphysicians of the present age have argued long and skilfully on this subject.

But if the perceptive Malebranche maintains the truth of all this, I am surprised that he agrees with René Descartes' first truth: 'I think, therefore I am.' For it should follow from the fact that God creates ideas in me that 'something thinks in me, therefore something exists. But in my thinking I discern no idea of body, therefore what thinks in me is unadulterated mind, i.e., God.' Unless, of course, the human mind should be so constructed that it achieves knowledge of God from things which it is completely unable to doubt, but after it has come to know Him it recognises as false even those things which it once held to be beyond all possible doubt. But in this case all ideas of created things would, in general, be in some measure false, when compared with the idea of Almighty God, because they are about things which, compared to [the idea of] God, are seen to be unreal, whereas the idea of the one God would be true because He is truly one. Thus, had Malebranche wanted his teaching to be consistent, he should have taught that the human mind gains from God its knowledge not only of the body whose mind it is, but also of its own self, in such a way that it does not discern itself unless it also knows itself in God. For since the mind manifests itself in thinking, and God thinks in me, I know my own mind in God. This would render Malebranche's doctrines consistent.[14]

We receive within ourselves [the knowledge] that God is the first author of all movements, whether of bodies or spirits. But here [we are in danger from] quicksands and rocks. For how can God be the mover of

---

[14] It would do so, however, only if one were to accept something like the causal argument for God's existence which Descartes offered, for example, in *Meditation III,* with its strongly inbuilt *a priori* element, which Vico, despite his earlier dismissal of *a priori* arguments for God's existence (see p. 65, above), uses in his own proof for God's existence (see p. 67, below).

the human mind, when so many sins, abominations, falsehoods and vices persist? And how can God's true and absolute knowledge coexist with man's free will to act? We know with certainty that God is omnipotent, omniscient and perfect, and that His understanding is true, His will good, His understanding absolute and immediate, His will fixed and ineluctable. Indeed, as the scriptures teach, 'no one can approach the Father, unless the Father has drawn him to Himself'. But how does He draw him if he whom He draws is a willing agent? Here Augustine replies: 'He whom He draws is not merely a willing, but even a rejoicing agent, and He draws him through enjoyment.' What could be more consistent both with the immutability of the divine will and the freedom of our will?

As a result, God is never absent from our sight even when we sin, since we embrace the false under the appearance of the true and evils under the semblance of goods. We see the finite, and we feel ourselves to be finite, but this is because we have the concept of the infinite. We seem to see movement aroused by bodies, and communicated to us by bodies, but these very movements and communications declare and confirm that God, and God as mind, is the author of movement. We see wrong as right, many as one, different things as the same and movement as rest, but since right, one, the same and rest do not exist in nature, the fact that man is deceived in these things means that even when he is ignorant or deceived about finite things, he contemplates Almighty God in these very representations.

Thus metaphysics treats of indubitable truth, since it concerns a subject about which one reaches certainty, whether one doubts, errs, or is deceived.

7

I *On faculties*

The derivation of *facilitas* – *Animae facultates* appropriately defined in the schools – Faculties relate to what we make – External senses – *Olere* applies to things, *olfacere* to men – Imagination – Internal sense – True intellect – Arithmetic, geometry and mechanics lie within human faculties – Physics lies within a faculty of God – In God the faculty is true – So that all things are truly *pensieri di Dio*

The term *facultas* was pronounced *faculitas* from which later arose *facilitas,* a kind of easy or ready skill, as it were, in doing things. Thus facility is that whereby a power is translated into an act. The soul is a power, vision an act, and the sense of vision a faculty. The Schools, therefore, speak with propriety when they call sense, imagination, memory and intellect *animae facultates* [faculties of the soul] but they destroy this propriety when they judge that colours, tastes, sounds and touch are in objects. For if the senses are faculties, we make the colours of things by seeing, their tastes by tasting, their sounds by hearing, and cold and hot things by touching. On this matter the views of the ancient philosophers of Italy survive in the words *olere* [to smell of] and *olfacere* [to perceive by smelling], for *olere* is applied to things and *olfacere* to living beings, implying that living beings make smell by smelling.

Imagination is a true faculty, because in using it we create images of things. Internal sense is another such faculty, for in battle men feel pain [only] when, having withdrawn from it, they notice their wounds. Similarly, intellect is a true faculty since, when we understand something by the intellect, we make it true. Thus, arithmetic and geometry and their offspring, mechanics, lie within human faculties, since in them we demonstrate the true because we make it. Physics, on the other hand, lies within a faculty of Almighty God, in whom alone the faculty is true, because it is in the highest degree easy and ready, so that what is a faculty in man is purest act in God.

From these considerations it follows that just as, by the application of his mind, man produces the modes of things and their images, as well as human truth, so God, through understanding, generates divine truth and makes created truth. Thus, where in the vernacular we improperly call statues and paintings *pensieri degli autori* [the thoughts of their authors], it may properly be said of God that all things are *pensieri di Dio* [the thoughts of God].

II *On sense*

In Latin, everything produced by the mind is *sensus* – This was a pagan metaphysics – Christian metaphysics teaches the opposite

In Latin the word *sensus* [sense] applied not merely to the external senses, e.g., the sense of sight, and the internal sense, which was called *animi sensus* [the sense of the spirit], e.g., pain, pleasure and annoyance, but also to judgements, deliberations and wishes. Hence, *ita sentio* meant 'I judge so and so'; *stat sententia* meant 'it is certain'; *ex sententia evenit* meant 'it happened as I desired'; and in legal formulae we find the phrase, *ex animi tui sententia* [in accordance with your judgment]. Is it the case, then, that the ancient philosophers of Italy believed, like the Aristotelians, that the human mind perceives nothing except through the senses? Or did they believe, as did Epicurus' followers, that the human mind is nothing but sense? Or did they believe, as did the Platonists and Stoics, that reason is a kind of ethereal and very pure sense? The truth is that none of the pagan sects believed that the human mind was completely incorporeal. Consequently they thought that everything produced by the mind was sense, i.e., that whatever the mind does, or undergoes, is a contact of bodies. But our religion teaches that the mind is absolutely incorporeal, and our metaphysicians confirm that the mind is moved by God on the same occasion as our sense organs are affected by bodies.

III *On memory and imagination*

The meaning of *memoria* – The meaning of *reminiscentia* – *Phantasia* means the same as the Latin *memoria* – Man can imagine nothing not given in nature – Why the Muses were the daughters of Memory

In Latin, *memoria* [memory], that which stores within itself the perceptions of the senses, is called *reminiscentia* [reminiscence] when it discloses them. But it also meant the faculty by which we form images, which the Greeks called *phantasia* [imagination] and we call *immaginativa*. For where we commonly say *immaginare* [to imagine], in Latin they said *memorare* [to remember]. Was this because we can neither imagine something unless we have remembered it, nor remember anything unless we perceive it through the senses? Certainly, painters have never depicted any kind of plant nor any living thing which nature has not produced, for their hippogriffs and centaurs are truths of nature mingled with what is false. Nor have poets thought up any form of virtue not to be found in human affairs. Rather do they extol, to an unbelievable degree, something selected from public life, and fashion their heroes in that mould. Through their fables, therefore, the Greeks handed down their belief that the Muses, which are virtues depicted by the imagination, were the daughters of Memory.

IV *On ingenuity*[15]

The meaning of *ingenium* – The derivation of the words *acutum* and *obtusum* – *Ingenium* and *natura* mean the same – Ingenuity is man's proper nature – Only

---

[15] Vico uses the term *ingenium* for this capacity, which is sometimes translated as 'inventiveness', 'wit', or 'genius', although none of these terms is wholly appropriate. *Ingenium*, as Vico uses it, involves the capacity to invent, as in a work of art, to synthesise from prior elements, as in geometry, to perceive relevant similarities, as when constructing arguments or applying theories of one science to another area of research, and insight into such vague properties as suitability, fittingness and proportion. Since no English word captures all of this, I have used 'ingenuity' because of its etymological relationship

man sees the symmetry or proportions of things – God is the artificer of nature, man is the god of artifacts – Why the word *scitum* is used instead of *pulchrum* – Why geometry and arithmetic are the best established branches of knowledge – Why *ingegneri* are so called

Ingenium is the power of connecting separate and diverse elements. In Latin it is described as *acutum* [acute] or *obtusum* [obtuse], terms which belong to geometry, because when it is acute it penetrates [things] more quickly and links different elements more closely, analogous to the connection of two lines at a point with less than a right angle [between them], whereas when it is obtuse it approaches things more slowly and leaves different elements more remote from their foundation, analogous to the connection of two lines at a point with more than a right angle [between them]. Thus, when obtuse, ingenuity links different things more slowly; when acute, it does so more swiftly.

Moreover, *ingenium* and *natura* meant the same in Latin. Is this because human ingenuity is man's nature, since its function is to see the proportion of things, what is suitable, fitting, beautiful and base, a power denied to animals?[16] Or is it because just as nature produces physical things, so human ingenuity gives birth to mechanical things, and just as God is the artificer of nature, so man is the god of artifacts? For 'science' and *scitum* [what is suitable] certainly have the same derivation, and the Italians translate *scitum,* with no less elegance, as *ben inteso* [the well-understood] and *aggiustato* [the well-adjusted]. Or is it because human knowledge consists solely in making things fit together in beautiful proportion, which only those of ingenuity can do? Thus the best established branches of knowledge are geometry and arithmetic, which teach these things, and those who excel in their use are called *ingegneri* [engineers] in Italian.

V *On the faculty peculiar to knowledge*

The three operations of mind: perception, judgement and reasoning – Their regulation by the three arts of topics, criticism and method – Why the ancients had no particular art of method – Intentions should not be formulated according to

with the Latin *ingenium,* the Italian *ingenio,* which Vico also uses, and the English 'genius', which is also occasionally appropriate. It should however be treated as a technical term. For helpful discussions of the importance of the concept in Vico, see E. Grassi's 'Critical philosophy or topical philosophy?' in *Giambattista Vico: An International Symposium,* and his 'The primacy of common sense and imagination' in *Social Research,* 43 (3), autumn 1976. It should not be thought, however, that the weight which Vico lays upon the need for a theory of invention means that he did not also see the need for a theory of criticism (see below, pp. 72–3).

[16]*Cf.* p. 51 above.

the geometric method – Nor should public speaking be controlled by it – Cicero's order of speaking – Demosthenes' confusion – But the power of Demosthenes' eloquence lies in his confused order of speaking – Method is not a fourth operation of the mind, but an art of the third – The division of all ancient dialectic into topics and criticism – In the absence of topics Cartesian critical dialectic lacks certainty – In what way Aristotle's categories and topics are useful for discovery – Arts are the laws of literate states – Why the Greeks divided them into topics and criticism – Ingenuity is the faculty proper to knowledge – In man it reveals itself from boyhood – What common sense is – Resemblance is the mother of all discovery – Why *argumentum* is so called – Who the *arguti* are – What ingenuity is – The discovery proper to ingenuity, its method and result – Ancient dialectic, induction and the comparison of similarities – What a syllogism is – What a sorites is – The precise and the acute methods of argument – Why the geometric method is useful for discovery in the field of geometry – In fields other than geometry it is useful for the arrangement of what has been discovered – Not the geometric method but the proof should be imported into physics – When geometry sharpens ingenuity – Synthesis discovers truths, analysis makes them – Imagination is the eye of ingenuity, as judgement is the eye of the intellect

The foregoing considerations offer us an opportunity to enquire what particular faculty has been given to man in order that he might attain knowledge. For man perceives, judges and reasons, but his perception is often false, his judgement rash and his reasoning defective. The Greek philosophers believed that these faculties were given to man in order that he might achieve knowledge, and that each was regulated by its own art: the faculty of perception by topics, that of judgement by criticism, and that of reasoning by method. But they left us no precepts on method in their dialectic, for boys learnt it more than adequately in practice, when they studied geometry. In matters other than geometry the ancients thought that the ordering should be entrusted to practical judgement, which is regulated by no art, and that is why it is practical judgement. For only those skilled in the arts teach one to arrange one thing in first place, another in second, and another elsewhere, a method which forms craftsmen rather than men of practical judgement.

Indeed, were you to apply the geometric method to life, 'you would succeed only in trying to be a rational lunatic', steering in a straight line amid life's curves, as though caprice, rashness, chance and fortune held no sway in human affairs. Moreover, to construct a public speech according to the geometric method would be to deny it effectiveness, and to demonstrate only what is quite obvious. It would be as though one were to present an audience with nothing not already chewed over, treating them like children: in a word, to act like a pedagogue rather than an orator when making a speech.

It is quite beyond me to understand why those who recommend the geometric method so highly in public speaking offer Demosthenes as the sole model for eloquence. For, please God, [they find] Cicero confused, irregular and disordered, yet this is the very Cicero hitherto admired by scholars for his fine order and for the great pains which he took to arrange things correctly. For his first point is unfolded in a certain way, and succeeded by the second in such a way that what he says next seems not so much to be spoken by him as to issue and flow from the subject itself. But if we turn to Demosthenes, what else does he offer but [a series of] hyperbata, as Dionysius Longinus, that most judicious of all rhetoricians, rightly noted? To which I would add that in the confused order of his discourse its whole enthymematic force is tautened like a catapult. For he offers first an exposition of his theme, so as to tell his listeners what he is talking about; he digresses next to some subject which appears to have nothing to do with the matter in hand, in order that his audience should to some extent become hostile and perplexed; and he turns finally to the analogy between the subject now under discussion and that first introduced, in order that the thunderbolts of his eloquence may strike the more heavily the more unexpected they are.

It should certainly not be thought that the method used by the whole of antiquity was rendered defective by its failure to recognise what is now called the fourth operation of the mind. For it is not by a fourth operation of the mind, but by an art belonging to the third, that lines of reasoning are put in order. The whole of ancient dialectic is divided into the art of discovery and the art of judgement, but the Academicians concentrated entirely on the art of discovery and the Stoics entirely on that of judgement. Both were wrong, for neither discovery without judgement, nor judgement without discovery, can be certain. For how can a clear and distinct idea in our mind be a criterion of the true unless we perceive everything in, or related to, the thing itself? And how can anyone be certain that he has perceived everything, unless he has pursued every question pertaining to the matter under consideration? First, [he should raise] the question whether it exists, lest he should be talking about nothing. Then the question what it is, lest his efforts be expended upon a name. Then how great it is, whether in extent, weight or number. Then what it is like, under which heading come colour, taste, softness, hardness and the other tactile sensations. Then he must ask when it was created, how long it lasts, and into what it changes as it decays. And proceeding thus through the remaining categories, he must connect it to all the things which are in any way related to it, whether they be its causes or effects, or those effects it has when combined with objects which are similar, dissimilar or contrary, or when combined with those which are bigger, smaller or equal.

Aristotle's categories and topics are therefore quite useless should anyone wish to discover anything new in them. For should anyone try to do so, he would, like some latter-day Lully or Kircher, resemble a man who knows the letters of the alphabet but cannot put them together so as to be able to read the great book of nature. But if the categories and topics are taken to be the indices and alphabets, as it were, of questions to be asked about the matter in hand, so that we have it in a clear perspective, nothing can be more fruitful for discovery. As a result, the best of observers can arise from the same source as the most fluent of orators.

On the other hand, anyone who is confident of perceiving something in a clear and distinct idea of the mind, is easily deceived, and he will often think that he knows a thing distinctly when he still has only a confused consciousness of it, for he has not learned all the elements which belong to the object and which distinguish it from everything else. However, if he ranges through all the general heads of topics with a critical torch, he will then be certain that he has a clear and distinct knowledge of the matter, because he has considered it in the light of all relevant questions. And by means of such thorough consideration, topics themselves will become critical.

For the arts are the laws of literate states, since they are the observations of nature, which all scholars accept, transformed into rules for the disciplines. Thus anyone who makes something by means of an art is certain that he has the agreement of all scholars. [But] should he not employ an art he will easily be deceived, since he will be relying on his own nature alone.[17]

Indeed, wise Paulus, you value these very things I am discussing. For when you instruct your prince, you do not teach him to approach the art of criticism directly, but inculcate him with many examples over a long period, before he is taught the art of forming judgements about them. Why else is this done but in order that his ingenuity may begin to flower before it is cultivated by the art of judgement? The divorce of discovery from judgement, which began with the Greeks, occurred only because they failed to attend to the faculty proper to knowing, the faculty of ingenuity, whereby man is capable of observing things and of imitating

---

[17] In denying the Cartesian conception of knowledge as an essentially private property, Vico is implicitly asserting its public character. This is much more fully developed in the new science, where, although not wanting to deny that individuals can have knowledge (see, for example, N.S.³ 349), Vico denies that it is essentially private, by his insistence that it is only available to an individual when a society has reached a certain state of development, i.e., the fully human age, in which concepts proper to the nature of things are available (see, for example, N.S.³ 326–7, 924, with special reference to the nature of law). The knowledge which an individual can thus possess is available to him, therefore, only insofar as public knowledge is well founded. It is not, therefore, essentially private, as Descartes implied.

them. Indeed, we perceive that in children, whose nature is purer and less corrupted by persuasion or prejudice, the first faculty to manifest itself is that of seeing likenesses. Hence they call all men 'fathers' and all women 'mothers' and they imitate them:

> aedificare casas, plostello adiungere mures,
> ludere par impar, equitare in harundine longa

[by building huts, yoking mice to a small cart, playing even or odd, riding on a long stick].

Moreover, similarity of customs gives rise to common sense in nations, while those who have written about inventors maintain that all the arts, and everything useful by which the human race has been enriched, have been discovered either by good fortune or by some resemblance revealed by the animal world or thought up by men's own efforts.

The traces of their language show that the Italic sect was acquainted with everything we have hitherto mentioned. For that relation which the Schools call the *medius terminus* [the middle term], they called the *argumen* or *argumentum*. Moreover, from the word *argumen* came the word *argutum* or sharpened; and the term *arguti* [penetrating] was applied to those who spot some common resemblance by which quite separate and different things are related, and, going beyond that which is close at hand, seek in remote places for adequate grounds for the things with which they are concerned. This type of ingenuity is also called *acumen*. Thus ingenuity is necessary for discovery, since the effort and work of making new discoveries in general belongs to ingenuity alone.

This being so, it is a likely conjecture that the ancient philosophers of Italy approved neither the syllogism nor the sorites, but used induction based upon resemblance in their arguments. A consideration of the times in which they lived suggests that this is so, for the most ancient dialectic of all was induction and the comparison of resemblances, which Socrates was the last to employ. Afterwards Aristotle argued by use of the syllogism, and Zeno by that of the sorites. But in using the syllogism one does not so much connect elements which are different, as draw forth from the depths of a genus itself a particular which the genus contains; whilst in using a sorites one connects cause with cause, each one with the nearest. In adopting either of these, [therefore], one does not so much join two lines at an acute angle as extend a single line, and in so doing one seems precise rather than acute. In using the sorites, however, one is more precise than in using the syllogism, in so far as genera are of wider extension than the particular causes of each thing.

Descartes' geometric method corresponds to the Stoics' sorites. It is useful in geometry, because geometry is suitable to it, since terms can here be defined and possibilities postulated. But when it is transferred from the field of three dimensions and numbers to that of physics, it is useful less for the discovery of new facts than for the orderly arrangement of those already discovered . . .

Our final conclusion is that it is not the geometric method that should be imported into physics, but the proof itself. The greatest geometers, e.g., Pythagoras and Plato among the ancients and Galileo in more recent times, have contemplated the principles of physics in the light of those of mathematics. Thus it is right to explain the particular effects of nature by particular experiments which are the particular works of geometry. In our native Italy the great Galileo and other outstanding physicists, who explained numerous great phenomena of nature by this method before the geometric method was introduced into physics, paid attention to this. The English also are careful to attend to it alone, and, for that reason, they are forbidden to teach physics publicly by the geometric method. This is how physics can be furthered. Accordingly, in my treatise *On method in contemporary fields of study,* I intimated that the difficulties of physics could be avoided by the cultivation of ingenuity, perhaps to the surprise of those who employ the geometric method. For in its concern with facility the method hinders ingenuity and in its attention to matters of truth it destroys curiosity. Geometry sharpens ingenuity not when it is taught by method, but only when it is put to use, by means of ingenuity, in many other diverse and separate fields. Accordingly, I wanted it to be taught by the synthetic, and not the analytic, method, so that we might demonstrate by synthesis, i.e., we should make truths rather than discover them. For discovery is fortuitous, whereas making is a matter of work. For this reason I wanted it to be taught not by numbers or genera but by forms, so that if ingenuity were less improved in the art of learning, imagination would nevertheless be strengthened, for imagination is the eye of ingenuity, just as judgement is the eye of the intellect. Indeed, it is possible for the Cartesians, whom you, Paulus, so aptly describe as 'Cartesians in letter, but not in spirit', to see that, although they deny what we say in words, they acknowledge it in fact. Apart from the truth which they seek from consciousness, 'I think, therefore I am', the truths which are the norm to which they refer everything else are borrowed from no other source than arithmetic and geometry, i.e., from the true which we make. And their contention that 'the true should be in the fashion of [the propositions] "three plus four equals seven", and "the sum of two angles is greater than the third" ' is tantamount to looking at physics from the viewpoint of geometry. And whoever postulates this is committed to the following: that physical things will be true only for whoever has made them, just as geometrical things are true for men because they make them.

8

I *On the supreme creator*

Numen, fatum, casus, fortuna

The four Latin words *numen* [divine will], *fatum* [fate], *casus* [outcome] and *fortuna* [fortune] agree with what we have maintained about the true and what is made: that the true consists in the collecting together of its elements – of all the elements in the case of God, but of the outermost elements alone in the case of man; that the word of the mind is made properly in God but improperly in man; and that the faculties have to do with the things which we make and which we make with skill and facility.

II *On the divine will*

Divine goodness makes things by willing them – Why poets and painters are called *divini* – What nature is

The name for the will of the gods was *numen,* as though Almighty God expresses His will by what He has made, with the speed and facility of the blinking of an eye. Thus Dionysius Longinus admires Moses for the worthy and sublime expression he gave to divine omnipotence in the phrase: 'he spoke and it was so'. The Latins, however, appear to have expressed both concepts by one word. For divine goodness creates the things which it desires by willing them, doing so with such facility that they seem to exist of their own accord. Accordingly, since Plutarch relates that the Greeks praised Homer's poetry and Nicomachus' paintings on the grounds that they appeared to have come into being of their own accord, and not to have been created by any art, I believe that it is because of this faculty for creating things that poets were called 'divine'. Consequently this divine facility for making is a natural property. In man it is that rare and splendid ability, difficult to find and worthy of the highest praise, which we call *naturalezza* [spontaneity]. Cicero puts it like this: 'a genus which has flowed forth of its own accord, and is in a certain way natural'.

III *On fate and outcome*

Dictum, certum, fatum – Dictum, factum, casus – Why fate is inexorable

In Latin, *dictum* [what is said] is the same as *certum* [what is certain]. For us what is certain is the same as *determinatum* [what is determinate].[18] Moreover, *fatum* [fate] and *dictum* are the same, while *factum* [what is made] and *verum* [the true] are convertible with *verbum* [the word]. In Latin when they wanted to indicate that a given thing had been effected quickly they said *dictum factum* [no sooner said than done]. In addition they used the same word, *casus,* for both the outcome of things and the case-endings of words. Accordingly, the Italian sages who first thought up these words called the eternal order of causes *fatum,* and the outcome of that eternal order of causes *casum.* Thus created things are God's words, the outcome of things are the case-endings of the words which He utters, and fate is the same as what is made. They therefore thought that fate was inexorable since what is made cannot be unmade.

IV *On fortune*

The derivation of *fortuna – Fortus –* What fortune is – The world is nature's republic – In what sense fortune is queen of everything

The word *fortuna* used to be applied to either good or bad fortune, yet it was derived from the word *fortus* which meant good. Later, therefore, to distinguish favourable and adverse fortune from each other, men used the expression *fortis fortuna* [good fortune]. But fortune is God, who works from certain reasons beyond all our expectation. Did the ancient philosophy of Italy therefore hold that anything whatsoever that God makes is good, and that everything true or everything made is likewise good, whereas we, because our iniquity leads us to consider only ourselves and not the universe, think that whatever is opposed to us is evil, although [the truth is that] such things are good in so far as they contribute to what is common to the whole world? The world, then, is nature's republic. For Almighty God, as ruler, has regard for the common good, while the individual person, as private citizen, is concerned with his own particular affairs. Thus private evil may be public good. Just as the welfare of the people in a state which has been founded by men is the supreme law, so, in this universe established by God, the queen of every-

---

[18]*Cf. N.S.*[3] 321, where *certum* is similarly characterised. For the much greater importance of the certain in that work, however, see 137–41, 163, 325. Since one of the fundamental presuppositions of the new science is that what men make in history is the certain, the problem of knowledge has become that of showing how the certain and the true can be synthesised.

thing is fortune, or rather God's will, by which, concerned for the welfare of the universe, He holds sway over all private goods or particular natures. And just as private welfare yields to public, so the particular good of an individual takes second place to the preservation of the universe.[19] In this way nature's disadvantages are good.

[19] Although stated only in the most general of terms, the view put forward here clearly foreshadows the theory of providence and of the heterogeneity of ends which is much more fully developed in The *New Science*. See above, pp. 15–16 and *N.S.*[1] 45–7; *N.S.*[3] 132–3, 341–2, 1108.

[*The First New Science*]

*The principles of a new
science of the nature of
nations leading to the
discovery of the principles of
a new system of the natural
law of the gentes**

Book I
The necessity to seek a new science and the difficulty of the means whereby it can be discovered

1 The reasons for meditating this work

8. The natural law of nations certainly arose with their common customs; nor has the world ever contained a nation of atheists, since all nations originated in some religion.[1] The roots of all religions, moreover, lie in the desire for eternal life, which is natural to all men. This common desire of human nature arises from a common sense, hidden in the depths of the human mind, that the human soul is immortal.[2] The more this sense is secret in origin, the more clearly does it have the following effect: that, in the last throes of death, we hope for a power superior to nature by which death can be overcome, a power which is to be found only in a

---

*Published in 1725. For its relation to the *Second New Science,* see above, pp. 12–13. The suggestion that the new science will lead to the discovery of the principles of the natural law of the gentes shows how closely Vico's desire to produce a science of the nature of nations was connected to a desire to produce a more plausible account of the nature of law than that which the natural law theorists had provided (see above, pp. 19–21). In the *Second* and *Third New Science,* a philosophy of law, although still important enough to be mentioned as one of the principal aspects of the science (cf. *N.S.*[3] 394–8) had ceased to be so central as to merit mention in the title of the works.

[1] The reference here is to Bayle, who had maintained the possibility of a society of atheists. On the view Vico puts forward, this is impossible, since, given the nature of (fallen) man, a society is impossible without relationships which depend upon the constraints put upon human behaviour by a belief in some god. Bayle is mentioned by name only once in the *First New Science,* at 476, where, it is claimed, '[the opinion of] Bayle, that nations can subsist without religion, is refuted by fact'. The same claim is repeated in the *Third New Science,* cf. *N.S.*[3] 334, 1110. Nevertheless, it is an important task of the new science to refute Bayle on this point, since Vico accepted Bayle's conclusion that if there were no beliefs common to different societies – and religious belief was generally accepted as the most viable candidate – historical knowledge of other societies would be impossible. For further discussion of this, see my *Vico: A Study of the 'New Science',* pp. 27–9.

[2] The suggestion that we have an innate desire for immortality is part of Vico's general view that we have some implicit innate ideas which develop and become explicit upon the appropriate occasions in history (cf. *N.S.*[1] 49). Vico seems to deny this in a passage in the *Third New Science,* not here translated (*N.S.*[3] 363), when he quotes with approval Aristotle's claim that there is nothing in the intellect which was not previously in the senses, but he shows that this is not so when he goes on to add, 'the mind uses the intellect when, from something which it senses, it gathers something which does not fall under the senses . . .'. It should be noted that Vico frequently uses the word 'sense' for beliefs and judgements. Cf. pp. 68–9 above; *N.S.*[1] 46; *N.S.*[3] 141–2. They do not, however, have to be consciously held, hence they are also described as an instinct (see *N.S.*[1] 27).

God who is not identical with, but superior to, nature, i.e., an infinite and eternal mind. [But] when men stray from this God, they become curious about the future.

9. Such curiosity, which is forbidden by nature, since it is proper only to a God who is an infinite and eternal mind,[3] occasioned the fall of the two founders of mankind. As a result God based the true religion of the Jews upon worship of His infinite and eternal providence and, as a punishment, because its first authors desired knowledge of the future, condemned the whole human race to work, pain and death. Hence all the false religions arose through idolatry, i.e., the worship of imaginary gods, falsely thought of as beings of supernatural power who supported men in the extremity of their ills. Idolatry shared its birth with that of divination – a vain science of the future, employing certain sensible intimations, believed to be sent to man by the gods.[4] Yet this vain science, in which the vulgar wisdom of all gentile nations must have originated, conceals two great principles of truth: that a divine providence must exist, which governs human beings; and that men must possess free will through which, if they so desire and should they make use of it, they can escape that [fate] which, without such provision, would otherwise be theirs. It follows from this second truth that men can choose whether or not to live in justice. Further proof of this common sense is [afforded by] the common desire which men naturally have for laws, when they are not influenced against them by feelings of self-interest.

10. This, and no other, is certainly the human nature which, at all times and in all places, has based its practices upon the following three common senses of mankind: first, that providence must exist; second, that men should beget certain children[5] by certain women,[6] with whom they must share at least the rudiments of a civil religion, in order that children be brought up by their fathers and mothers in a spiritual unity in conformity with the laws and religions amongst which they were born; third, that the dead should be buried.[7] Hence not only has the world never contained a nation of atheists, but neither has it contained a nation in which it has not been the duty of women to adopt the public religion of their husbands. And if there has been no nation which lived in total nakedness, still less has there been one in which bestial and shameless sex

---

[3] *Cf.* p. 54 above.   [4] *Cf. N.S.*[3] 177–88, 374–9.
[5] Children with certainty of descent, i.e., in a context which allows for the establishment of lineage.
[6] Rather, for example, than by women held in common, as Plato had suggested (see *N.S.*[1] 13).
[7] *Cf. N.S.*[3] 130, 332–7.

and casual matings have been practised in front of others. Nor, finally, has there been any nation, however barbaric, in which the unburied corpses of its members have been left to rot above ground, for such would be a nefarious state, i.e., a state sinning against the common nature of men. To avoid falling into such a state, all nations preserve their native religions by [the observation of] inviolate ceremonies and, with refined rites and solemnities, celebrate marriage and burial above all other human practices. This is the vulgar wisdom of mankind, which originated in religions and laws and reached its completion and perfection in the sciences, disciplines and arts.[8]

2 Meditation of a new science

11. All the sciences, disciplines and arts have been directed towards the perfection and regulation of man's faculties. Yet none of them has so far contained a meditation upon certain origins of the humanity of nations from which, beyond doubt, all the sciences, disciplines and arts have arisen; nor, through these origins, established a certain ἀκμή [acme], or state of perfection, which would enable them to judge the stages through which the humanity of nations must pass and the limits within which, like everything mortal, it must terminate. From this they might have gained a scientific grasp of the customs by which the humanity of a nation, as it develops, attains this perfect state and those by which, as thence it wanes, it is reduced to its former condition. This state of perfection would consist only in the following: first, that the nations would be established upon certain maxims, both demonstrated by immutable reasons and practised in common customs, by means of which the recondite wisdom of the philosophers would aid and direct the vulgar wisdom of nations, so that agreement would exist between the most distinguished members of the academies and all wise statesmen; second, that knowledge of civil things divine and human or of religion and of law – which constitutes a theology and a mandatory morality acquired through custom – should be supported by knowledge of natural things divine and human – which constitutes a theology and a rational morality acquired through reason – so that to live without such maxims would be the real [state of] error or estray not merely of men but of beasts.

[8]*Cf. N.S.*[1] 46–7; *N.S.*[3] 141–6.

3   The defects of a science of this sort if based upon the maxims of the Epicureans and Stoics and the practices advocated by Plato

12. But the Epicureans and the Stoics, following paths which were not merely different, but quite opposed to each other, have unhappily set themselves at a distance from, and abandoned, vulgar wisdom. In the case of the Epicureans this is a consequence of the following doctrines: that chance exercises a blind control over everything human; that the human soul dies with the body; that, since only the existence of the body is allowed, the bodily senses must regulate the passions by means of pleasure; and that an ever-changing utility is the rule of justice. The Stoics, on the other hand, decree a fatal necessity which drags everything, even the human will, in its wake, while conceding a temporal life to the soul after death. But, although they preach an eternal and immutable justice, and claim that honesty should be the norm of human actions, they reduce human nature to nothing, by wanting it to be insensible to the passions. Moreover, they drive men to despair of the possibilities of living a virtuous life by their maxim, which is harder even than iron, that all sin is equal, so that it is as much a sin to beat a slave slightly in excess of his deserts as to kill one's father. Hence, the Epicureans, with their ever-changing utility, undermine the first and most important foundation of this science, the immutability of the natural law of the gentes; and the Stoics, with their iron severity, deny natural law the benign interpretation[9] in which compensation and punishment are determined in accordance with the three celebrated categories of crime. So far do these sects of philosophers concur with Roman jurisprudence that the one destroys the most important maxim, and the other renounces the most important practice, involved in its principles!

13. The divine Plato alone contemplated a recondite wisdom for the regulation of man in accordance with maxims which he learned from the vulgar wisdom of religion and the law. For he is wholly committed to [the ideas of] providence and the immortality of the human soul, he locates virtue in the moderation of the passions, and he teaches that it is

---

[9] *Cf. N.S.*[3] 327, 940.

one's duty as a philosopher to live in conformity with the law even when, for some reason, the latter has become excessive in its severity. Here his example is that which his master, Socrates, gave with his own life: for, when he was declared guilty, Socrates preferred to submit to his punishment and drink the hemlock, despite his innocence. Yet Plato lost sight of providence when he perpetrated a common error of the human mind, that of judging the scarcely known natures of others according to oneself. For he elevated the barbaric and rough origins of gentile humanity to that perfect state of exalted, divine and recondite knowledge which he himself possessed, when, on the contrary, he ought to have descended or sunk from his 'ideas' back to those origins. Hence, through this scholarly blunder,[10] which is repeated to this day, he found it necessary to prove that the first authors of gentile humanity were the possessors of recondite wisdom in the highest degree, whereas, in fact, as races of impious and uncivilised men, such as those of Ham and Japhet must once have been, they could only have been beasts consumed by wonder and ferocity. As a result of this erudite error, instead of meditating upon that eternal state, and those laws of an eternal justice, in accordance with which providence ordered the world of nations and governs it through the common needs of mankind, he meditated upon an ideal state and a purely ideal justice by which the nations would be led not only not to be ruled and guided by the common sense of the whole of mankind, but, alas, even to neglect and do violence to it. Such for example, is that [rule of] justice, enjoined in his *Republic,* that women should be [possessed in] common.

4 This Science is meditated upon the basis of the Roman jurists' idea of the natural law of the gentes

14. In the light of all this, what is here required is precisely the science of the natural law of the gentes which the Romans inherited from their ancestors, defining it as 'a law, ordered by divine providence together with the dictates of human necessities or utilities, which is observed equally among all nations'.

---

[10]Cf. *N.S.*[1] 20. This is the error of conceptual anachronism which lies behind Vico's criticism of the natural law theorists and which he later called 'the vanity of scholars' (*cf. N.S.*[3] 127–8, 329).

5   The defects of a science of this sort if based upon the systems of Grotius, Selden and Pufendorf

15. Our own times have given birth to three celebrated men, Hugo Grotius, John Selden and Samuel Pufendorf, headed by Grotius, each of whom has meditated on a system of the natural law of nations of his own. All the rest who have subsequently written about the natural law of the gentes have simply added, as it were, a few adornments to Grotius' system. But all three princes of this doctrine fell into error: for they did not think to base the natural law of the gentes upon divine providence and were not, therefore, beyond doing harm to the Christian people, whereas the Roman jurists, in the midst of their paganism, recognised that great principle.

16. Grotius' altogether excessive zeal for truth led him to commit an error which is quite unpardonable, both in connection with this kind of subject and with metaphysics. For he claimed that his system would hold good and stand firm even were all knowledge of God set aside, whereas men have never come together as a nation without some worship of a divinity.[11] For just as it is impossible to have certain knowledge of physical things, or of the movements of bodies, without the guidance of the abstract truths of mathematics, so it is impossible to have knowledge of moral things without the guidance of the abstract truths of metaphysics and, therefore, without a demonstration of God. In addition, as a Socinian, holding that early man was good rather than wicked, Grotius supposed that he was solitary, weak, and lacking in all his needs, and that he entered society when the tribulations of bestial solitude made him aware [of all this]. Hence the first men were solitary simpletons and their later entry into social life was dictated to them by utility. This, in truth, is [nothing but] Epicurus' hypothesis.

17. Next came Selden, whose quite excessive love for Jewish learning, in which he was highly versed, led him to locate the origins of his system in the few precepts which God gave to the sons of Noah. But, omitting here the difficulties which Pufendorf raises in this connection, of these sons only Shem continued in the true religion of the God of Adam. And from Shem came not a law in common with that of the gentes founded by Ham and Japhet, but a law so peculiar [to his own nation] that it was

[11] See p. 81, n. 1, above.

the basis of the celebrated separation of the Jews from the Gentiles. This separation endured until the Jews' later times, in which Tacitus refers to them as 'unsociable men', and, since their destruction by the Romans, they have remained exceptional in living diffused amongst [other] nations without forming part of them.

18. Finally there is Pufendorf, who, however much he may mean to serve providence and to take pains on her behalf, employs a hypothesis quite indistinguishable from those of Epicurus and Hobbes, which are identical in this matter, in which man is cast into this world bereft of divine care and assistance. Hence, Pufendorf's destitutes, no less than Grotius' simpletons, must be classed with those violent, dissolute men on the basis of whom Thomas Hobbes counsels his citizen to disregard justice and to use force in the pursuit of utility. Thus fit are the hypotheses of Grotius and Pufendorf to establish an immutable natural law!

19. Hence, since none of the three considered providence when establishing his principles, they failed to discover the true, hitherto concealed, origins of any of the parts which go to make up the entire economy of the natural law of the gentes – the origins, that is, of religions, languages, customs, [positive] laws, societies, governments, kinds of ownership, occupations, orders, authorities, judiciaries, penalties, wars, peace, surrender, slavery and alliances. And because they failed to discover the origins of these things, they all committed the following three serious mistakes.

20. First, since they appeal to the rational maxims of moral philosophers, theologians and, to some extent, jurists, to establish their natural law, and since natural law is, in truth, eternal in its idea, they believe that it has never been practised together with the customs of nations. They failed to notice – and here their reasoning is inferior to that of the Roman jurists, who appreciated the fundamental point that natural law is ordered by providence – that this law arose with the customs of nations. Nor did they notice that it is an eternal law among all nations in [the sense] that, originating with the birth of religion, and passing through certain 'sects of times',[12] as the jurists themselves often call them, it proceeds through the same stages in all nations and attains a certain limit of clarity whence, in order that it should attain its perfection or [proper] state, it remains only that some sect of philosophers should complete and

---

[12] These are the three stages through which, in accordance with the three types of human nature which develop historically in each nation, each fundamental sphere of human activity develops and acquires certain characteristics, founded upon certain doctrines or beliefs. It could have been translated as 'temporal conceptual schemes' but I have retained Vico's technical term in order not to lose the force of his suggestion that the characteristic doctrines of certain sects of philosophers are to be found in the common sense beliefs of the times in which they live.

consolidate it by rational maxims derived from the idea of an eternal justice.[13] Hence, in all those matters in which Grotius criticised the Roman jurists over many particular examples or cases of this law – and he did this in disproportionate number and in a manner unbecoming to a philosopher, whose concern should rather be with the principles of things – his blows fell on empty air. For the Roman jurists had in mind the natural law of nations practised by the sect of their times, but Grotius the natural law reasoned by the sect of moral philosophers.

21. Second, the authorities by which each of the three supports his system – in respect of which Grotius, more learned than the others, seems to have an inexhaustible fund – supply neither science nor necessity for the origin of the historical era which, because of its barbarity, is heavily cloaked in fable in all nations. This applies even more to the fabulous era and most of all to the obscure era. For they failed to meditate how, upon the occasion of certain human necessities or utilities, together with certain modes,[14] and with everything [arising] in its proper time, divine providence ordered this universal state of mankind in accordance with the idea of its eternal order. Nor [did they consider] how providence dictated a law which is universal and eternal in [the sense] that it is uniform in all nations wherever, notwithstanding their differences in time, the same occasion of the same human needs occurs, rendering the origins and progress of the nations invariable. Consequently they lacked knowledge of those things which it was necessary to establish if they were to use the authorities they had collected with certain science

---

[13] This is one example of the doctrine of the implicit ideality of certain fundamental notions (see above, pp. 21–3). Cf. *N.S.*[1] 48–54; *N.S.*[3] 218–19, 319–29.

[14] Vico uses the Italian word *guisa* here and throughout all versions of the new science. Although it can mean 'way', 'manner' or 'guise', I have treated it as a technical term and translated it in most cases as 'mode' for the following reasons. In *On the ancient wisdom of the Italians* Vico uses the Latin *modus, forma* and *genus* interchangeably. In his *Reply to the second objection* (1711), which is in Italian but not here translated, he not only describes the forms which exist in God's mind as *guise* or *forme* but also identifies them with *generi* and *modificazioni*. This suggests that a *guisa* is not a way or manner but a form, mode or, in the sense in which Vico approves, genus. In the *First* and *Third New Science* (*N.S.*[1] 40; *N.S.*[3] 147–8) the identification of *guisa* and *modificazione* is maintained, but it is there made clear that what is referred to is a modification of the human mind – a form or mode of mind, that is, in virtue of which human institutions and practices take on a certain character (*N.S.*[1] 27; *N.S.*[3] 374). Additional support is given to this interpretation by the fact that Malebranche, whose works were known to Vico, used the terms *modification* and *mode* interchangeably and regarded the senses, the imagination and the understanding as three different modes of thinking substance.

Vico sometimes also uses *guisa* to refer to the way or manner in which something is done. In most such places, however, it would seem that the way derives from the prevalent mode of mind – the different forms of religious practice, for example, derive from different prevalent modes of understanding. Thus the way or mode *in* which something is done depends upon the mode or modification *under* which it is done.

(*scienza*). For example, they were ignorant of the [kind of] natural law of the gentes which obtained in the period when the Law of the Twelve Tables was given to the Romans, yet it is necessary to know this if we are to have scientific knowledge of that [part of their] law which the Romans shared in common with other nations and that which was peculiar to them. Nor did they know what [kind of] natural law of the gentes obtained in the times of Romulus, yet this is necessary for scientific knowledge of the natural law Romulus might have introduced into his new city from the other nations of Latium and what he might have ordered that was peculiar to it. For they would [then] have noted that the customs which were observed in Rome in the time between Romulus and the decemvirs, which were codified in the Twelve Tables, were identical with the law of the gentes which obtained in that sect of time in Latium; and that [the things which were] peculiar to Roman law were the formulae and interpretation appropriate to that law. Hence it was called the civil law, or the law appropriate to the citizens of Rome, not so much for its excellence, as has hitherto been believed, as for its propriety, as we have shown in a work already published.

22. Their third and last common error is to have dealt with considerably less than half of the natural law of the gentes, for they omit all discussion of that part which has to do with the individual preservation of nations and include only that part which is concerned with the preservation of the whole of mankind in common. Whereas the natural law which was introduced separately into [different] cities must have been that which so trained and conditioned peoples that, when they later came into contact with one another, they should find themselves in possession of a common sense through which, without previous knowledge of one another, they [had] made and accepted laws in conformity with the human nature which belonged to them all.[15] And by means of such a common sense they must have recognised them as laws dictated by providence and hence their reverence for them must have rested upon the true belief that they were dictated by God.

6 Reasons why this Science has hitherto been lacking among philosophers and philologists

23. The unfortunate reason for this lack is that we have not hitherto possessed a science which constituted both a history and philosophy of

[15]Cf. *N.S.*[3] 141–6.

humanity together. For the philosophers have meditated upon a human nature already civilised by the religions and laws in which, and only in which, philosophers originated, and not upon the human nature which gave rise to the religions and laws in which philosophers originated;[16] while, because of that fate common to everything ancient, that when anything has receded too far from us we lose sight of it, the philologists have handed down vulgar traditions which are so disfigured, mutilated and displaced that, unless their proper appearance is restored to them, their fragments are pieced together and they are returned to their [proper] places, no serious thinker can believe them to have been created thus. This applies as much to the [philosophical] allegories which have been superimposed on them as to the vulgar beliefs with which, much later, they have come down to us through the hands of rough, wholly illiterate, peoples.

24. In the light of this reflection, we may safely assert that the fables, in which lie the beginnings of all gentile history, could not have been the spontaneous inventions of the theological poets who, from Plato to our own times – that is, those of the celebrated Bacon of Verulam (*The Wisdom of The Ancients*) – have been thought of as particular individuals, steeped in recondite wisdom, skilled in poetry, and first authors of gentile humanity. For 'vulgar theology' is nothing other than the beliefs the vulgar entertain about the divine. Hence, since the theological poets were men who created deities with their imagination, if each gentile nation had its own gods, and as all nations originated in some religion, then all were founded by the theological poets, that is, by the vulgar who founded their nations with false religions. These principles of gentile theology are both more appropriate than the ideas aroused by the words which descended from it, and more suitable to the early days of nations whose origins were quite barbaric and lacked the magnificent and enlightened features imagined by men such as Voss (in his *Theology of the Gentiles*), after all the mythologies which they had considered. For the ambitious, who hunger to become lords of the cities, open the road to this by siding with the masses and flattering them with a semblance or illusion of liberty, something which they must do when men have already become civilised and accustomed to the servitude of law and misgovernment by the powerful. Or, [if we are not prepared to admit this] and omitting other insuperable difficulties raised elsewhere, are we to believe that, accompanied by the sound of the lute, songs telling of the scandalous activities of gods – the adulterous Joves, the chaste Junos, their sterile and abused wives, the unchaste and fecund Venuses, and others foul and filthy –

[16]*Cf. N.S.*[3] 138–41, 328–9.

should induce men who were complete savages, born and reared in a state of unbridled liberty, to cast off their natures and from their state of bestial lust to be led into the modesty of marriage in which, as all philosophers are agreed, the first human society originated? Surely these examples, relating as they do to the gods, ought rather to have confirmed such men in their native bestiality.

7 The human, as well as doctrinal, necessity that the principles of this Science be derived from holy scripture

25. Since all gentile histories have similar fabulous origins – a clear example of which is provided by Roman history, in which the rape of a Vestal virgin gave rise to the [very] Romans who later substituted a great dispute for this rape – and since we have abandoned all hope of discovering the first common principles of humanity from anything Roman, which, in relation to the world's great age, is of comparatively recent origin, or from the vanities of the Greeks, the remains of the Egyptians, such as their pyramids, and even from the total obscurities of the East, let us seek them among the principles of sacred history. The philologists corroborate the need to proceed in this way, since they are agreed that, being still a human faith, Christianity is older than the fabulous faith of the Greeks. We confirm their shared belief by the following demonstration: that sacred history offers a more intelligible description than any gentile history of an original state of nature, or era of families in the beginning, in which fathers ruled under the government of God, which Philo has elegantly named Θεοκρατία [theocratia or theocracy]. Such a state and era must certainly have been the first in the world, for the philosophers all agree, when they discuss the origins of politics, i.e., the origins of the rights which governments possess, that the cities all arose from the state of families. And because of the two periods of slavery which the Jews suffered among the Egyptians and Assyrians, sacred history offers a weightier account of the antiquities of Egypt and Assyria than does Greek history. It is, moreover, beyond doubt that the nations which spread themselves to populate the whole earth came from the East and that they must have adopted the same routes as those followed by the worshippers of the God of Adam as they wandered into impiety. Thus, as the first monarchy to appear in history is that of Assyria, so the first sages, the Chaldeans, also appear there.

8   *The impossibility of discovering the principles of development and continuity [proper to this Science]*

26. Grotius postulated a state in which man was solitary and hence weak and lacking in all his needs; Hobbes postulated one in which all was allowed to all against all; while Pufendorf postulated one in which man, having been thrust into the world and abandoned on his own, lacked God's care and assistance – a principle upon which Christian philosophers and philologists are agreed and which, since it is Christian, is a matter not of hypothesis but of fact. But how did man's impiety lead him into such states and how did false religions later lead him from them into civil life? Here, indeed, the very nature of antiquity, that in everything she keeps her origins concealed, makes us fear for the discovery of the modes which would constitute the principles of the world of gentile nations. For thus is it arranged by nature: that men should first have done things because of a certain human sense, without conscious consideration of them; that then, very late, they should have applied reflection to them; and that by reasoning about their effects they should have contemplated them in [the light of] their causes.[17]

9   *Either from the philosophers . . .*

27. Hence one cannot imagine more than two kinds of mode from which the world of gentile nations might have originated: either a few sages gave it order through reflection, or some bestial men were brought together by a certain human sense or instinct. But we cannot accept the first view, since it is the nature of origins that in respect of everything they should be simple and crude. Hence, simple and crude must have been the origins of gentile humanity in which, as it has hitherto been believed, the likes of Zoroaster, Hermes Trismegistus and Orpheus arose and existed, possessed of the highest and most recondite wisdom, with which they founded the humanity of the Assyrians, Egyptians and Greeks. And if they did not, as they should not, wish to posit the eternity of the world, scholars should have meditated upon origins of this kind,

[17]*Cf. N.S.*[3] 236.

in order to base the science of humanity, i.e., the science of the nature of nations, upon certain first principles beyond which it would be foolish curiosity to seek others, which is the true characteristic of science.

28. Neither the oracles ascribed to Zoroaster, nor the poetic fragments of Orpheus, in any way compel us to believe that their authors were the authors of the humanity of their nations. We have elsewhere raised many a serious doubt about this, including, amongst others, that of the great difficulty and length of time required for the formation of articulate languages in nations which were already founded. In addition, however, as we shall show in this book, it is impossible to understand how a language could express abstract things in terms which are also abstract, unless the language belongs to a nation in which skilled philosophers have existed for a long time. A proof of this is afforded by the Latin language which, because it made late contact with the thought of Greek philosophy, expresses itself in the sciences in an impoverished and positively miserable fashion. This leads to the important thesis that Moses did not utilise the recondite wisdom of the Egyptian priests. For his narrative is woven entirely from words which have much in common with those used by Homer who, since we have located him as contemporary to Numa, existed some eight hundred years later [than the Egyptian priests]. Moreover, in sublimity of expression, Moses often surpasses the priests, while, at the same time, concealing meanings which, in sublimity of understanding, surpass all metaphysics. Such, for example, is the expression with which God describes himself to Moses, *Sum qui sum* [I am who I am], which Dionysius Longinus, prince of critics, admires as the sublimity of poetic style. But Greece needed to reach the summit of its learning, and in that state to produce a Plato, to attain metaphysical sublimity, through the abstract idea by which, when God is meant, he calls Him το ὄν, or *ens* [being]. So late were the Latins to express this idea that their word for it belongs not to pure Latin but to low Latin, i.e., to the times in which Greek metaphysics was celebrated among the Romans. This comparison provides an indefeasible proof of the antiquity and truth of sacred history.

29. These reasons force us to conclude that [the other] such verses were created by the last Greek metaphysicians, for they contain nothing about divinity which is not present in the thought of Plato and Pythagoras. This should serve to warn us of the determinacy of the limits of human knowledge and of the vanity of the desire to discover the wisdom of the ancients. For these [later] verses themselves make it manifest that they were written in the same style as is to be found in Pythagoras' *Golden Verses* and that they must have been written thus by certain people in order that their doctrines should be thought to be both very old

and religious. For if one compares these verses with Geronimo Benivieni's Platonic poem 'On love', which Pico della Mirandola found worthy of note, the latter will be found much the more poetic. Thus much do the former smack of scholarship! For these reasons we conclude that they must have been the forgeries of scholars, as Francesco Flusso Candella proved beyond doubt with regard to the *Poimander*.

30. Accordingly, since it is denied by the nature of their languages themselves and opposed by [metaphysical] criticism, there is no need to affirm, on the strength of these verses, that the founders of the gentile nations were the possessors of a recondite wisdom. We are unable, therefore, to consider the origins of the humanity of nations in terms of the reasons which philosophers have so far adduced. These reasons go back to Plato, who, believing perhaps in the eternity of the world, took his start from the humanity of his own times, in which philosophers from other civilised nations must [already] have tamed the human race which remained elsewhere in a state of savagery. And this was perhaps the reason for the scholarly fiction of a succession of schools in which learning was transmitted from Zoroaster, through Berosus, Trismegistus and Atlas, successively, to Orpheus, while the Christian critics (of whom Peter Daniel Huet is the latest, though second to none in erudition), whom Selden must have followed, would have the founders of the gentile nations issue in a state of complete learning from the school of Noah. The complete irrationality of these beliefs will be shown in the following section.

31. Here we shall confine ourself to the observation that Plato, accepting with too much trust the vulgar tradition of his [own] Greece, failed to reflect upon the fact that this showed humanity arising in Thrace, when, rather, it was such as cruel Mars who came from there. And so far was this country from fostering philosophers that the word 'Thracian' has survived in Greek, with the meaning 'one of obtuse ingenuity', as a means of reproach, thus constituting to this day a public judgement on an entire nation. This amounts to a philological demonstration, contrary to Plato and the whole of gentile philosophy, that the Jewish religion was founded with the creation of the world in time by the true God.

10   *Or from the philologists . . .*

32. Having rejected the sages [of the philosophers], it remains to think about the brutes posited by Grotius and Pufendorf as the first men from whom gentile humanity must have arisen. And here, since we are unable to accept the reasonings which the philosophers have adduced, we are

constrained to consider the authorities presented by the philologists, taking the latter to include poets, historians, orators and grammarians, the last of whom are commonly called 'scholars'. But nothing is enshrouded in such doubt and obscurity as the origins of languages and the principle of the propagation of nations. So great is the uncertainty which these matters breed that the philologists still confess openly that universal gentile history possesses neither certainty of origin nor any certain, or determinate, continuity with sacred history.

33. For the world certainly did not come into existence at the same time as Rome, which was a new city founded in the midst of a large number of lesser, but older, peoples in Latium. Hence Titus Livy does well to excuse himself from offering to guarantee the truth of the whole of ancient Roman history. [Indeed] he later states openly that his account of Roman history contains more truth when it reaches the Carthaginian wars, while still confessing with candour that he does not know at which point of the Alps Hannibal made his great and memorable passage into Italy, whether it was over the Cottian or Apennine Alps.

34. Everything we have inherited relating to antiquity we owe to the Greeks,[18] yet they were shockingly ignorant of their own early times. We can offer three weighty proofs of this, of which two are drawn from Homer, the earliest certain Greek author and the earliest certain father in the whole of Greek learning. First, there is a public admission, by all the Greek peoples, that none of them knew Homer's native land, for each people claimed him as their own citizen, although the long dispute was finally settled in favour of Smyrna. The second proof rests upon another public confession, [this time] by the philologists: their beliefs about the time at which Homer lived vary so greatly that a difference of four hundred and sixty years can be calculated between the period of the Trojan war, in which some would place him, and that of Numa, preferred by others. Their ignorance of such important things in connection with the celebrated Homer inspires us to pity the vain diligence of the critics, [which has been] so detailed as to determine not merely the country but the very stones and fountains, not merely the century but the very month and day, of the most insignificant things belonging to the most distant and obscure past. The third proof is provided by the evidence of Thucydides, the first truthful and serious historian to write about Greece, who testifies at the beginning of his account that the Greeks of his time knew nothing of their own early history prior to the times of their fathers. And this when Greece, with its two empires of Sparta and Athens, was in its most enlightened period, that of the Peloponnesian War,

[18]*Cf. N.S.*[3] 171.

which Thucydides described as a contemporary! And this, moreover, was the state of affairs twenty years before the Law of the Twelve Tables was given to the Romans![19] What more can be done to show that prior to this time the Greeks knew little or nothing of anything foreign?

35. The first nations must certainly have retained much of their savage origins for very long and hence they must normally have remained within the boundaries of their lands, unless they were provoked by insult and fearful of injury. Such a nature [as this] is proved by the cause of the Tarentine War, for the Tarentines attacked not only the Roman ships, as they drew up on their shores, but the Roman ambassadors as well, believing that they were perhaps pirates and excusing themselves by claiming, in the words of Florus, that *qui essent aut unde venirent ignorabant* [they knew neither who they were nor whence they came]. Yet this occurred within a stretch of mainland as short as that between Tarentum and Rome, at a time when the Romans were already a force in the land and their fleets were scouring the whole Tyrrhenian and touching on the Adriatic! But, much more than a single people, entire nations confirm that such was the nature of their ancient customs, as, for example, in the case of the nations of Spain. Here neither the ferocious burning down of Saguntum, which was so troublesome to Hannibal, nor the long, heroic defence of Numantia, which had already given the Romans so much concern, could stimulate the nations of Spain to form a league against their enemies. These events later led the Roman historians to pronounce it an unhappy virtue that 'the nations of Spain failed to realise their unconquered strength until they had been conquered'.

36. This public evidence, drawn from entire peoples, considerably strengthens the private judgement which Livy passed on the vulgar tradition that Pythagoras was Numa's teacher. For, despite his belief that Pythagoras was contemporaneous with Servius Tullius, who lived a hundred and fifty years before the Tarentine War, Livy nevertheless judged that it would have been impossible in such times for Pythagoras, not only in person but even in name, which was that of a most distinguished philosopher, to have penetrated from Crotona to Rome, passing through the many nations of different language and custom which lay between them. Further substantial support is added to this private judgement by another very enlightening item of public evidence relating to the Roman people. This is to be found in St Augustine's *City of God,* in which he states that, under their kings, the Roman people engaged in wars for a period of two hundred and fifty years, subjugating twenty or more peoples, without extending their rule by more than twenty miles —

---

[19] Vico's thesis is that the Law of the Twelve Tables was not imported to Rome from Greece but that it was a codification of ancient Roman customs.

and Roman miles were very much shorter than ours. The first thing this passage reveals is just how impenetrable were the first small nations, no matter how proximate they were to one another. In addition it subverts all the grandiose ideas we have hitherto accepted about the early days of Rome and, in similar fashion, about all the other empires of the world.

37. This passage from Livy, and these facts of Roman history, which provide incontrovertible proof that it is proper to nations to pass their early days in savagery and seclusion, do much to discredit Pythagoras' voyages: to Thrace, to visit the Orphic school; to Babylon, to learn from the Chaldeans at the school of Zoroaster; and to the Indies, to learn from the Gymnosophists. Further voyages include passing from the Near East through Egypt, where he was taught by the priests, and through Africa, to the school of Atlas in Mauritania in the farthest West, and then returning across the sea to Gaul to learn from the Druids. But these journeys are all fictions [which arose] because a resemblance was later discovered between some of Pythagoras' doctrines and those of the vulgar sages of these nations, separated as they were by immense stretches of land and sea. An example of such a doctrine is that of the transmigration of the soul, which still occupies an important place in the religion of the Brahmins, who were the ancient Brachmani or Gymnosophists, the philosophers of India. The existence of such serious doubts about the journeys Pythagoras made, in order to gather together and carry back to Greece the very best of the world's humanity, forces us to deny all credence whatsoever to Hercules' travels, some seven hundred years earlier, in which glory alone spurs him to kill the monsters and tyrants of nations and to introduce Greek eloquence into Gaul and Greek humanity into the other nations. We are given even more cause to doubt Homer's visits to Egypt by a passage in which he describes the island of the pharos as lying as far from [that part of] the mainland where Alexandria was later founded as an unladen Greek ship could travel in a day when the north wind blew, that is to say, with the wind at her stern. And this the little island so close to the mainland that the port of Alexandria later finished up on it, as one can still see! So close is it, indeed, that had Homer ever set eyes on Egypt, he would certainly never have told a lie of this magnitude, and had the Greeks of his time enjoyed trade with Egypt, everything else he wrote would have been thrown into total discredit.

38. Apart from the consideration that the first contacts between nations come with the outbreak of wars, a further point, upon which all scholars are agreed, which upsets, and militates against, the above beliefs, is this: that Psammetichus was the first king to allow the Greeks access to Egypt, though only the Greeks of Ionia and Caria. If, therefore, at the time of Tullus Hostilius, with whom Psammetichus was contemporaneous, a nation of such humanity had hitherto observed the practice of

keeping its frontiers closed to overseas nations, what are we to believe of other, absolutely barbaric, nations? Hence it is rightly asserted that the first person to write about Persian things with some distinction was Xenophon, the immediate successor to Thucydides, himself the first to write about Greek things with certainty. For Xenophon was the first Greek captain to lead a Greek army into Persia, whence he made that memorable retreat. Moreover, the Greeks were ignorant of Assyrian things prior to the conquests of Alexander the Great, and Aristotle, who accompanied him, noted, as he wrote later in his *Politics,* that the Greeks had previously written [only] fables about them.

39. These difficulties close with the most relevant of all: that in all ancient nations the priestly orders kept all religious things hidden from the plebs of the cities in which they lived, and these therefore retained the name 'sacred things', hidden, i.e., from the profane. The Greek philosophers themselves long concealed their wisdom from the vulgar of their own nation, so that only after many years did Pythagoras admit even his own disciples into his secret audience. Are we then to believe that individual foreigners made safe and swift journeys, within the forbidden confines of distant nations, in order that the priests of Egypt or the Chaldeans of Assyria should profane their religion and their recondite wisdom [by communicating it] to them, in the absence of interpreters and of any long-standing linguistic intercourse between them? And are we to believe this, above all, of the Jews, ever unsociable towards gentile nations?

11   *The need to seek the principles of the nature of nations by means of a metaphysics elevated to contemplate a certain common mind possessed by all peoples*

40. Amid all these uncertainties we are obliged [to explain] how, liberated from servitude to the religion of God, creator of the world and of Adam, which alone could hold them within duty and, hence, within society, the impious ways of those first men, from whom the gentile nations later arose, led them to dissipate themselves in a ferine migration, in which they penetrated the great forests of the earth, when it had cooled after the creation and become thick with woods after the waters of the Flood; and how, constrained to seek food, water and much else to pre-

serve themselves among the wild animals which must have been abundant in the great forest, the frequent desertion of women by men and of children by mothers, with no possibility of their reuniting, gradually, through the generations, caused them to forget the language of Adam; and how, again, lacking language and with thought of nothing but the satisfaction of hunger, thirst and the impulses of lust, they reached a state in which all human sense was stifled. In view of all these uncertainties, when meditating upon the principles of this Science we must, with very great effort, clothe ourselves in a nature in many ways similar to that of those first men. Hence, we must reduce ourselves to a state of extreme ignorance of all human and divine learning, as if, for the purposes of this enquiry, there had been neither philosophers nor philologists to help us.[20] And whoever wishes to profit from this Science must reduce himself to such a state, in order that, in the course of his meditations, he should be neither distracted nor influenced by preconceptions for long held in common. For all these doubts combined can cast no doubt whatsoever upon this one truth, which must be the first in such a science, since in this long, dense night of darkness, one light alone glows: that the world of the gentile nations has certainly been made by men. Hence, in this vast ocean of doubt, one small island appears, upon which we may stand firm: that the principles of this Science must be rediscovered within the nature of our human mind and in the power of our understanding, by elevating the metaphysics of the human mind – which has hitherto contemplated the mind of individual man, in order to lead it to God as eternal truth, which is the most universal theory in divine philosophy – to contemplate the common sense of mankind as a certain human mind of nations, in order to lead it to God as eternal providence, which should be the most universal practice in divine philosophy. In this way, without a single hypothesis (for metaphysics disowns hypotheses) this Science must, in fact, seek its principles among the modifications of our human mind in the descendants of Cain, before the Flood, and in those of Ham and Japhet, after it.[21]

12 · *The idea of a jurisprudence of mankind*

41. By means of [the method of] division, we must proceed from cognition of the parts and thence of their composition, to achieve cognition

[20]*Cf. N.S.*[3] 330.
[21]See the corresponding version of this famous passage at *N.S.*[3] 331.

of the whole which we wish to know. In this manner, to give, by way of example, the most perspicuous of all the parts which compose the whole we seek, we arrive at the fact that Roman jurisprudence is a science of the mind of the decemvirs concerning civil utilities in the severe period of the Roman people. At the same time it is also a science of the language with which they conceived the Law of the Twelve Tables, described by Livy as the 'source', and by Tacitus as the 'end', of Roman justice as a whole. When public and private civil transactions took place in other circumstances and in times of more enlightened ideas, which were accordingly themselves more human, this science contributed to the ever-increasing development of the mind of the decemvirs, supplying it with the things it lacked by reducing [the importance of] the propriety of the words of the law, modifying their harshness and giving them a more benign sense.[22] And all this occurred in order that the decemvirs should preserve that choice or selection of the public good which they had proposed, which was the welfare of the Roman city. Hence the jurisprudence of the natural law of nations should be considered a science of the mind of man set in solitude (like the man of Grotius and Pufendorf, but understood by us, as stated above, in conformity with catholic doctrine), who desires the preservation of his nature. Such a science must show how, upon the occasion of different human necessities, the mind of solitary man must develop through different states, upon the basis of his primary aim of preserving his nature, by the preservation first of the family, then of the city, next of the nation and finally of the whole of mankind. It must be shown that through this aim, and by making use of certain marriages, providence drew impious man from the state of solitude into that of the families, from which the first gentes were born, i.e., the clans or houses which later gave rise to the cities.[23] And this science must begin with these first and oldest gentes, since it is with them that its subject matter or material began. And in all this it must follow the celebrated rule, the universal foundation of all interpretation, which the jurist has suggested to us in the wisest of sayings: *Quotiens lege aliquid unum vel alterum introductum est, bona occasio est cetera, quae tendunt ad eandem utilitatem vel interpretatione vel certe iurisdictione suppleri.* [Whenever something or other is introduced by law, the occasion is good for the introduction of other things which tend towards the same utility, either by the interpretation or by the certain administration of justice.] The word *caussa* is not used here, for the cause of the just is not variable utility [itself] but eternal reason which, in immutable geometric and mathematical proportions, distributes the variable utilities upon the

---

[22]Cf. N.S.[3] 321–8.   [23]See the corresponding version, N.S.[3] 341.

occasion of different human needs. Thus, with indispensable necessity, our reasoning about the natural law of nations must proceed in accordance with the natural order of ideas,[24] and not in accordance with the beliefs of those who, while conferring grandiose titles upon the most enormous tomes, collect in their works nothing that is not commonly known.

13 The extreme difficulty of discovering [the principles of the nature of nations]

42. But even a first glimmer of understanding of the modes [from which these ideas arose] seems beyond hope, while to explain them we should require the science of a language common to all the first gentile nations. For we have to judge the life of mankind, which is that of men who grow old over the years, so that we ourselves are [to be counted among the] old while the founders of nations are [among the] young.[25] But children who are born into nations in which speech already exists possess, by the age of seven at the most, a large vocabulary, so that, when any vulgar idea is awakened in them, they skim quickly through this vocabulary, immediately finding the correct word for communicating the idea to others, while every word which they hear awakens the idea to which it is tied.[26] Hence, when composing speech, they employ a certain geometric process of synthesis, by means of which they skim through all the elements of their language, selecting those that they require and instantaneously uniting them. Thus each language is a great school for making the human mind dexterous and swift. Moreover, [children with such minds] learn how to count much better than do the children of less civilised nations, counting being such an abstract and spiritual activity that, in recognition of a certain excellence [proper to it], it is called 'reasoning'. This was why Pythagoras located the whole essence of the human mind in numbers. A practice of a different kind, which nevertheless resembles geometry, is literature, or the school of reading and writing, in which children's imaginations are refined beyond belief by means of those slender, delicate forms which we call 'letters'. For, when they read or write some word, children skim through the elements of the

---

[24]Cf. *N.S.*[1] 55–6. Utility is the occasion of new conceptions of justice, but not the cause. The cause is the ideal – equity – which, in the course of human history, men become increasingly able to understand and implement. See pp. 20 and 22 above.
[25]Cf. *N.S.*[3] 212, 216.
[26]Cf. pp. 38–9, 71–3 for some partial anticipations of these claims.

alphabet, selecting those that they need and putting them in the order required for reading or writing them. Literature is, however, more sturdy and stable than words, while numbers are more abstract than letters and sounds. For letters leave traces of the impressions which they have made upon the eye, sight therefore being the sharpest sense for learning and retention. But words are composed of air, which strikes upon the ear and then vanishes, while the odd and even numbers, for instance, affect no sense whatsoever when numerical calculations are made. Hence we can scarcely understand and are totally unable to imagine either how the first men of the impious races must have thought, in that state in which they had yet to hear a human word, or the coarseness with which they must have given form to their thoughts and the disorderly way in which they must have connected them.[27] In these matters we are unable to draw a single comparison, not only with our own idiots and illiterate rustics but with the most barbaric inhabitants of the polar regions and of the African and American deserts, whose customs, according to reports given by travellers, are so extravagant by [the standards of] our own civilised natures as to excite horror in us. For such people are at least born among languages, no matter how barbaric in kind, and they must have some ability to reckon and to reason.

43. In face of all these extreme doubts, and the almost insurmountable difficulties which such a project encounters, in which we know neither from which first real men nor, consequently, in which first parts of the world the gentile nations originated, we shall trace in thought the ferine wanderings of men of the sort we have outlined above in the *Idea of this Work*. We therefore put forward for consideration our book, the theme of which may be summarised in the saying: *Ignari hominumque locorumque erramus* [When neither places nor men are known we go astray].

[27]Cf. *N.S.*[3] 338.

Book II
The principles of this science drawn from ideas[28]

[Introduction]

44. Since we have hitherto lacked any information about the first world of the gentile nations, and can form no idea of it [by projection] from our own human world, we now propose for its discovery the following principles, which are divided into two classes – of ideas and of languages. And, as the mind governs each and every part of the body, so these principles, singly or in numbers, sub-divided or in groups, directly or through their consequences, inform and establish this Science, both in its parts and in its total complexity, as a system, whether for the comprehension of it as a whole or piece by piece, even in the smallest parts of the sections which compose it.[29] It will accordingly be possible to understand, one by one, all the things we have already mentioned, as well as many others which, given the opportunity, we shall propound below, including even the confusing world of the dictionary. And we shall do so without suffering the discomfort which arises from the need to adopt some tedious method, or even no method at all, if such books [dictionaries] are meditated in accordance with the exact order in which they are written. Only here, in confirming effects through their principles, we shall adduce as examples one, two, or at most three, effects, appropriate to each principle, in order that they be understood as principles. If one wishes to see them confirmed in their almost innumerable consequences, it will be necessary to consult other works which we have already published or which are about to appear in print. Here it will suffice, to pass judgement on the rest, that the principles should be reasonable as causes and that the examples fit them as effects, for it is the principles of doctrines which are the most difficult part to think out and which therefore contain, as Socrates said, more than half the science.

[28] In the list of amplified titles at the start of the work, this is given as: *Principles of this science [drawn] from the ideas of a provident divinity upon whose worship, warnings and commands all nations have arisen.* In fact, however, the book contains considerable discussion of other ideas than that of a provident divinity, although the latter is certainly very prominent.

[29] *Cf.* N.S.[3] 119, 330.

1   *The first principle of nations is providence*

45. Now, to commence these principles with that idea which is paramount in any work whatsoever, the architect of this world of nations is divine providence. For men cannot join together in human society unless they share a human sense that there exists a divinity who sees into the depths of their hearts.[30] For a society of men can neither come into being, nor sustain itself, without a means whereby some should rely upon the promises of others and be quietened by their assurances concerning secret matters. For the giving and accepting of promises is a frequent necessity of human life, while things often occur which, though secret, are not misdemeanours, with respect to which it is necessary to offer people assurances without its being possible to supply any human evidence for them. Were it to be suggested that this could be attained [only] through the rigour of penal laws against lie-telling, it would be attainable [only] in the state of the cities and not in that of the families from which the cities arose. For in the state of the families there was as yet no civil or public rule, to the armed, legal force of which two fathers of the families, for example, could be equally subject in law. Those who think along the above lines, of whom John Locke would be one, could fall back on the suggestion that man might develop the habit of being obliged to believe [something] as soon as another asserts that he is promising or talking truly. But were they to do so, they would presuppose an idea of the true such that the revelation of something true is enough to oblige people to believe it without [requiring] any human evidence. This idea can be nothing other than the idea of God in the attribute of providence, that is, an eternal and infinite mind which comprehends and foresees everything. And by its infinite good, insofar as this pertains to our topic, whatsoever particular men or particular peoples order for their own particular ends, proposals which would be the principal cause of their ruin, it orders towards a universal end beyond, and very often contrary to, their every aim; and through this universal end, using their particular ends themselves as means, it preserves them. It will be shown throughout the whole of this work that under this aspect providence governs the entire natural law of nations.[31]

---

[30]See p. 81, n. 1, above. For the fulfilment of the social necessity which Vico ascribes to religion lower in this paragraph, see p. 22 above.
[31]Cf. *N.S.*[3] 132–3, 341, 1108.

2   *The rule of the world of nations is vulgar wisdom*

46. This divine architect has sent forth the world of nations with vulgar wisdom as its rule. Vulgar wisdom is a common sense possessed by each people or nation, which regulates our social lives, in all our human activities, in such a way that they should be in accord with whatsoever everyone in the people or nations feels in common. The concordance of these common senses among all peoples or nations is the wisdom of mankind.[32]

3   *The artificer of the world of nations is human will regulated by vulgar wisdom*

47. Subservient to the divine architect, the artificer of the world of nations is human will. Otherwise by nature extremely uncertain in particular men, it is determined by the wisdom of mankind through the judgements of human utilities and necessities uniformly common to all the particular natures of man. These human necessities or utilities, thus determined, are the two sources which the Roman jurists assert for the whole natural law of the gentes.[33] This leads us to meditate upon the state of solitude in which Grotius situates man, in which his solitude renders him weak and lacking in all his needs. This is the state into which the race of Cain must immediately have fallen, followed gradually by that of Seth. And after the Flood the races of Ham and Japhet must also immediately have fallen into it, followed gradually by that of Shem. This must all have occurred after the time when, solely in order to free themselves from the servitude of religion, which alone could preserve them in society, and bound by no other restraint, they turned their backs upon the true God of their fathers, Adam and Noah, and wandered in bestial liberty, dispersed through the great forest of the earth, losing their language and suppressing all social customs. This would be the state described by Pufendorf, in which man has come into the world and been abandoned there, without prior care and assistance from God. From here we continue our meditation by considering which first necessities or utilities common to the nature of such wild and brutish men must have been

[32]Cf. N.S.³ 141–5.   [33]*Ibid.*

felt in order for them to be received into human society. Selden failed to consider this, for he proposed origins common to the gentile and Jewish nations, without distinguishing between a divinely assisted people and others completely lost. Pufendorf did take it into consideration, but erroneously, for his hypothesis runs counter to the fact of sacred history. While Grotius sinned most of all, proposing the Socinian hypothesis that [early] man was a simpleton, and then completely neglecting to reason it out.

4   *The natural order of human ideas of an eternal justice*

48. We have shown that the natural law of the gentes was ordered by providence through the dictates of human necessities or utilities. To complete the remaining part of the definition left us by the Roman jurists – that the natural law is observed equally among all nations – let us now consider its two principal properties, immutability and universality.

49. As for the first, the natural law of the gentes is an eternal law which traverses time. But just as within us lie buried a few eternal seeds of truth, which are cultivated gradually from childhood until, with age and through [various] studies, they develop into the fully clarified notions which belong to the sciences, so, as a result of [human] sin, within mankind were buried the eternal seeds of justice which, as the human mind develops gradually according to its true nature from the childhood of the world, develop into demonstrated maxims of justice.[34] The following difference must, however, always be observed: that this occurred in one, distinctive way among the people of God, and in a different, ordinary way among the gentile nations.

50. In this connection we adduce the following examples. In the oldest period of Greece, when the Athenians had consecrated all the lands of Athens to Jove and lived under his rule (as the history of the obscure period of Greece relates), one could own a farm only if Jove's auspices allowed it. In another age, such as later among the ancient Romans, because of the Law of the Twelve Tables, a solemn consignment, known as a 'bond' (*nodo*), was needed. But in another age, which endures to this day among nations, the real consignment of the farm itself is enough. All three of these ways of acquiring ownership rest upon this [principle of] eternal justice: that one cannot become the proprietor of something

---

[34] See pp. 21–2 above.

which belongs to another without the will, which must be secured in advance, of the master of that thing. Finally came the philosophers, who understood that in its essence ownership depends absolutely on will and that it suffices that there be clear signs that the owner has decided of his own will to transfer his ownership of some particular thing to another, be these signs straightforward words or mute acts.

51. It will be one of the continuous tasks of this Science to show in detail how, with the development of human ideas, laws and rights emerged first from the scrupulousness of superstitions, then from the solemnity of legitimate acts and the limitations of words, and finally from any of the physical aspects which were believed at first to constitute the very substance of the matter; and how they must be led to their pure and true principle, their proper substance, which is human substance: our will determined by our mind through the power of truth, which is what we call 'conscience'. And all this because the natural law of the gentes is a law which has arisen with the natural customs of nations, based upon their ideas of their [own] nature.

52. We may add to this example, which relates to private justice, another, which is drawn from public justice. It follows from the above principles that were there some distant time in which men possessed bodies of disproportionate strength and minds of equally disproportionate stupidity, it would have been dictated to them, in accordance with their having the idea of such a nature, that God be feared as [possessing] a strength superior to anything human. They would have believed this god to be their divine law and, consequently, have based that justice entirely upon strength. Precisely this is acknowledged by Achilles, greatest of the Greek heroes, whom Homer, by his invariable use of the epithet 'irreproachable', set before the Greek people as the paradigm of heroic virtue. For this divine law led Achilles to profess to Apollo that he believed him to be a god because of his superior strength, as is shown when Achilles stated that, were his own strength equal to that of a god, he would not hesitate to enter combat against Apollo. In speaking thus he seemed to show the same reverence for the gods as Polyphemus, who claimed that had he the strength he would join battle with Jove himself. Moreover, augurs, who could not have existed among atheists, existed even among the giants, for one of them had predicted to Polyphemus the fate that he was later to suffer at the hands of Ulysses! Indeed, this divine law even led Jove to set himself above the likes of Achilles and Polyphemus, as is shown by the great chain which he proposed, from one end of which he alone would drag along all men and gods, who were holding on at the other end, in order to prove, through his superior strength, that he was the king of men and of gods.

53. We claim also that it is as a consequence of this divine law that, when Hector wants to reach agreement with Achilles over his burial, in the event of his being killed in that battle in which he was later killed, Achilles replies that there is no equality of right between the weak and the strong, for men have never made pacts with lions nor have lambs and wolves ever shared any uniformity of desires. Here we meet the law of the heroic gentes, based upon the principle that the nature of the strong was believed to be of a different and more noble kind than that of the weak. This is the source of the law of war, by which the victors should forcibly deprive the defeated of all rights to natural liberty, as a result of which the Romans took slaves rather than things. Providence administered this custom in order that, since men of such a ferocious kind had not been brought to heel by the rule of justice, they should at least fear the god of strength and accordingly measure justice by strength, so that, in such fierce times, killing should not breed killing and lead to the extermination of mankind. This would constitute the history, as it does the philosophy, of what Grotius calls 'the external justice of wars'.

54. If, finally, in times when human ideas are fully developed, men should no longer judge themselves to possess a nature different from, and superior to, that of others because of [differences in] strength, but should recognise that all are equal in respect of their rational nature, which is the proper and eternal human nature, the law of the human gentes will obtain among them all. This dictates to men the equal communication of utilities, with the sole reservation that, in order that equality be preserved, a just difference be observed in matters of merit. This law is shown to be the natural law of the gentes which the Roman jurists reasoned out and which, in defining the law of the gentes of his time, Ulpian significantly describes as the law of the 'human gentes'. But in doing so he means to distinguish it not from the law of the barbaric gentes beyond the Roman empire, with which the Roman laws of private justice had no connection, but from the law of the superseded barbaric gentes [within Rome].

5   The natural order of human ideas of a universal justice

55. The foregoing principles, which have enabled us to affirm one of the two most important properties of the natural law of the gentes, its immutability, allow us in addition to affirm the other, its universality, by meditating [upon the fact] that there is only one possible way in which

we can understand how the progress of human ideas of natural justice occurred. In a state of solitude – the state of Grotius' lonely, weak and indigent man and of Pufendorf's man, bereft of the care and assistance of others – such progress of human ideas must have originated in the most inborn of necessities and this, in such a state, could only have been man's need to propagate his species by uniting with a woman who would provide him with company, care and assistance. This was a natural monastic or solitary, and hence sovereign, law. Because of this law of the cyclopes – Plato mentioned it fleetingly in connection with Homer's Polyphemus – it must have been just that men should use force to seize vagabond women and keep them captive in their dens. This is the time in which the first principle of just wars with the first just acts of plunder began to develop, since the wars that were waged to found gentile mankind were no less just than those waged later to preserve it. Thus here what Grotius calls 'the internal justice of wars', the true and proper justice of arms, begins to emerge.

56. As a result of these first just acts of plunder, the first men acquired a cyclopic power over their wives and thence over their children, precisely as, in Homer, Polyphemus recounts to Ulysses, thus preserving the earlier custom by which children inherit their mother's status. This custom belonged to the first period of bestial communion but it was impossible to change it all at once in order to adopt that quite contrary custom of the gentes, which we still retain, whereby children born in wedlock inherit their father's status. Accordingly, in the state of the families, upon the occasion of family utilities and necessities, this monastic law developed into a natural economic law. Later, when the original stock had ramified into further families, upon the occasion of needs common to whole clans, i.e., the ancient houses or tribes which preceded, and were the basis of, the cities – these were the houses which the Latins first and properly called 'gentes' – the economic law must have disseminated itself into a natural law of the gentes which were, for the first time, properly named and referred to by the Latins as the 'greater gentes'. Later, when the houses or tribes came together in cities, the natural law of the greater gentes must have been elevated into the natural law of the lesser gentes, i.e., the private law of peoples pertaining to the civil necessities or utilities of each city. This must be the natural civil law which, because of the uniformity of its causes, was born in common in each age in each part of the world, as for example in Latium, and which was, at the same time, proper to every city, no matter how many there were, when Romulus later founded Rome among them. Finally, after the cities had become known to one another, through the common business of wars, alliances and commerce, the natural civil laws were recognised, though much

wider in extension than the earlier ones, in a natural law of the second gentes, i.e., a natural law of nations united together as in one great universal city. This is the law of mankind.

6   The natural order of gentile human ideas of God through which, according as they are separate or communicated, the nations are separate from or in communication with one another

57. The Roman jurists establish that the first and principal part of the natural law of the gentes was worship directed towards God. For when, in the absence of the rule of law and the force of arms, a man is in a state of complete freedom, he can neither enter into a society with another, nor remain there with him, other than through fear of a strength superior to both of them and therefore of a god common to them. Such a fear of god is called 'religion'.

58. Now, since we agree with Grotius and Pufendorf in beginning our Science with man in solitude (though only in connection with the origins of the gentiles), it is quite impossible to understand the awakening and later development of the idea of God in the minds of the gentile nations other than through the following natural order. First came the idea of a strength superior to anything human, which these men, living alone and separate, imagined to be divine and which each man believed to be his own individual god. The first human society brought together by religion was therefore a society of marriages, which certain men must have contracted when, in fear of some god, they must have abandoned their life of ferine migration. And, hidden among the caves, they must have held captive with them women, whom they had dragged there by force in order to mate with them free of the fear aroused in them by the countenance of the sky, which, on certain occasions, they had imagined to be a god, as we shall demonstrate below in the appropriate place. For fear redirects those spirits which are required for such mating. In such mode, from this sense of bestial lust, providence first tinged the face of these lost men with the blush of shame, and certainly no nation has ever existed which did not blush, for human matings occur in all nations. But in the case of Adam and Eve this came about in a distinctive way for, since they had already fallen from contemplation of God as punishment for their

sin, at the moment of their fall they became aware of their corporeal nature, noticed their nakedness and hid those parts which it is unseemly not only to see but even to mention. And Ham, who in jest insisted upon seeing the [private] parts of Noah, his father, as he lay asleep, carried God's curse with him into the bestial wilderness for his lack of piety. This is one of those origins beyond which it is foolish curiosity to seek anything earlier, which is the most important mark of the truth of origins. For if, going back before Ham and Japhet, we do not stop our enquiry with Noah after the Flood and, before Cain, with Adam and a God who is the creator both of him and of the world, the following question raises itself: at what point did men begin to feel ashamed of themselves in that state of bestial freedom in which they were able to feel shame neither before their sons, to whom they were by nature superior, nor before one another, when they were both equal to one another and equally incited by the promptings of lust? Hence, if we do not bring our enquiry to a halt [when we arrive] at shame felt before a God – but not the likes of naked Venus, Hermes or Mercury or obscene Priapus – humanity could never have arisen from the men of Hobbes, Grotius and Pufendorf.

59. Such being the origins of human things, the first men must have confined the first women within the religion of a god who prohibited carnal indulgence under the open sky, whence it remained the custom in all nations that women should adopt the civil religion of their husbands, which, as we see clearly from their family sacrifices, the Romans did. From this first and oldest principle of all humanity began the communication of ideas between people, husbands and their women commencing, before any other, with the idea of the god who had united them in the first society, which was certainly that of marriages. Next, in the state of the families, these deities peculiar to each father, linked in whole clans, became the gods of the fathers, *divi parentum,* as they continued to be called in the Law of the Twelve Tables, in the section *On Parricide.* Later, when the families came together in cities, they became the gods of each fatherland, the paternal gods, who were called *dii patrii* and were therefore believed to be the gods proper to the fathers, i.e., to the order of patricians. After this, when the uniformity of ideas in a single language led a number of different cities to become whole nations, they became the gods of nations themselves, such as the oriental, Egyptian and Greek gods. Finally when the nations came to know one another through wars, alliances and commerce, they became the gods common to mankind. As such, they were not the Juno of the Greeks or the Venus of the Trojans but that which, in their mutually exchangeable oaths, the Greeks and Trojans meant through their Juno and their Venus: a god who is Jove to everyone.

60. Two things are demonstrated by this. First, that the whole of humanity is contained within the unity of God, originating in a single god separately in each nation, and terminating in a single universal god. Second, the truth, antiquity and continuity of the Christian religion; for it came into existence with the world from a single God, nor, with the passing of years and of nations, let alone customs, has it ever produced a plurality of gods.

7

I *The natural order of ideas of the law of nations [as it develops] through the religions, laws, languages, marriages, names, arms and governments proper to them*

61. But if the gentes were, first and properly, original stocks which had branched out into different families, it is absolutely impossible to understand the origin and progress of the law of the gentes other than in accordance with the following natural order of ideas. First, and before all else, it was a law which came into existence together with the customs of certain stocks, which, under the fathers of the world, had branched out into many families, prior to coming together in cities, the clans of which were called the greater gentes. In these cities Jove, for example, was called the god of the greater gentes, because he had been imagined by the first fathers and was accepted as god by whole families whose common stock and sovereign principles lay in the fathers. It was necessary, therefore, that each of these clans should have a language proper to it, invented for the internal communication of the laws which, from what was said in the preceding section, must have been the laws of the auspices which were believed to be divine. As a result of this the gentile nations gave providence the name 'divinity', derived from *divinari* [divination]. They must therefore have believed that these divine laws were proper to them, and through these laws they believed that the Jove, which each clan had invented as its own god, commanded to them all human matters, of which the first and most important is undoubtedly marriage. By virtue of such religions, laws and languages proper to them, they must naturally have celebrated among themselves marriage under the auspices of their gods.

62. Now, let us assume for a moment what will soon be shown [to be true] in fact: that, long afterwards, others were received from the state of bestial intercourse into that of social life, in areas of land already occu-

pied and cultivated by men who, at some earlier time, had abandoned their ferine migrations. Such foreign vagabonds, bereft of religion and language when admitted – and, similarly, their offspring, as long as they remained ignorant of the religions, languages and laws of those who had taken them in – must naturally have been denied the contraction of marriages with the clans who already had languages, laws and gods proper to them. This must have been the first and oldest natural law of the gentes in the state of the families, common to gentiles and Hebrews alike, but observed more thoroughly by the Hebrews than by the gentiles, since the people of God possessed the true merit, in connection with the impious vagabonds who had turned to them, of not profaning the true religion.

63. Meanwhile, when these clans had come together in the first cities, on certain occasions which we shall show in the correct place, the natural law of these gentes must have been a law preserved along with the customs of the orders thus formed, the latter being called the 'lesser gentes'. Hence Romulus, for example, was referred to as the god 'of the lesser gentes', because he was a god which their order had imagined. This is certainly how Proclus Sabinus, who belonged to the order of senators, described him in a public pronouncement to the Roman plebs. Consequently, a long time after the foundation of the cities, a law of the gentes of the kind which had previously belonged to the clans must have belonged to the orders of noble families. This is shown all too clearly by Roman history which – we rely now more heavily upon Livy than the rest – as a result of other erroneous [accounts of the] origins of humanity, has hitherto been lacking in either science or usefulness.

64. In order that Roman history be guided by the things we have meditated, it will be helpful now to give some brief consideration to the vulgar belief that the Phrygians and Arcadians were admitted in large numbers to Romulus' asylum from overseas, though their marriages, languages and gods were unknown. We shall ignore here many others one might take into account who, with absolutely no gods, no languages nor any human feature, and having split up over certain ultimate necessities, abandoned their [state of] bestial solitude and took refuge in the little cities of Latium, rather as wild beasts are sometimes led to take refuge in inhabited places to save their lives when the winters are harsh or hunters give pursuit. [In this connection] certain Roman history informs us that when the plebs seek marriage, or the right to contract marriage (for this is what, in correct jurisprudence, the Latin *connubium* means), and when they seek the auspices of the gods, with which the fathers or nobles celebrated marriage, they are refused them. For the nobles contend, with reasons stated in the full propriety of the words of such times, which Livy has faithfully reported to us: *confundi iura gen-*

tium, se gentem habere and *auspicia esse sua.* By these expressions
they meant first that the rights of kinship would be adulterated. Secondly,
they meant that they alone had certain descendants, through which they
were safeguarded by marriage from those nefarious relationships in
which sons would lie with their mothers, fathers with their daughters,
and a number of brothers with a single sister. For, as the young understand almost as soon as they begin to learn Roman law, solemn marriage
alone establishes certain fathers, hence certain sons and certain brothers.[35] Consequently the nobles were innocent of nefarious incest, the
effect of which is to terminate rather than disseminate the human species,
since children return to the origins whence they came, and close blood
relationships are compounded, since they are blended together rather
than diversified, this being the natural evil of such incestuous unions.
And in this very dispute, indeed, the nobles censured the plebeians for
this evil, with the words, *agitarent connubia more ferarum* [they practised marriage in the manner of wild animals]. Finally, they meant also
that they understood the language of their gods who, through the pro-
nouncements and commands of auspices which were believed to be
divine, gave them control over all human things, of which marriage was
the first and most important.

65. In accordance with this natural order of ideas the natural law of
the heroic gentes is disclosed through that difference of nature, as great
as that between men and wild animals, by which the nobles believed
themselves superior to the plebs of the first cities, which corresponds to
the superiority between the strong and the weak, ascribed by Achilles to
lions and men. Thence is disclosed the natural origin of the concealment
of religions and laws within the orders of nobles, sages or priests, and the
natural origin of sacred or arcane languages throughout all nations,
which, in the case of Rome, have hitherto been commonly believed to be
an imposture practised by the patricians or nobles.

66. Much later, when these strangers or, more accurately, their
descendants, had been admitted into the first cities, they gradually
became accustomed to worshipping and fearing the gods of the lords of
these cities. During a long period of subservience they learned the language of religion and of the law and, following the example of the nobles,
contracted natural marriages with women who were naturally, or in fact,
certain. And just as, through the truth of [their] nature,[36] they reached a
state of humanity, their nature led them also to desire equality with the

---

[35] Throughout this passage, 'certain' descendants, 'certain' brothers and so on, are legally
    ascertainable descendants, brothers and so on.
[36] *Per verità di natura.* This probably means 'through the truth of their birth or parentage',
    taking *natura* in the sense in which Vico explains it lower in the paragraph.

nobles under the natural law of the gentes, by the lawful route of sharing their marriages and their gods. Hence the nobles finally gave them legal access both to the gods and to marriage, six years after the Law of the Twelve Tables was given to the Romans, as is clearly stated in Roman history. In this way, as the light of certain Latin history dispels the darkness which has hitherto shrouded the fabulous history of the Greeks, we discover that it was by fear of the gods that men such as Orpheus tamed these beasts and subjugated them in the cities. Hence, from that state onwards, the natural law of the gentes was a law common to all who were born of free men in the same city and because of this 'nature', or kind of birth, it was later called the 'natural law of nations'. Thus we can understand how solemn marriages were proper to Roman citizens as against the conquered gentes, as earlier they had been proper to the Roman patricians as against the plebeians. And this must be [the true explanation of] the civil law of the Roman people, rather than that the citizens of other nations, of their own power and in their civil liberty, did not celebrate solemn marriage among themselves.

67. In more recent times, having, during long periods of subjugation to dominant nations, gradually disregarded their own defeated gods, lived in fear of the victorious gods and, with the passage of many years, allowed their own languages to fall into disuse, defeated nations have come to celebrate the language of the dominant religions. Thus they naturally reached a state in which it was possible for the gods and marriages of the ruling peoples to be extended to them and with this extension the natural law of the gentes was judged according to the ideas of human necessities and utilities belonging to entire nations, each of which was unified by the bond of sharing the same religion and the same sacred language.

68. Such a sacred language of worship, in this case that of the Latin and Greek Church, unites all Christian peoples into one nation, as against the Hebrews, Mohammedans and heathens, thus explaining the natural sin of unions between men and women of these different nations. A much greater degree of sin, however, is the natural sin which attaches to carnal unions with women who are Christians, if these are made without the solemnity of marriage, for they must issue in children whose parents are unable to teach by example the first of all the laws of humanity, from which humanity itself was born: the fear of a god which must be felt when a man mates with a woman. Thus, when they indulge in uncertain promiscuity, they sin naturally by sending their offspring, insofar as they are theirs, into a state of bestiality.[37]

---

[37] *Cf. N.S.*[3] 336.

69. All this is based upon the second of the three principles which apply to the whole of humanity, which we proposed above: that men should unite with women only within the principles of a common religion, through which, with the addition of a common language, children may learn those things which pertain to their religions and laws and thus preserve and perpetuate their own nations. A number of distinguished philosophers of our age should therefore be careful lest, in their unbridled enthusiasm for philosophy, they condemn the study of the learned languages, i.e., those of the Far East and of Greece and Rome, upon which our holy religion and laws are founded, and are thus led, without their realising it, to undermine the most highly cultivated of all the nations in the world. For that nation is unique in the heights it has achieved because the religious and legal practices of the Christian peoples have forced them to cultivate the most brilliant languages of antiquity.

70. Finally, when wars, alliances and commerce brought many nations of different languages to share uniform beliefs, the natural law of mankind was born of ideas, uniform in all nations, concerning the human necessities or utilities proper to each of them.

71. For all these reasons the principle of natural law is that of a single justice, i.e., the unity of the ideas of mankind concerning the utilities or necessities common to the whole of human nature. Hence Pyrrhonism destroys humanity since it fails to provide a single justice, Epicureanism dissipates it since it would leave the judgement of utility to the sense of each individual, while Stoicism annihilates it since it neglects the utilities or necessities of bodily nature in favour exclusively of those of the mind, of which only the Stoics' own sage is allowed to be the judge. Plato alone favours a single justice for he believes that that which seems one or the same to everybody should be adopted as the rule of truth.

72. Thus the natural order of ideas concerning the law of the gentes must have progressed through the religions, laws, languages and marriages by which the gentes were founded and disseminated. Let us now consider, in the rest of this chapter, by what names the gentes were distinguished and by what arms and governments they were preserved.

73. If names were first and appropriately applied to the gentes – and in Rome they did so by adding the suffix *ius* [right] (such as *Cornelius*, which was widely diffused over many noble families, the most distinguished of which was that of Cornelius Scipio) – and if among the ancient Greeks they developed by means of patronymics, which are properly the names of fathers (whose antiquity is also very well attested because they have been preserved by the poets), it follows that the first gentes must have been confined to the descendants of noble houses, for the nobles alone were born of just or solemn marriages. HEnce when the

words 'Roman', 'Numantian' and 'Carthaginian', for example, were used to signify the *gens,* they must first have applied only to the noble orders of these nations. And since they alone understood the divine language of the auspices, the administration of all public business to do with peace and war must have been confined to them. Roman history has proclaimed this at well-nigh excessive length in its account of the dispute between the plebs and the fathers over the communication of marriage, consulship and priesthood.

74. From these things, i.e., the right to names among the Romans and to patronymics among the most ancient Greeks, and other equivalents among other nations, was born the natural law of the first gentes, which was protected by all three principles from which, as we suggested above, humanity emerged. The first of these was the correct universal belief that providence exists. Our second principle was that men should contract lawful marriages with certain women, with whom they should share common religions, laws and languages, in order to beget certain children, and that these should be brought up in religion and instructed in their native laws so as to be able to establish their certain fathers by names and patronymics and thus bring about the perpetuation of nations. (The Latins therefore first and properly called such children *patricii* while the ancient Greeks called them εὐπατρίδαι [eupatridai], both in the sense of 'nobles'. Hence, according to what is numbered as the eleventh of the Twelve Tables, in the chapter entitled *Auspicia incommunicata plebi sunt* [The exclusion of the plebs from the auspices], the Roman patricians confined the auspices exclusively to themselves.) And our third principle was that the dead should be buried in their own grounds which were assigned to that purpose. Hence by means of their genealogy or series of ancestors, [the practice of] burial must have ascertained their sovereign dominion over their lands, which they must have recognised through the auspices of their gods, by means of whom their original stock had first occupied them. Thus was distinguished the dominion of land by propriety where formerly all dominion had been common to all mankind by usage. This is the original dominion, the source of all sovereign dominion and hence of all sovereign empires, all of which, beginning with these first and oldest auspices, come from God.

75. All this gives us reason to think that, of the [kind of] men posited by Grotius and Pufendorf, some must have reached the human condition earlier than others. Moreover, the great principle of the first division of fields, which providence ordered by means of auspicial religion and burial, is revealed and, hence, the principle whereby all cities arose on the basis of the two orders of nobles and plebeians. An even more sublime discovery is that the world of nations has been ordered by God, perceived

principally in the attribute of providence, because of which He is worshipped everywhere through the idea of divinity, the idea, i.e., of a mind which sees into the future (for such is the meaning of *divinari*). Thus was the important custom of burying the dead (the Latin for 'to bury' being *humare*) taught to humanity. From these two great principles the science of divine and human things must make its start.

76. It follows from the fact that in the earliest times the word 'Roman', for example, applied only to the fathers or nobles, that this custom must have spread to Rome from a law, common to the gentes of Latium, [to the effect] that in the oldest assemblies the nobles alone should be called *quirites*, a word derived from *quiris,* meaning a spear. For *quirites* certainly meant 'the armed gentes of the assemblies' (just as, in our barbaric times, only the nobles were called 'men of arms'), since it was never applied to people when not in assembly or when they were few in number. This persuades us that since only the nobles had the right of arms, and therefore of force, which in the cities is called 'civil power', and since they alone belonged to the gentes, they must naturally have treated the law of the gentes as something belonging to themselves. We have shown elsewhere that the law of the Roman gentes must have remained within the confines of the order of fathers until the law of the dictator Philo. But since by then, after many a long struggle, the fathers had communicated marriage, sovereign command of arms and priesthood to the plebs, entitlement to the majesty of Rome was finally extended to everyone in the large assemblies in which, from then on, they were all referred to as Roman *quirites.* Hence, after that time, the name 'Roman' signified 'the nation of those born of free men in Rome, with the right to [decide] peace and war in the assemblies'. The provinces proper lacked a name for this right, for the Roman victories had deprived them of the sovereign right of arms. They thus had no appropriate name for the Roman citizens, just as earlier the Roman plebs had had no name for the fathers. Here we discover the origin of the law of the Roman gentes which, with differences to be reasoned out below, spread to the lands they conquered in Latium, Italy and the provinces.

77. It remains, finally, in accordance with the correct order of nature, to trace the development of the ideas which pertain to the natural law of the gentes in [their bearing on] the extremely important topic of governments, the last of the seven points proposed above. This has cost us the greatest effort in these meditations, the effort required to enter, through the force of our understanding, the nature of the first men, in whom all speech was lacking. For we finally discovered that through the same natural causes which produced the sacred language of hieroglyphics or mute characters in the first nations (as we shall explain more fully below),

which were known to the nobles alone and not to the vulgar among the plebeians – upon which language, believed divine, the oldest laws were dependent – it naturally came about that the first governments in the first world of nations were composed entirely of aristocrats, or orders of nobles. And these are shown to have been the heroes, Roman, Greek, Egyptian and Asian, in their age of barbarism. But as, little by little, vocal languages were formed and vocabularies grew among nations (and we argued earlier that these constituted a great school for rendering the human mind quick and deft)[38] the plebeians came, through reflection, to recognise in themselves a nature equal to that of the nobles. And, having recognised this true human nature, their eyes were opened to the vanity of heroism and they wished for equality with the nobles in their right to the utilities. Hence they decreasingly tolerated the bad government which the nobles had exercised over them, grounded upon the vain belief that their heroic nature was different in kind from that of man, until, on the ruins of the natural law of the heroic gentes, in which things were judged according to superiority in strength, the natural law of the human gentes (as Ulpian names and defines it) was finally erected, in which things were judged according to equality of right. Consequently, at the same time as the peoples had already naturally, or as a matter of fact, come to be composed of nobles and plebeians, and with a larger proportion of plebeians than nobles, and as the peoples had become masters of language through ideas created by the masses, they naturally came to make themselves masters of the laws in the popular states, whence they passed naturally to monarchies in which the laws are dictated in the common languages of nations.

78. Thus in the persons of monarchs were united the oldest auspices (called 'the fortune of leaders'), the names of nations (which are 'the glory of family coats-of-arms') and, as a result of auspices and names, the supreme command of arms, through which the religions and laws proper to nations, which distinguish and preserve them, are defended. Mastery of the hieroglyphic language of the first gentes was thus preserved intact, both among the free peoples of the assemblies and among the monarchs, who were restricted to a certain armorial language, a language of coats-of-arms and flags, through which the nations communicated with one another in wars, alliances and commerce. This language is here revealed to be the principle of the science of heraldry as well as that of medals. Moreover, it provides the underlying reason why, in nations which already possess conventional languages, governments can change from monarchies to popular governments and vice versa, whereas

[38] N.S. 1 42.

in certain history, for all nations and in all times, we never read that, in any human and cultivated era, either of the two changed into an aristocratic government. Thus can we understand how much science is contained in philosophers' meditations on the principles of civil governments and how much truth there is in Polybius' reflections upon their changes!

II *Corollary: a practical test comparing [the results of] rational principles with the vulgar tradition that the Law of the Twelve Tables came from Athens.*

79. The foregoing alone should suffice to alert us not to entrust ourselves in future to those authors who have based their theories of the origins of the natural law of the gentes and of Roman civil law upon vulgar traditions. Since, however, one who criticises the entire systems of other thinkers has a duty to replace them by one of his own, the principles of which provide a happier support for all the effects [to be explained], we shall pursue our meditation further in order to fulfil this duty. We believe it worthwhile, however, before continuing upon the journey we have already begun, to offer a test of the truth and utility of this new Science, in order [to decide whether] we should persevere further with it or abandon it upon its very conception.

80. The test is this: whether, in the foregoing reasoning, based upon principles laid down solely by the force of our understanding, we have entered the nature of the first men who founded the gentile nations so that, by means of the order of ideas we have devised, these principles should have led the nations to that state of completion in which we have inherited them from our ancestors. Let us compare the following: [first] the mode in which, contrary to our normal ingrained habits, and having by a supreme effort divested ourselves of that humanity of nations to be found in the theories of philosophers and the descriptions of philologists, we found origins, which were both reasonable as causes and appropriate to [their] effects; [second], on the other hand, by an effort which runs counter to these few, new and unusual, notions and which, by comparison, is bound to be very easy, let us try, if we can, to forget these origins, so that in what follows we allow ourselves, in the manner [which others have] hitherto adopted, to rely with tranquil mind upon the vulgar traditions which the ancients have left us in written form. If we are precluded from so doing, this will be a true test that the things which we have here conceived must be identical with the innermost substance of our soul, that is, that we have done nothing more than express our reason, so that it would be necessary to dehumanise oneself in order to deny them. This would constitute that innermost philosophy from which

Cicero wished to produce the science of law. It will be a true test, more-over, that the principles meditated so far were truths hitherto enclosed within us, which have either been overwhelmed by the burden placed upon the memory by having to retain innumerable, unsystematic things which are of no help to the understanding whatsoever, or truths which have been transformed in our imagination by our picturing them in accordance with our present ideas and not in accordance with the origi-nal ideas proper to them.[39]

81. So, setting aside what we have so far argued about the origins of false religions, of the gods born of them, of laws, of their first sacred language, and of the heroic customs and governments, so that these things might seem to be quite unknown – as, for thousands of years, they have indeed been unknown – let the things which belong to certain Roman history be agreed, the most certain of which is the dispute between the plebs and the fathers over the contracting of marriages through common auspices. This is the divine law which the jurist Modes-tinus made the first and most important part of the just or solemn mar-riages contracted by the Romans when he defined them thus: *sunt omnis divini et humani iuris communicatio* [the sharing of all rights, divine and human]. This dispute took place in Rome, three hundred and six years after her foundation, and thus three years after the Law of the Twelve Tables was given to the plebs. [But] here we must reflect that in those times the plebs had no gods in common with the fathers, which is tantamount to saying that the plebs constituted a nation of men entirely different in kind from the order of nobles, since it is certainly the unity of religion which unites a nation.

82. What dense nights of darkness must our minds encounter, in what abyss of confusion must they not be lost, as they search for the nature, the customs and the kind of government which ancient Rome must have had, unable to draw upon any likeness, no matter how remote, with our own nature, customs and governments? Let even our most ingenious [scholars] employ all their acuteness, or rather sharp-wittedness, to sup-port the reliability of our recollections, which are indeed of great age, of the following matters: that under the kings the government of Rome was an admixture of monarchy and popular liberty; that with the expulsion of the kings of Rome Brutus established popular liberty there; and that the Law of the Twelve Tables came from Athens, certainly a free city at that time, and that this Law established equality in Rome. For against all this the public evidence of incontestable history provides us with the fol-

---

[39] Cf. pp. 28–9 above for a suggestion how to interpret this passage. See also my 'Imagi-nation in Vico' in *Vico: Past and Present,* vol. 1, pp. 162–70, in which I argue that reflection rather than imagination provides the epistemological basis of the new science.

lowing: that until six years after the Law of the Twelve Tables not only
were the plebeians not Roman citizens, like those who did not share
divine things with the nobles, but they were not even part of the Roman
nation, for the fathers objected that they themselves, who were nobles,
were of a *gens,* which was certainly the Roman *gens.* On the contrary,
astonishing though it may be, they were held to be of a different species
from man, for *agitarent connubia more ferarum* [they practised marriage in the manner of wild animals], lasting only as long as their
cohabitation with their women. But unless we are to accuse Modestinus
of giving a false definition of marriage, and also to deny the common
custom of nations that their cities should not be divided into regions
according to [different] gods (for cities divided by religion are either already in ruins or close to ruin), and to disregard the all too strident evidence which certain Roman history provides of a three-year period of
dispute involving public debates and popular movements over [the matter of] some right, the above things force us or, better, allow us the freedom, not to place overmuch trust in the accuracy with which each critic
has affixed his own heading to each of the Laws of the [Twelve] Tables.
Hence [we must not place too much trust in] the heading whereby the
plebians might be fathers of families, since this is possible only for citizens; nor in that whereby they might make solemn testaments and create
guardians for their children, since this is permissible only to fathers of
families; nor in that whereby their inheritances might descend *ab intes-
tato* [as a result of intestacy] to their heirs or, failing that, to their male
relatives or, finally, to their gentes. For these, we assert, are the inheritances of plebeians who, until three years after this law was [supposedly]
given to them, belonged neither to gentes nor to houses!

83. But what perverse diligence [does this not reveal] when the doubts
about the law [said to have] come from Athens to Rome are such that it
is quite impossible not to pay heed to them? For, from within our own
minds, warnings press in upon us as to the wild and isolated nature of
the first nations, between whom linguistic intercourse was possible only
after occasions of war, alliance and commerce. Hence, like claps of thunder in our heads, [the questions ring out]: if, as Livy resolutely asserts, it
was impossible, only eighty-six years before his time and in a stretch of
land as small as Italy, for the famous name of Pythagoras to have reached
Rome from Crotona, [passing] through so many [intervening] nations of
diverse language and custom, how could the fame of Solon's wisdom
have come overseas to Rome all the way from Attica, the part of Greece
furthest from us? And how could the Romans have had such detailed
knowledge of the quality of the Athenian laws as to judge them adequate
to settle the disputes between the plebeians and the nobles no more than

twenty years after Thucydides wrote that the Greeks' knowledge of their own affairs went back no further than their fathers' memories could reach? And how had the Greeks come to be known to the Romans, and by means of what linguistic commerce and through what embassies, when, a hundred and seventy-two years later, because they were unknown in Italy, and in the absence of any linguistic commerce, the Romans' ambassadors were maltreated by the Tarentines and it was as a result of this that the Greeks and Romans came to know each other? Is the answer, perhaps, that, in the absence of linguistic commerce, the Roman ambassadors (Grotius' real simpletons, Accursius' truly ridiculous ambassadors, who unhappily discredit the highly renowned wisdom of the decemvirs) carried the Greek laws home with them in ignorance of their contents, so that had the authors of this fable not, in the meantime, also imported Hermodorus the Greek to Rome, to spend his exile there, they would not have known what to do with these imported laws? [But] how [in that case] could Hermodorus have translated the laws into a Latin so pure that Diodorus Siculus judges it 'to lack the faintest trace of Greek', a Latin so elegant, we assert, that no subsequent Latin author, no matter how well versed in Greek, was able to match it in his Latin translations of Greek authors? And how did he dress up Greek ideas in words so properly Latin that the Greeks themselves, including Dio [Cassius] claimed that in the whole of Greece there existed no similar words to express them, such as, for example, the word *auctoritas* [authority], which, as we shall show below, contains one of the most important elements, if not perhaps the whole or sole content, of the [corresponding] law [in the Twelve Tables]?

84. We have shown elsewhere, throughout two complete books, the fabulous nature of this vulgar tradition, when we revealed that the advice which the embassy gave forth, under the pretext of [being in the interest of] Rome, was, in fact, intended to hold the plebs at bay for three years. Here, however, faced with the attacks of those who would rather not understand than forget, we would take shelter in the shadow of Cicero, who was never prepared to believe this fable and who stated so openly. For prior to Cicero no Greek or Latin author mentions such a fact in Roman history, unless we are willing to give credence to a letter which Heraclitus wrote to Hermodorus, in which he rejoices in Hermodorus' dream that the other laws of the world had all come to adore his own laws. But the letter is the true dream, written in a part as remote as Ephesus or the desert into which Heraclitus later withdrew to escape the unjust hatred of the Ephesians, [and sent] to another in Rome via those places through which, as we said, Pythagoras [supposedly] had made his most distant journeys throughout the world. It is, moreover, a letter quite

unworthy of such an important philosopher [as Heraclitus] and of Hermodorus, a leader of such worth that Heraclitus himself thought that the Ephesians should be strangled to the last man for driving him from their city. For whatever the one said [in the letter] was received by the other with such delight and bare-faced adulation [as to imply] that the glory of good laws ought to belong to a translator, much as if one were to say that the glory for a great peace ought to redound to its interpreters! For if such praise were due him as the author who, as Pomponius believed, was sent to Athens for the laws of liberty, he seems utterly unworthy of it, since although, according to Diogenes Laertius, he was the most important citizen of Ephesus, he knew, to his own cost, neither those laws of liberty which led to his banishment by the Ephesians and that of the righteous Aristides by the Athenians, nor even those which, a few years earlier, had led to the exile of the valiant Coriolanus from Rome. This piece of nonsense must therefore be regarded as a forgery like the oracles of Zoroaster and the *Orphics,* or fragments of verse of Orpheus.

85. Of the rest, the earliest authors to mention such a fact are Titus Livy and Dionysius of Halicarnassus, so that none of the others who came later merit any more trust than these two writers. Here, however, [we must make an exception of] Cicero, who was more of a philosopher and a philologist than either of them and certainly lived before them. Moreover, as an extremely learned consul of the Republic he knew much more about the history of its laws than either a private citizen from Padua or a Greek with an interest in the fame of his vainglorious nation. In an erudite argument, which constitutes the subject of the three books, *De oratore,* he introduces Marcus Crassus to discuss Roman law in the presence both of Quintus Mucius Scaevola, prince of the jurists of his age, and of Servius Sulpicius, who (as the jurist Pomponius relates in his short history of Roman law) was taken to task by this same Scaevola for the fact that, although he was a patrician, he was ignorant of the laws of his own country.[40] Ever the most careful of all in observing decorum in his dialogues, Cicero makes Marcus Crassus state in the presence of these men (for it would otherwise have been an incredible impudence) that the wisdom of the decemvirs, who gave the Law of the Twelve Tables to the Romans, surpasses greatly that of Lycurgus, who gave them to the Spartans, and of Draco, and even of Solon himself, who gave them to the Athenians.

86. We shall reveal below those bases of truth which explain why, with the greatest inconsistency, the Law of the Twelve Tables was said to

[40]*Cf. N.S.*[3] 284.

come now from other cities of Latium, such as those of the Aequi, now from the Greek cities in Italy, now from Sparta and finally from Athens, where the fame of her philosophers eventually brought this wandering to a halt. We shall see here that the Law of the Twelve Tables suffered the same fate as the travels of Pythagoras, belief in which arose because the Greeks later found ideas similar to his in nations scattered through the length and breadth of the universe. For, going beyond those parallels which some Attic scholars have drawn between the Law of the Twelve Tables and some unimportant Athenian customs, and others between it and some equally unimportant Spartan things, and the parallels which the Christian scholars have drawn between some still minor laws and the Mosaic laws, we shall show in these books that the whole body of Roman law provides the most complete and certain public evidence in the whole of gentile antiquity (hitherto obscured by the foregoing vulgar belief) by which we can establish the law of the gentes of Italy, Greece and the other ancient nations. Here we have suffered greatly from the desire to match the vanity of the Greeks, to which the Romans were led by their love of pomp. For the Greeks vaunted, as the founder of their nation, an Orpheus rich in recondite wisdom and, to enhance him yet further, ascribed a wealth of such wisdom to Trismegistus and Zoroaster, from whom, by way of Atlas, Orpheus the philosopher must have descended. Hence, since, as we shall show below, the Romans lacked in Italy a founder for the laws which providence dictated to them – for Livy denies that Numa was taught by Pythagoras, however much the Romans may have boasted of this – they ascribed their authorship to Solon, prince of the sages of Greece.

87. This false belief had the same effect in the case of the Law of the Twelve Tables as in that of the wisdom of Zoroaster, Trismegistus and Orpheus, to whom were accredited works of recondite wisdom, which came [in reality] not only a long time after vulgar wisdom but as a result of the vulgar wisdom of Zoroaster, Trismegistus and Orpheus. For since it was believed that the Law of the Twelve Tables came all at once from Athens, while she was, at that time, a city of perfected liberty, many laws and rights were attached to it which the nobles had extended to the plebs [only] much later and after many disputes. This happened, for example, in the case of the right of marriage, which was extended to the plebs six years after the Law of the Twelve Tables and which, together with the auspices, was reserved to the fathers in the Eleventh Table. And on this depends paternal authority, testaments, guardianship, agnation, owner-ship and membership of the gentes.

88. Hence we must make a choice. Ought we, in this dense night, in these rough seas, surrounded by so many dangerous reefs, to continue to

sail in this merciless storm, which leads to the total subversion of all human reasoning, in order to defend the shadows of the obscure age and the fables of the heroic age, which were invented later rather than born thus from the very start? Or ought we to apply our reason to the fables, whose every interpretation has hitherto been quite arbitrary, to give them those senses which reason demands, and make ourselves possessors of the things of the distant past which have hitherto belonged to nobody, ownership of which can consequently be conceded legitimately to whoever occupies them, so that, in such fashion and by means of the principles of heroic nature proposed above, we may illuminate these dense nights, calm these storms and escape these dangerous reefs? We refer here to heroic nature, not as reasoned in accordance with the ideas of philosophers, nor as imagined in accordance with those of the *romanceros,* but insofar as it pertains to those origins which Homer, the first author of all profane learning, has faithfully narrated for us. This is the heroic nature uniformly revealed in the likes of Achilles and Polyphemus, which conforms to one of Lycurgus' laws or, rather, a Spartan custom, according to which the Spartans were forbidden any knowledge of letters. Since the Spartans accordingly remained in a state of ferocity, their government continued to be aristocratic, as, on the whole, most political thinkers recognise. It was a state of government, moreover, quite dissimilar to our own, even to those which have endured from the last barbaric age, which must therefore, in our present condition of highly cultivated humanity, be preserved with consummate wisdom. But because of its ferocious nature, the Spartan state retained a great many of the oldest heroic customs of Greece, such as, for example, as all philologists agree, that there was a ruling order of Heraclids or Herculean races, headed by two kings, whom this order elected for life. The Roman government will be found to have had precisely this form during the period in Rome when, in the absence of any letters at all or as long as only the nobles were literate, the state of ferocity endured.

89. Heroic nature, which lay halfway between the divine and human things of nations, has been largely unknown until now, because we have either relied on memory alone or imagined it other than it was. It has thus concealed from us the divine things of nations, from which it originated, while leaving us without a science of human things, all of which were born of divine things. Thus the material for working out not merely the systems of the natural law of the gentes but the whole science of human learning, divine and gentile, has come down to us in a distorted and despoiled form. Having, with this example, subjected our thoughts about the things under meditation to a severe examination, let us now return to our original path.

8 The idea of an ideal eternal history traversed in time by the history of all nations which have certain origins and certain continuity[41]

90. By means of the foregoing properties we have established the eternity and universality of the natural law of the gentes. Since this law emerged with the common customs of peoples, which are themselves the invariable creations of nations, and since human customs are practices or usages of human nature, which does not all change at once but always retains an impression of some former habit or custom, this Science must provide, at one and the same time, both a philosophy and a history of human customs, which together comprise the kind of jurisprudence with which we are concerned, i.e., the jurisprudence of mankind. It must provide these, moreover, in such fashion that the first part unfolds a linked series of reasons while the second narrates a continuous or uninterrupted sequence of the facts of humanity in conformity with these reasons, [rather] as causes produce effects which resemble them. In this way the certain origins and the uninterrupted progress of the whole universe of nations should be discovered. And in conformity with the present order of things laid down by providence, this Science comes to be an ideal eternal history, traversed in time by the history of all nations. From this alone can we obtain scientific knowledge of universal history with certainty of origins and continuity, the two most important characteristics which, up to the present day, men have so greatly desired.

9 The idea of a new art of criticism[42]

91. This same Science can provide us with an art of criticism applicable to the authors of the nations themselves and should give us rules for the

---

[41]Cf. *N.S.*[3] 245, 294, 349, 393. The meaning and significance of the notion of the 'ideal eternal history' is one of the most debated issues in contemporary Vichian scholarship. For one interpretation, see *Vico and Herder*, by Isaiah Berlin, pp. 64–7 and 80–2. Although acknowledging the importance of the 'ideal eternal history' in Vico's own estimation, Berlin nevertheless thinks it 'the least interesting, plausible and original of his views' (*op. cit.*, p. 64), implying, though not actually asserting, that it belongs to the 'chaff' rather than the 'grain' of the new science (*op. cit.*, p. 67). For two alternatives which attach great importance to the 'ideal eternal history', see W. H. Walsh's 'The logical status of Vico's ideal eternal history', in *Giambattista Vico's Science of Humanity*, and my *Vico: A Study of the 'New Science'*, pp. 97–128, 144–5, 156–8.

[42]Cf. *N.S.*[3] 348, 351–9.

discernment of the truth in all gentile histories, which, during the barbaric origins [of nations], became intermingled, to a greater or lesser degree in different cases, with fables.

92. For even learned historians are obliged to narrate the vulgar traditions of the peoples whose histories they write, in order that they be accepted as truths by the vulgar and [thus] be useful to the states for whose continuous existence they are written, leaving the assessment of their truth to scholars. But when facts are problematic they should be taken in accordance with laws, while when laws are problematic they should be interpreted in accordance with nature, whence we must accept such problematic laws and facts as create neither absurdity nor impropriety, much less impossibility. [Again,] problematic peoples must have acted in accordance with the forms of their governments, the forms of problematic governments must have been appropriate to the nature of the men governed, and the nature of problematic men must have been determined in accordance with the nature of their [geographical] locations. They must therefore have been of one kind on islands and of another on mainlands, for on the former they became more withdrawn and on the latter more sociable. They differ again in inland and maritime countries, becoming farmers in the one and merchants in the other. And there are further differences between those who live in hot, volatile climates and those in cold, sluggish climates, for in the former their ingenuity is acute and in the latter obtuse.

93. These rules of interpretation, which are applicable even to new laws and recent facts, enable us to understand the vulgar traditions we have inherited pertaining to the humanity of the obscure and fabulous periods which, in the form in which they have lain so far, have seemed absurd and even impossible. The reverence to which their antiquity entitles them is, however, ensured by the following maxim: that communities of men are led naturally to preserve the memory of those customs, orders and laws which hold them within this or that society.[43] If all gentile histories have therefore preserved their fabulous origins, and the Greeks more so than any others (for the Greeks are the source of all that we possess about gentile antiquity), the fables must uniquely contain historical accounts of the oldest customs, orders and laws of the first gentile nations.[44] This will be the guiding principle for the whole of this work.

[43]Cf. *N.S.*[3] 201.   [44]Cf. *N.S.*[3] 202.

10 First: by the use of certain kinds of evidence synchronous with the times in which the gentile nations were born

94. First, where the fabulous traditions, in which are strewn all the origins of the gentile histories, are found to be uniform among many ancient, gentile nations, separated from one another by immense stretches of land and sea, they must have been born of ideas which were naturally common to them.[45] Such traditions must constitute evidence which is synchronous, or contemporary, with the origins of the natural law of the gentes. An example here is the fable of the heroes who were born of the union of gods and [mortal] women. Since this fable is uniform among the Egyptians, Greeks and Latins (the last of whom relate that Romulus was the son of Mars by Rhea Silvia), it is necessary to meditate upon the idea, naturally common to these three nations, which gave rise to their heroic age.

95. And here appears the first special difference between the origins of sacred and of profane history. For although, in its account of the giants, sacred history contains the expression 'the sons of God', which Bochart explains as referring to the descendents of Seth, it remained free, nevertheless, of the filth contained in the account which profane history offers when it describes lascivious relationships between gods and women. The suggestion that the giants may have been the offspring of demonic incubi must therefore be emphatically rejected, for sacred history is not contaminated by the slightest taint of the paganism which possibly led the Greeks to name their demonic incubus Πάν, i.e., the god Pan, signifying a poetic monster whose nature was part man and part goat. We shall show here that this refers to men living in [bestial] communion, born of nefarious intercourse.

11 Second: by the use of certain kinds of medals belonging to the first peoples, through which the Flood is demonstrated

96. As public medals are the best ascertained documents of certain history so, for [the period of] fabulous and obscure history, their place must

---

[45]Cf. N.S.[3] 144.

be taken by various marble remains. These establish the common customs of the first peoples, of which the following is the most important.

97. A poverty of conventional languages led all the first nations to
express themselves by means of objects, which at first must have been
natural, and later carved or painted. Olaus Magnus asserts this of the
Scythians and Diodorus Siculus has written it of the Ethiopians, while we
certainly have the Egyptian hieroglyphics depicted on their pyramids.
Fragments of antiquity, moreover, are everywhere to be found with characters [formed] of carved objects of the same kind as the magical characters of the Chaldeans must have been. Additionally, the Chinese, who
boast in vain of enormously ancient origins, write in hieroglyphics, thus
proving that their origin was not more than four thousand years ago.
This is confirmed by the further consideration that, having remained
closed from contact with foreign nations until a few centuries back, they
have no more than three hundred articulate sounds with which, by enun-
ciating them in a variety of ways, they express themselves. This demonstrates the great length of time which must pass, and the extreme difficulty nations must experience, before they can furnish themselves with
articulate languages, a point to be discussed more fully below. It has been
noted also by travellers in most recent times that the Americans write in
hieroglyphics.

98. This poverty of articulate languages among the first nations, which
was common throughout the universe, proves afresh that the Flood
occurred prior to them. Moreover, in demonstrating this point we provide a true resolution of Thomas Burnet's fantasy of a capricious revo-
lution of the earth, the grounds of which he derived first from Van Hel-
mont, then from Descartes' *Physics*. According to Burnet, because the
Flood dissolved the Southern part of the earth more than the Northern
part, the latter retained more air in its bowels and was therefore more
buoyant and on a higher plane than the former. The Southern part therefore sank into the ocean, thus causing the earth to incline away from a
plane parallel to that of the sun. [But this cannot be correct,] for Idanthyrsus would not [then] have replied in hieroglyphics when Darius the
Great sent his men to declare war on him.[46] Moreover, granted the
assumption, which we shall prove later, that, among all ancient nations,
the science of such characters was concealed within the order of priests,
and that Moses gave the law which God had written to the people to
read, we can provide a demonstration of this truth of the Christian reli-

---

[46] Vico's argument is that if the Northern hemisphere had been preserved from the Flood,
Idanthyrsus, king of Scythia or Russia, would have had a much more developed language
than hieroglyphics with which to reply to Darius. For Idanthyrsus' reply in the language
of objects, see *N.S.*[3] 435.

gion: that Noah and his family were preserved from the Flood and that their antediluvian literature was preserved by the people of God, even during the period of slavery in Egypt.

99. This kind of proof, [drawn] from the whole of human nature, establishes both the principles of this Science and the truth of the Christian religion, without relying solely upon the authority of writers who have inherited highly distorted traditions in things profane.

12   Third: by the use of physical demonstrations, which establish the giants as the first principle of profane history and of its continuity with sacred history

100. In addition, proofs can be provided by means of physical demonstrations, from which a proof of the nature of the first nations can be derived.

101. Thus, nothing in nature precludes the existence of giants, men of huge body and disproportionate strength. Such, indeed, were the ancient Germans, who retained a large measure of their most ancient origins, both in custom and language, because they never allowed any civilised nations to exercise foreign control within their boundaries. Moreover, even today giants are still born at the foot of America. Hence arose those meditations on the physical and moral causes relevant to the ancient Germans, produced first by Julius Caesar and then by Cornelius Tacitus, which, in the end, reduce to the ferine upbringing of their children.[47] For this left them free to wallow in their own filth, even were they children of princes, free from any fear of a master, even were they children of the poor, and free to develop their bodily strength as they wished. But these same causes were much more potent in the case of the races of Cain, before the Flood, and of Ham and Japhet after it. For these races were cast into a state of impiety by their authors and thence, some time later, went into one of bestial liberty, brought about by themselves, whereas the ancient Germanic children stood in fear of their gods, i.e., their fathers.

102. Thus the giants become true. Sacred history relates that they were born of the confusion of the human seed of the sons of God (identified by Samuel Bochart as the descendants of Seth before the Flood, to whom

[47]*Cf. N.S.*³ 170, 243.

we would add those of Shem after it) with the daughters of men (identified by Bochart as the descendants of Cain before the Flood, to whom we would also add those of Ham and Japhet after it) and describes them as 'the celebrated strong men of their age'. Declaring also that it was Cain who founded the cities before the Flood and Nimrod the giant who erected the great tower [of Babel] after it, sacred history sets forth a fully developed case to show that both before and for a long time after the Flood, the world was divided into two nations. One was composed of non-giants, its members having been brought up in cleanliness, in fear of God and of the fathers. This was the nation of those who believed in the true God, the god of Adam and Noah, who were scattered over the immense lands of Assyria (as, later, the ancient Scythians, an extremely lawful nation, were scattered through their immense lands). The other was a nation of idolatrous giants (like the ancient Germans) divided by city, who later, through their terrifying religions and frightful paternal powers (which are described below) and finally through the political nature of their upbringing (which perhaps explains why the Greek πόλις [polis] or city and the Latin *polio* and *politus* have the same origin) were gradually reduced from their disproportionate size to our correct stature.

103. This meditation opens the only way, hitherto closed, by which to discover the certain origins of universal profane history and its continuity with sacred history, which is older than any profane history. The two can be connected by means of the start of Greek history, the source of all we possess about profane antiquity, which begins by mentioning Chaos which, as we shall show below, must first have meant the confusion of human seed, then that of the seed of the whole of nature. Near the time of the Flood it tells of the giants and, through the giant Prometheus, of Deucalion, grandson of Iapetus and father of Hellen, founder of the Greek gentes, who gave his name to the Hellenes. This must have been the Greek race, descended from Japhet, which went on to populate Europe, as Ham populated Phoenicia and Egypt and, through them, Africa. But, because the traditions which Homer inherited were corrupt, Chaos was taken for the confusion of the seeds of nature, the Ogygian and Deucalionian floods were thought to be individual floods, when they could only have been mutilated traditions of the Universal Flood, and the giants thought to have possessed bodies and strength considered impossible in nature. The origins of profane history and its continuity with sacred history have therefore lain unknown until now.

13 Fourth: by the use of physical proofs drawn from fables, which show that the principle of idolatry and divination, common to the Latins, Greeks and Egyptians, was born at a certain determinate time after the Flood, after they had been born by a different principle in the East

104. [The foregoing account of] these origins can be given further support by proofs of physical history drawn from the fables themselves. For example, [our knowledge of] physical causes makes it reasonable [to believe] that for a long period after the Flood the earth ejected neither dry exhalations nor burning matter into the air to generate thunderbolts,[48] and that whether thunder struck in the sky sooner rather than later depended upon whether the region in question was nearer to the heat of the equinoxes, as in the case of Egypt, or further from it, as in the cases of Greece and Italy.

105. Accordingly, the many gentile nations originated in worship of as many Joves, of whom the earliest was Jove Ammon in Egypt. This profusion of Joves, which has caused so much amazement among philologists, can be resolved by our principles, for in every gentile nation a god was imagined in the same way when thunderbolts struck in the sky.[49] Such a large number of Joves offers physical confirmation of the Flood and establishes the principle common to the whole of gentile humanity, for the impious giants are laid low by Jove in the sense of the word *atterrare* in which it means 'to drive underground'. Hence, as will be shown in general below, the war in which the giants piled mountain upon mountain, in their attempt to drive Jove from the heavens, is certainly a fantasy created by poets subsequent to Homer, in whose time it sufficed that the giants should merely shake Olympus, upon whose peaks and ridges, as Homer constantly asserts, Jove and the other gods lived.

106. It is possible – and from the effects to be worked out in connection with the mode of the division of the fields [we shall show that] it happened in fact – that when Jove's first thunderbolts struck not everybody was laid low and that the more alert, and hence more advanced, who had taken refuge in the caverns throgh fear of the thunderbolts,

[48]*Cf. N.S.*[3] 192.   [49]*Cf. N.S.*[3] 193, 377.

began, in that state of stupor, to feel human or modest desire. For since their terror prevented them from indulging their desire under the gaze of the heavens, they used force to seize women and drag them into caves, where they kept them. Hence the first virtue in men begins to reveal itself, with which they correct the natural fickleness of women, leading to the natural nobility of the virile sex, the cause of the first authority, that of men over women. And through this first human custom, certain children were born, from whom came certain families, which were the basis of the first cities and, thence, of the first kingdoms.

107. Here, among Egyptians, Greeks and Romans, divination is born identically, based upon the observation of thunderbolts and eagles, the weapons and birds of Jove. These were certainly the two things most observed by the Romans in divinity and thus the first and most important divine things in Roman law. This explains why the Egyptians – and from them, it is believed, the Romans via the Etruscans – retained eagles on top of their sceptres, why the Greeks retained wings on Mercury's sceptre and why both the Greeks and Romans kept carved or painted eagles among their military insignia. Among the orientals, however, it gave birth to a more refined kind of divination: the observation of shooting stars. The reason for this difference lies solely in the fact that the Assyrians came from the disavowed descendants of Shem and were able to learn the strength of society, before the heavens rang with thunder, from believers who, not that much earlier, had been united by a religion. The Chaldeans therefore developed wisdom more rapidly than did the Egyptians, as is shown by the fact, with which philologists agree, that the use of the quadrant and of the altitude of the pole-star passed from the Chaldeans to the Egyptians via the Phoenicians. Hence, if the Chaldeans were the first sages of the gentile world, and recondite wisdom therefore passed from them into Phoenicia and Egypt and thence into Greece and Italy, and since the whole of mankind spread over the earth from the East, we owe the occasion, at least, if not the principle, of all recondite wisdom, to worship of the true god, i.e., God, the creator of Adam.

14   Fifth: by the use of metaphysical proofs, which reveal that the whole of gentile theology owes its origins to poetry

108. The greater part of our proofs are metaphysical and we always use these when we are deprived of all other kinds of proof as, for example, in the following case.

109. False religions cannot have arisen other than from the idea of a body of strength and power superior to anything human which, because they were by nature ignorant of causes, men imagined as possessing intelligence. This is the origin of all idolatry.

110. In keeping with such a human habit, when men are ignorant of causes, their natural curiosity awakens in them a desire to know the significance of anything unusual in nature which arouses wonder in them.[50] This is the universal origin of the whole of divination, throughout the innumerable different kinds which have been practised by the gentile nations.

111. These two origins [of idolatry and divination] are based, as can be seen, upon this metaphysical truth: that when man is ignorant he judges what he does not know in accordance with his own nature.[51] Idolatry and divination are thus inventions of a poetry which is, as it must be, entirely imaginative, both coming into existence with the following metaphor, the first to be conceived by the civil, human mind and more sublime than any formed subsequently: that the world and the whole of nature is a vast, intelligent body, which speaks in real words and, with such extraordinary sounds, intimates to men those things which, with further worship, it wishes them to understand.[52] This is the universal origin of sacrifices amongst all the gentiles who procured or sought the auspices superstitiously in their ceremonies.

15   By the use of a metaphysics of mankind the great principle of the division of the fields and the first outline of kingdoms is revealed

112. Just as, by dint of a civil metaphysics, an [account of the] particular jurisprudence of a people, for example that of the Romans, must enter the mind of her legislators and take note of the customs and government of that people, in order to reach a proper understanding of the history of the civil law by which that people was, and still is, governed, so a jurisprudence of mankind must be directed by a metaphysics, and thence by a system of morals and politics, of mankind itself, in order to gain scientific knowledge of the history of the natural law of nations.

113. Before all else the metaphysics of mankind enables us to discover

---

[50]*Cf. N.S.*[3] 184.   [51]*Cf. N.S.*[3] 120, 180–1.   [52]*Cf. N.S.*[3] 375.

the great principle of the division of the fields, which is the source of Grotius' 'original dominion' and from which all the domains and kingdoms in the world derive, so that it will be found that the origin of kingdoms came about in the same mode as the division of the fields. Hence, to his credit, Hermogenianus begins his account of the entire history of the natural law of the gentes with the division of the fields. But the manner in which he and the other Roman jurists received it from the earliest jurists, and transmitted it to us, gives rise to infinite difficulties in seeking the mode [appropriate to it]. Did the first men, for example, divide the fields amongst themselves when there was an abundance of the uncultivated fruits of nature or when there was a scarcity of them? If they did so when there was an abundance of these fruits, how, in the absence of any harsh necessity, did they divest themselves of that equality, and hence that liberty, which was natural to them, and which to us, in this servitude to law in which we are born and grow up, seems as sweet as nature herself? But if they did so when there was a scarcity of such fruits, how could this have happened without even greater squabbles and killings than those which are said to have given birth to community itself? For just as an abundance of the necessities of life leads men naturally [to a state in which they are inclined] to be moderate and well disposed to one another, in which they concern themselves with nothing other than those necessities, so a scarcity, on the contrary, particularly of the ultimate necessities of life, turns men, be they human or savage, such as those violent men of whom Hobbes speaks, into wild beasts.

114. These grave difficulties may perhaps explain why it has hitherto been possible to imagine that the division of the fields took place through one of the three following modes alone: either Grotius' simpletons voluntarily allowed themselves to be guided by some sage of the sort Plato demands; or Pufendorf's abandoned souls were forced to agree to it by their fear of one of Hobbes' violent men; or men enriched by the virtues of a golden age in which justice reigned on earth, but foreseeing the disorders to which community could give rise, were themselves the benevolent arbiters in the separation of their boundaries, in such ways as to ensure that not all the fertile lands should go to some and the infertile to others, nor all the absolutely arid lands to some and those rich in perennial springs to others, and, having thus established the boundaries, then preserved them with supreme justice and good faith until the rise of the civil kingdoms. Of these three modes, the last is wholly poetic, the first wholly philosophical, and the other the product of treacherous politicians who, to establish their tyrannies, secured themselves a following by favouring liberty and bringing the disinterested to accept the idea of the common good. But, as Polyphemus tells Ulysses, the cyclopes had already

separated from one another; and it was normal practice for each to remain alone and isolated in his cavern where he looked after his family of wife and children, with a complete lack of interest in the affairs of others. Hence, in matters of utility, it remained the practice in Roman private law that nobody should have access to the law through some other person, so that only very late on was the contract of procuration understood, while, even when the resounding defeats of Saguntum and Numantia were imminent, the Spanish failed to realise the strength which alliances provide, so as to unite together against the Romans[53] – practices totally compatible with an origin of bestial solitude, in which men had no understanding of the strength of society. And since, as a result, they lacked awareness, nobody was able to take account [of anything] unless it pertained to himself in particular.

115. These difficulties drive us to seek [the principle of] the division of the fields exclusively in religion. For when men are ferocious and wild, and in such properties of their nature lies their only equality, and when neither the force of arms nor the rule of law exists, should they ever come together this can only be through belief in the strength and power of a nature superior to anything human and through the idea that this superior strength compels them to unite.

116. This leads us to meditate upon the long and deceptive workings of providence, whereby those of Grotius' simpletons who were more awakened in that state of stupor were stirred, when the thunderbolts first struck after the Flood, believing them to be the commands of a divinity who was the product of their own imagination. Hence they took occupation of the first empty lands, and here they stopped with certain women and, having settled down, begot certain races, buried their dead and, upon certain occasions which religion afforded them, burned down the forests, ploughed the land and sowed it with wheat. Thus they established the boundaries of the fields, and invested them with fierce superstitions, which led them, in savage defence, to protect their clans with the blood of impious vagabonds who, ignorant of the strength of society, came, alone and separate, to steal the wheat, and were killed in the course of their theft. The latter, the descendants of those who had not at first awakened to become aware of God (as had those from whom the lords of the fields were descended), and who were therefore unaccustomed to understanding His commands, came to humanity within these boundaries only after long and great experience of the great evils which the violence of Hobbes' licentious men caused in their [state of] bestial communion. Whereupon, to escape these evils, Pufendorf's destitutes

---

[53]*Cf. N.S.*[1] 35.

were naturally led to take shelter within the boundaries of the fields established by the pious who, thanks to providence, already had the advantage over the rest of being lords of the fields and sages of an imaginary divinity. Pomponius states precisely this when, in describing the origins of lordship in the history of Roman law, he elegantly asserts: *rebus ipsis dictantibus regna condita* [kingdoms are founded by the dictation of things themselves].

Book III
The principles of this Science drawn from language[54]
[Introduction]

248. The foregoing meditations upon the principles of ideas provide both a philosophy and history of the law of mankind. To complete the other side of the jurisprudence of the natural law of the gentes, we must now seek the science of a language of this law common to the whole world of human generation.

1 New principles of mythology and etymology

249. The definition of μῦθος is 'true narration' but it has continued to mean 'fable', which everybody has hitherto taken to mean 'false narration', while the definition of λόγος is 'true speech', though it is commonly taken to mean the 'origin' or 'history of words'. [Hence] the etymologies which we have inherited are highly unsatisfactory for understanding the true histories of the origins of the things signified by words. In the following meditation we shall therefore reveal new principles of mythology and etymology, showing that fables and true speech meant the same thing and that they constituted the vocabulary of the first nations.

For a poverty of words naturally makes men sublime in expression, serious in conception, and acute in understanding much in brevity, which are the three supreme virtues of language. This reveals the origin of the sublimity of the Spartans' words, for by one of Lycurgus' laws the Spartans were forbidden knowledge of letters. It reveals further the origin of the brevity and seriousness of ancient laws, such as the Law of the Twelve Tables, for this was committed to writing when the Romans were still in extremely barbaric times. Finally, it reveals the origin of the acuteness of Florentine aphorisms, which were born in the Old Market in Florence in the most barbaric of Italian eras, from the ninth to the twelfth centuries. The three most important virtues of poetic language are: that

[54] In the amplified titles given at the beginning of the volume, this reads: *The principles of this Science [drawn] from a language common to all nations.*

it should heighten and expand [our powers of] imagination; that it should give brief expression to the ultimate circumstances by which things are defined; and that it should transport the mind to the most remote things and present them in a captivating manner, as though decked out in ribbons.

251. Later, the necessity to express themselves for the communication of their ideas with one another, when their spirit is much preoccupied with this problem because of their lack of words, makes these mute men naturally ingenious and they express themselves by means of things and actions which bear a natural relationship to the ideas they wish to signify. We thus find that the first words of the earliest nations were mute. The earliest Greeks must have referred to them by the word μῦθος, meaning 'fable', which would be the Latin *mutus*. We find also that the word *fabula* remained in Italian as *favella* [language][55] and that the fables were the first *fas gentium* [religious dictates of the gentes], an immutable word. Hence from *for* [I say] came Varro's *formulam naturae*, meaning 'fate', the eternal word of God, and the Romans' communal *fasti* [court-days], both those of the proctors, who used immutable formulae to administer justice in times of peace, and those of the consuls, who employed heraldic formulae for it in times of war.

252. Finally, an absence or scarcity of reasoning brings with it a strength of the senses which, in turn, leads to vividness of the imagination, and a vivid imagination is the best painter of the images which objects impress on the senses.

2   New principles of poetry

253. On the basis of these truths, which are compatible with the man posited by Grotius, Pufendorf and Hobbes, new principles of poetry are revealed, which are not merely different from, but are quite contrary to, those which have been believed since Plato and his pupil, Aristotle, up to those of men such as Patrizzi, Scaliger and Castelvetro in our own day. For poetry is shown to have been the first common language of all ancient nations, including the Hebrews, though with certain differences which stem from the distinction between the true religion as held by the gentiles and as held by Adam who, though he lacked words, yet remained inspired by the true God.

---

[55]Cf. N.S.[3] 401 for a parallel passage.

3 Establishment of the birth of the first fable which gave rise to idolatry and divination

254. When men wish to create ideas of things of which they are ignorant they are naturally led to conceive them by means of resemblances with things which they know.[56] And when there is not an abundance of the latter they judge things of which they are ignorant in accordance with their own nature.[57] And since the nature which we know best consists of our own characteristics, men ascribe to brutish and insensible things, movement, sense and reason, producing the most luminous works of poetry. But when these characteristics give them no assistance, they conceive things in accordance with intelligent substances, which is the human substance proper to us. This is the supreme, divine artifice of the poetic faculty, by means of which, in a God-like manner, by our own ideas we give being to things which lack it.

255. This reveals the first, great principle of poetic fables, for, since they are characters for corporeal substances which are imagined to possess intelligence, their corporeal aspects must be explained by means of the modifications of our human minds. Moreover, we disclose the first fable of all, explaining the mode by which, and the time in which, it was born:[58] how, in the state of bestial solitude men, like children, were all force and expressed their feelings by shouts, grunts and murmurs, doing so only under the impulse of the most violent of passions. And since, in such a state, they were ignorant of the causes of thunderbolts, those of them at least who were more alert in their stupor imagined that the sky was a vast, animate body which, with shouts, grunts and murmurs, was talking and wishing to say something to them. Here we meditate upon the modes [involved in this], which are the very same as those through which both the [present-day] Americans believe that everything they see which is new or great is a god,[59] and the Greeks, in their times of superstition, regarded those who made discoveries useful to mankind as having a divine aspect, and in this way, created their imaginary gods.

256. From these origins of Greek humanity and, following her example, of the humanity of all other gentile nations, a continuous proof commences, running through the whole period of the foundation of nations, [which shows] that men are led naturally to revere providence and that providence alone must therefore have founded and ordered the nations.

[56]*Cf. N.S.*[3] 122.   [57]*Cf. N.S.*[3] 120, 181–2.   [58]*Cf. N.S.*[3] 147–8.   [59]*Cf. N.S.*[3] 375.

4   The fundamental principle of divine poetry or gentile theology

257. Thus was born the first fable, the fundamental principle of the divine poetry of the gentiles or of the theological poets. Its birth was wholly ideal, as that of the best of fables must be, for, from his own ideas, the poet gives to things which lack it the whole of their being. Thus it is as masters of the art themselves assert: that it is entirely a product of the imagination, be it the art of the painter of non-pictorial ideas or of the painter of representations. This resemblance to God the creator explains why poets, like painters, are called 'divine'.

258. The first fable was born with its three fundamental properties:

1. of being a credible impossibility. For it is impossible, since it gives mind to body, yet it is, at the same time, credible, insofar as those who imagined it believed it;
2. of inspiring awe and perturbation to excess for, from then on, it made men feel ashamed of venery under the open sky and forced them to hide in caves to indulge in it;
3. of [possessing] the highest sublimity, such as belongs to Jove, the hurler of thunderbolts, greatest of all gods.

259. It was born, finally, fully directed towards the instruction of the ignorant vulgar, which is the principal end of poetry; so that by means of this first fable, the first ignorant men of the gentile world taught themselves a civil theology which included idolatry and divination.[60]

260. We are persuaded that this origin of poetry, narrated with simplicity and clarity, is both more reasonable [in itself] and more appropriate to the origins of humanity (which above all are naturally rough and crude) than Plato's suggestion that the theological poets took Jove to be a mind, the principle of the movement of ether, which penetrates, agitates and moves everything. Such a theory was necessary to Plato to provide a foundation for his Republic, but not for the simpletons and destitutes through whom Grotius and Pufendorf respectively founded gentile mankind. For in the movements of those bodies, which the theological poets imagined to be innumerable, individual gods, Plato saw a single, infinite mind, the principle of movement. But this mind was not itself a body, since it is characteristic of body to be susceptible to movement and hence divisible, but not to cause movement and division, which is a property of something other than body.

[60]Cf. N.S.[3] 376.

5 Discovery of the origin of the poetic characters which constituted the vocabulary of the gentile nations

261. Upon the basis of what we said at the outset – that we can scarcely understand and are absolutely unable to imagine how the man of Grotius, Pufendorf and Hobbes must have thought, let alone have spoken – after a continuous and severe meditation, which has occupied us for twenty-five years, we finally discovered the principle which is as fundamental to this Science as vocabulary is to grammar and geometrical shapes to geometry.[61] For just as the letter 'a', for example, is a grammatical character invented to render uniform the infinite number of different vocal sounds, of open or closed accent, which are thus enunciated, or, to give another example, the triangle is a geometrical character designed to render uniform the innumerable figures of different-sized angles which are formed by the juncture of three lines at three points, so the poetic characters are found to have been the elements of the languages in which the first gentile nations spoke.

262. For if, by reason of its limited understanding, a nation is unable to name some abstract, or general, property, it must, upon the first occasion it becomes aware of the property, name some particular man who possesses it, in accordance with that aspect of the property under which the nation first observed him.[62] It may be, for example, in accordance with the aspect of a man who performs great labours under the demands of family necessities, and becomes famous for these labours since they preserve his house or race and, through his descendants, mankind itself. In this case he will be called 'Hercules' from Ἡρας κλέος [Hēras kleos] or 'the glory of Juno',[63] Juno being the goddess of marriage and therefore of the family. Such a nation, from all the things which, at other times, other men will be seen to have done as a result of this same property of labour, will certainly name these other men after the man who was first named for this property. Thus, to keep to the same example, all these other men will be called 'Hercules'. Moreover, such a nation, which we assume to be crude, and therefore also stupid, will become aware of only the most exceptional events and will therefore connect all the most striking actions of the same general kind, performed by different men and at different times, to the name of the first man who was named by that

---

[61]Cf. *N.S.*[3] 338.   [62]Cf. *N.S.*[3] 206, 412.
[63]Juno was the Roman equivalent of Hēra.

property. Thus, in our example, it calls all men who have performed great labours, under the demands of family necessity, by the common name 'hero'. And because their nature was of this sort, all the first gentile nations will be found, in respect of this side of things, to have been composed of poets.

263. Many and evident are the vestiges of the first nature which we have inherited in the vulgar languages. Latin is a case in point. When the Romans, for example, were ignorant of strategies of war, of pomp and of luxurious living, and first became aware of them by contact with the Carthaginians, Capuans and Tarentines respectively, they called everyone in whom they then encountered these practices 'Carthaginian', 'Capuan' or 'Tarentine'. Thus the antonomasia which has hitherto been taken to be a capricious invention of individual poets arose from a necessity of nature, common to all gentile nations, to think and express oneself in such a way. The vocabulary of all the first gentile nations will therefore be found to consist of such characters and will explain the language of the origins of the natural law of the gentes.

264. From these things, and starting first with language, a distinction begins to manifest itself between the gentile nations and the people of God, whose authors, though they suffered from a similar poverty of speech, were still enlightened by knowledge of the true God, the creator of Adam. They must therefore, even if not expressly ordered by God, have directed everything conducive to their continued existence, which other nations at different times had arranged differently, towards a single, provident and eternal god. Thus it comes about that in the Hebrew language, although it is wholly poetic and surpasses in sublimity that of Homer himself, a fact recognised even by philologists, one finds not a single mention of polytheism. This, itself, must be a demonstration that the fathers of sacred history really existed for the many centuries which it recounts.

6   *Discovery of the true poetic allegories*

265. The meanings of words at first must appropriately have been constituted by allegories, a word by which the Greeks still mean *diversiloquia*, i.e., words embracing different people, facts or things. [This explains why it is that] when mythologists sought univocal rather than analogical meanings for them, they ended up with results of such vagueness that the fables seem to have come down to us as basic material for all the interpretations of scholars learned in the fields of logic, physics

and metaphysics. Moreover, these interpretations, which, be they concerned with morality, politics or history, have been constructed by analogy with contemporary customs, governments and deeds, fail entirely to reflect the fact that, by a necessity of nature, the customs, governments and deeds of the humanity furthest from us must have been very different. Thus the mythologists seem, rather, to have been poets, inventing so many different things on the basis of the fables, and the poets, who meant their fables to be true narrations of the things of their own times, were the real mythologists.

266. But since it is impossible to create false ideas, for falsity consists in an incoherent combination of ideas, no tradition can be created, however fabulous, which did not originally have some basis of truth. And since we have shown above that the fables must have been histories of the oldest human events of Greece, the most difficult part of our work has been to meditate upon the bases of truth from which these fables sprang. These bases will provide us, at one and the same time, with the true principles of mythology and of the histories of the barbaric ages.

7   *The idea of a natural theogony*[64]

267. The discovery of poetic characters enables us to meditate upon the occasion of which human necessities or utilities, and in what times, there arose within the Greek mind the bases of truth from which, before anything else, they imagined the characters of their false gods. These characters are shown to have been histories of the oldest superstitious customs of the peoples of Greece, and a natural theogony of them is traced, which explains the modes of their generation, that is, as we have seen in the case of Jove, how they were born naturally of the imagination of the Greek gentes.

[64] Cf. *N.S.*³ 392.

8   The idea of a rational chronology, running from the fables of the gods, through those of the heroes, to the things of certain history, which is responsible for the continuity of the causes which influenced effects in the known gentile world[65]

268. A rational chronology is one which is guided by natural order, in accordance with the series of common ideas concerning human necessities or utilities. With such a chronology, the origins of which are themselves obscure and fabulous, we can assign to the gods and heroes the times in which the Greek imagination must have given birth to them. And, since we have inherited the tradition that the heroes were the sons of the gods, the gods must have preceded the heroes. Hence, since we have discovered that the heroic fables were histories of the heroic customs of Greece, our work must contain a continuous allegory of the whole of fabulous history, commencing with the gods and continuing with the heroes until it links up with the certain historical period of the nations.

269. This brings into view, from its very start, all the parts which go to make up the whole economy of the natural law of the gentes, almost all born at once, like the men whom Epicurus and Hobbes believed were born as cicadas and frogs respectively, and which all grew together into a huge monarchical body, that of Ninus, with which history begins. The omission of this crucial aspect led Grotius, Selden and Pufendorf, in despair, to treat of much less than half of the natural law of the gentes, that is, to concern themselves solely with that part which is relevant to the preservation of individual peoples, from which the natural law with which they did concern themselves must have developed.[66] Moreover, their ignorance of these origins led Epicurus, Machiavelli and Hobbes, in turn, to deal with the other half in such a way as to be guilty of impiety to God, to bring disgrace to the princes and to do injustice to the nations. In addition, both Plato, in founding republics which could not be put into practice,[67] and Polybius, who based his accounts of earlier states upon that of Rome, lost sight of providence. Hence, because neither of

[65]*Ibid.*   [66]*Cf. N.S.*[3] 394.   [67]*Cf. N.S.*[3] 131.

them considered [the role of] providence in the practice of human things, they both erred over two of the three completely universal principles of the humanity of nations which we put forward earlier.[68] For Polybius believed in the possibility of a nation in the world, which, while it contained sages, lacked any civil religion,[69] and Plato believed in the possibility of a republic of sages whose women were held in common.

40   The idea of an etymologicon common to all native languages[70]

381. The second principle [which follows from our account of the origin of articulate language] is that of an etymologicon common to all native languages. For the principles of things are wholly of that from which their composition arises and that into which they ultimately resolve themselves. And since we have shown above that the original words which the Latins uttered must all at first have been monosyllabic,[71] [we suggest] on the basis of this example, [that] it is in such monosyllables that the origins of native languages must everywhere be found. Moreover, since words are articulated human sounds, and children are led naturally to express things by imitating their sounds, the majority of words in all languages must owe their origins to onomatopoeic monosyllables of this sort. For example, a consideration of these same origins which we have discussed first in connection with the Latins and Greeks, shows that Jove, the first of all gods, was called Ζεύς by the Greeks, after the hiss of the thunderbolt and *Ious,* the genitive of which is *Iovis,* by the Latins, after the roar of thunder.

382. Such an etymologicon must be made to proceed constantly in accordance with the natural order of ideas. And since the forests came first, followed by isolated huts, then fields, flocks and herds, next cities and nations, and philosophers last of all, the etymologicon of each language must explain the origin and development of its words through these stages. Hence, for example, *lex* was originally a collection of acorns. Then they said *ilex,* as in Plautus' *lectus ilex,* in the same way as *aquilex* was a collector of water. Then *lex* became a collection of vegetables, from which vegetables themselves were called *legumina.* Next it

[68] N.S.[1] 45.
[69] The criticism of Polybius is the same as that of Bayle. See p. 81, no. 1, above.
[70] Cf. N.S.[3] 145, 161–2, 354.
[71] See N.S.[3] 447 for the way in which this is developed.

became a collection of men: originally of the rebellious clients, to whom the first agrarian laws were granted, then of the citizens in parliament, this being necessary, before the invention of writing, in order that citizens be informed of public decisions. After the invention of writing, *lex* was a collection of letters, whence the vulgar *legere* [to read] which still survives and from which the written law was finally called *lex*.[72]

41   *The idea of an etymologicon for words of foreign origin*

383. The third principle is also etymological. Since inland nations arose first everywhere, to be followed by maritime nations,[73] and since, as we established earlier, the first Latin words contained nothing of Greek origin – even though Magna Graecia was flourishing on the shores of Italy at the time when Latium still existed in Italy and Rome was still in its early days – words of indisputably foreign origin must be secondary words, introduced after nations come to know one another upon the occasion of wars, alliances and commerce. This principle allows us to settle many serious difficulties encountered in ancient Roman history.

384. For the common poverty of the first languages, together with the difficulty the first peoples had in abstracting qualities from their subjects, necessitated the antonomasia in which the names of nations, which were distinctive by virtue of certain qualities, were used to signify all men later observed to possess these qualities. Thus when the Romans were ignorant of refined practices and first came across them in the Tarentines, they used the word 'Tarentine' for 'refined', while when they were ignorant of pomp and first encountered it in the Capuans they used the word 'Capuan' for 'proud', and so on with other similar cases of antonomasia. This is what happened, for example, when Ancus Marcius, the first to extend the boundaries of Rome to the sea on the nearby shores of Ostia, first filled Romulus' asylum with Phrygians from overseas. Since the Romans were ignorant of their own origins – being in this respect no more fortunate than the Greeks – when they later came into contact with the Greeks and learned from them that these [coastal] settlements had come overseas from Phrygia (a fact which in later times was to provide grounds for the belief that the Roman race was descended from the Trojan Aeneas) they named Romulus' inland settlement [as though it were] an overseas Phrygian settlement. In this way we overcome that great

[72]*Cf. N.S.*[3] 237–40.   [73]*Cf. N.S.*[3] 298.

Roman misfortune: that in her own number there were not to be found men fit to choose as king, since [we read that] Numa and Ancus Marcius were Sabines, Servius Tullius was Greek ànd that an aristocratic kingdom was governed by a woman. For [in reality] all these must have been cases of antonomasia: Numa and Ancus, who resembled his uncle closely in piety, must have been called 'Sabines' because of the religious habits of the Sabines, Servius Tullius called 'Greek' because of the astute ingenuity in which the Greeks excelled, and Tanaquil a 'woman' because of his effeminate ways. And for the same reason effeminate men are called 'women' even today.

42   The idea of a universal etymologicon for the science of the language of the natural law of the gentes

385. The foregoing discoveries, [necessary] for the completion of the linguistic side of this Science, point towards this end: that just as, for example, the Roman jurists possessed the science of the languages of civil law and the history of the times in which the words of the Law of the Twelve Tables changed in meaning, jurists of the natural law of the gentes should possess it by means of a universal etymologicon. The model for such an etymologicon is given by the nature of proverbs, which are certain maxims of life, proven useful by the wisdom of mankind but expressed differently by the [different] nations because observed under different aspects.[74] In the same manner as proverbs, different words must have been given to men, events or things which, though identical in their nature, were observed under different aspects by [different] nations. Thus, for example, to this day, the very same cities of Hungary are called one thing by the Hungarians, another by the Germans and yet another by the Turks, using words which sound quite different in each case, because these three nations are accustomed to naming cities according to three different aspects. Hence it is that many barbaric cities are named in Roman history in a Latin of such elegance as to seem to be cities founded in Latium. Moreover this principle enables scriptural critics to circumvent the many difficulties which arise for them from observation of the infinite variety of names which profane history gives to the persons who are correctly named in holy language. Thus that mightiest king of Egypt,

[74]Cf. N.S.[3] 161.

who, according to Tacitus, was called 'Ramses' by the [Egyptian] priests
[when they spoke] to Germanicus, must have been the famous 'Sesostris'
of the Greeks, who subjugated the other three Egyptian dynasties to his
own Theban dynasty. In exactly the same manner the God Fidius, the
Romans' Hercules, was one of the Hercules the Greeks observed in every
ancient nation, of whom Varro diligently enumerated as many as forty.
The Latins called him 'Fidius' under the aspect of faith, the first and most
important foundation of nations, whence he was their god of oaths. But
when the Latins had come into contact with the Greeks, the habit of
taking pleasure in foreign things led them to use the name 'Hercules' for
this same idea. The same is true of Castor and Pollux who, among the
Greeks, must have been divine witnesses of oaths in addition to Hercules.
As a result the words *mehercules, edepol, mecastor* and *mediusfidius,* all
of which were formulae for oaths, survived among the Romans, the first
three being foreign, and only the last being an indigenous word. And in
the same way as the Latin Fidius survived in its changed Theban [form of]
Hercules, the heroic character of the gentes of Latium in the age of the
fields, who must have had some other indigenous name, was changed to
Evander, the Greek Arcadian who gave shelter to Hercules five hundred
years before even the very name of Pythagoras could penetrate to Rome
from Crotona, passing through so many nations diverse in language and
custom. This occurred also in the case of the major deities whom the
Chaldeans affixed to the stars, which certainly had different names in the
East. After the Phoenicians had traded much in Greece, they found native
gods there ready to lend their own Greek names to foreign gods. This
occurred without doubt after Homer, for in his age the gods were [still]
living on the summit or ridge of Mount Olympus [rather than in the
skies].

386. This [combination of the] certain history of the Latin and
rational history of the Greek languages sheds certain light upon the
origins of the Graeco-Neapolitan language. This must have been some
kind of Hellenistic language, involving native Syriac or Egyptian elements, which intermingled with a foreign Greek element after the Greeks
went [to Naples] to trade there, with the result that Tiberius took more
pleasure in Neapolitan Greek than in the Attic Greek of Athens. Thus,
with this kind of change of proper name by nations according to the
diverse aspects [of things], is revealed the principle of the eternal shadows
scattered over the civil history and geography of the ancients as well as
the principle of the natural history of fossils, plants and animals.

43   *The idea of a dictionary of mental words which is common to all nations*[75]

387. We conclude our book on language with the idea of a dictionary of, so to speak, mental words, which is common to all nations. By expressing the uniform ideas of substance (*sostanze*) through which, by means of the various modifications, the nations thought about the same human necessities or utilities common to all, but looking at them through different properties according to their diversities of place, climate and, hence, nature and custom, this dictionary must narrate the origins of the different vocal languages, all of which share a common ideal language.

388. To adhere to the same examples proper to our principles, let us enumerate all the properties of the fathers in the state of the families and in that of the cities to which they gave rise:

1. of imagining deities;
2. of begetting certain children by certain women under certain divine auspices;
3. of being, therefore, of heroic or Herculean origin, [for the following reasons];
4. for their possession of the science of the auspices or of divination;
5. for the sacrifices they made in their houses;
6. for their infinite power over their families;
7. for the strength with which they killed wild animals, cultivated the wild land and defended their fields against the impious vagabonds who would steal their crops;
8. for their magnanimity in allowing the impious vagabonds, endangered by the quarrels of Hobbes' violent men in the state of bestial communion, to take refuge in their asylums;
9. for the high repute which their capacity to crush the violent and support the weak brought them;
10. for their sovereign dominion of their fields, acquired naturally by the foregoing feats;
11. for their sovereign powers of arms, which accompanies sovereign dominion of the fields;
12. and, finally, for their sovereign choice of law, and therefore of punishment, which accompanies sovereign power of arms.

389. From the foregoing it will be found that the Hebrews called the fathers 'levites' from *el* which means 'strong', the Assyrians called them

[75]Cf. *N.S.*³ 162.

'Chaldeans' or wise men, the Persians 'magi' or diviners, and the Egyptians, as everybody knows, 'priests'. The Greeks had various names for them: 'heroic poets' from [the practice of] divination, whereby the poets were called 'divine' from *divinari* [to divine]; 'heroes', because they were supposed to be children of the gods, including, among these children, Orpheus, Amphion and Linus; 'kings', because of their infinite power, from which point of view Pyrrhus' ambassadors spoke of having seen a senate of kings in Rome; ἄριστοι from Ἄρης, i.e., Mars, like 'the martial ones' from whom, because of their strength, after the first cities were composed of them, the first civil governments were born in the form of aristocracies. Moreover, throughout the whole of Saturnia, i.e., Italy, and in Crete and Asia, from their aspect as armed priests they were called *curetes*, though first, with great exactness, throughout all Greece they were called 'Heraclids' or members of the Herculean tribes, a name which survived later among the Spartans, who certainly armed themselves with spears and whose government was without doubt aristocratic. In exactly the same way, among the Latin gentes they were called *quirites*, or priests armed with a spear called a *quir* – these are the *curetes* whom the Greeks observed in Italy. They were also called the *optimi* [the best] in the sense of the *fortissimi* [the strongest], for the old word *fortus* had the same meaning as *bonus* today, and the states which were composed of them were later called '[states of] optimates', corresponding to the aristocratic or 'martial' Greek states. For their absolute power over their families they were called *heri* or lords, which still sounds like 'heroes', and their patrimony after death was called their *hereditas*, i.e., sovereignty, from which the Law of the Twelve Tables left intact to the gentes the custom of making dispositions like sovereigns, as was shown above. They were also called *viri* for their strength, again corresponding to the Greeks' heroes, hence *viri* survived as the name for husbands by solemn marriage, these being the only nobles in Roman history until six years after the Law of the Twelve Tables. Others who were called *viri* were the magistrates, as in *duumviri* and *decemviri*, the priests, as in *quindecemviri* and *vigintiviri*, and the judges, as in *centumviri*. Thus this one word expressed wisdom, priesthood and rule, which, as we showed earlier, were one and the same thing in the persons of the fathers during the state of the families. Hence, with the highest possible degree of propriety, the Latin gentes called them 'fathers', because of the certainty of their children, while, for the same reason, the nobles were called 'patricians', in precisely the same way as they were called εὐπατρίδαι [wellborn] by the Athenians. In the times of the recurrence of barbarism they were called 'barons', and Hotman notes, not without surprise, that in feudal law vassals were called *homines*. [But] this is precisely the difference which survived among the Latins between *vir* and *homo,* the former, as we have seen, being a word which denotes a man of civil power, the latter denoting a man of ordinary nature, obliged to follow others who have the right to lead, called βάς by the Greeks, *vas* by the Latins, and *wass* by the Germans, whence came *vassus* and *vassallus.* From these origins the Spanish word *varon,* meaning male, must have survived, as well as the Latin *vir,* to distinguish male from female. Similarly, *homagium,* as if it were *hominis agium,* which was precisely the heroic law of bondage, the source of all the disputes described above in early Roman history. This shows how much science there is in the accounts of the origins of the fief given by Cujas and others!

Book IV
The ground of the proofs which establish this Science

390. This is the universal language of the universal law of the gentes observed in this great city of mankind. For it explains the modes by which are born all the parts which compose the entire economy of the nature of nations, since science consists solely in the cognition of the mode; it exhibits the times in which the first things of each kind were born, since it is the distinguishing mark of a science that it should reach starting points such that it is foolish curiosity to seek others earlier;[76] it discovers the eternal properties [of things] from these same times and modes of their birth, which alone enable us to ascertain that their birth or nature was thus and not otherwise;[77] and, from their first beginnings, it traces [their history] by means of an uninterrupted, that is to say continuous, succession of things, in accordance with the natural progression of human ideas.[78] Hence in the *Idea of the Work* we conceived this book primarily by means of the expression *leges aeternas* [eternal laws], which philosophers of law apply to the parts of law treated here. In addition, however, by means of the foregoing meditations, mythologies, which are histories of fact, and etymologies, which provide knowledge of the origin of things, are brought into agreement with one another; the remnants of antiquity, which have hitherto lain disordered, broken up and displaced, are clarified, recomposed and restored to their proper places; and reverence is preserved for vulgar traditions by the discovery of the basis of their truth and of the reasons why they have since reached us cloaked in falsehood. Moreover, everything that pertains to philology is governed with certain and determinate meanings by philosophy, each thing being presented thus both within the parts and within the whole of the system of these principles.

391. This Science has two practical aspects, which are arranged in accordance with the foregoing types of proof. One is a new art of criticism, which serves as a torch by which to discern what is true in obscure and fabulous history.[79] The other is, as it were, an art of diagnosis which, regulated in accordance with the wisdom of mankind, gives the stages of

[76]*Cf. N.S.*³ 346.   [77]*Cf. N.S.*³ 147–8, 346.   [78]*Cf. N.S.*¹ 90.   [79]*Cf. N.S.*¹ 91–3.

necessity or utility which belong to the order of human things and hence provides the principal end of this Science, which is recognition of the indubitable signs of the state of the nations.[80]

392. An example here is the mode by which some men were led from the practice of bestial mating to that of human mating.

393. The time in which this first came about was that in which, after the Flood, the sky first hurled its thunderbolts among the Egyptians, Greeks and Latins.

394. Its nature was that, because of their properties, the fathers were sages, priests and kings [at one and the same time] in the state of the families.

395. Continuity of succession is [to be found in the fact] that the first kings, who were certainly monarchical, were the fathers in the state of nature, so that it is in the full sense of the word that Homer gave the name 'king' to the family father who, with his sceptre, orders the sharing of the roasted ox among those who harvest the fields, [an event] which appears before [the rise of] the cities on Achilles' shield, on which the entire history of the previous world is described. Next, the kings were everywhere aristocratic. Finally, monarchical kings were established and monarchies everywhere, in both size and duration, were and are the most celebrated [form of government] in the world.

396. The eternal properties are as follows: that the natural law of the nations should be the concern only of the civil authorities, who should either be composed of a sovereign order of sages, as in the aristocratic states, or be under the control of a senate of sages, as in the free states, or have the assistance of a council of sages, as in the monarchies; that the civil authorities should be revered as sacred persons who recognise no superior other than God, as in the case of the first fathers in the state of the families, and, finally, that they should govern the peoples like the fathers of large families; that they should have the right of life and death over their subjects, as was exercised by the first fathers over their children; and that their subjects should, like children, acquire [property] through such fathers of their states – Tacitus, in his history of the *Lex Caducaria*, still refers to the Roman leader as *omnium parentem* [the father of all] – in order that the fathers should preserve the freedom of great families on behalf of both their nations and their children. This is the genesis of the eminent dominion of the civil authorities to which, in the face of public needs, the sovereign and despotic dominion which the fathers of families have over their patrimony must give way. How much truth there is in Bodin's claim that [the rise of] one sovereign dominion

---

[80] These are the stages of the 'ideal eternal history' (see *N.S.*[1] 90). For the 'principal end' of the science, see *N.S.*[1] 11.

under another sovereign dominion was an invention of the last barbarians, [we can see from the fact] that the first states arose upon the sovereign dominion of the first fathers and that civilisation arose with them!

397. The stages of utility are as follows: first, the necessity that states should worship a provident god; next, the certainty of clans by solemn marriage; finally, the necessity of the distinction of terrestrial domains through burial of the dead – a human custom which leads citizens to construct magnificent palaces and embellish their cities with public buildings for the brilliance and splendour of their descendants – whence the public desire for immortality flowers among nations. Hence, above all others the following three human practices are protected in all nations with the highest of ceremonies and refined solemnities: native religions, marriage within their own people and burial within their own lands. For this constitutes the common sense of the whole of mankind: that the nations should be steadfast in [their adherence to] these three customs, rather than to any others, in order that they should not relapse into the state of bestial freedom, for all three customs have arisen from a certain heavenly shame felt by the living and the dead.[81]

398. In the same way the stages of usefulness of recondite wisdom are shown, for recondite wisdom must be at the service of vulgar wisdom, since it is born of it and kept alive by it, in order that it should correct and support vulgar wisdom when it is weakened, and guide and lead it when it goes astray. Accordingly the rule for judging the state of nations should be whether the peoples are drawn closer together or driven further apart by these three maxims and whether philosophers assist them [in the former] or abandon them [to the latter].[82]

[81] These are the 'first three principles' of his science, which Vico discusses at length at *N.S.*³ 333–7.

[82] *Cf. N.S.*³ 129–30. For a translation of a development of the concept of a practical aspect of his science, which Vico wrote in 1731, but did not include in the *Third New Science*, see 'Practic of the New Science', translated by T. G. Bergin and M. H. Fisch, in *Giambattista Vico's Science of Humanity*. For discussions of the concept see 'Prudence and providence: the *Pratica della Scienza Nuova* and the problem of theory and practice in Vico', by Alain Pons, and 'Vico's *Pratica*', by Max H. Fisch, in the same volume.

[The Third New Science]*
*Principles of a new science
concerning the common
nature of nations*

Book I
The Establishment of Principles[1]
[Section II] Elements

119. To give form, then, to the materials laid out above in the Chronological Table,[2] we propose at this point the following axioms, some philosophical, others philological, a few reasonable and moderate postulates, and some clarifying definitions which, like blood in a living body, must flow through and give life to this Science in all its reasonings concerning the common nature of nations.

I

120. Because the human mind is of indeterminate nature, whenever it sinks into ignorance man makes himself the measure of the universe.

121. This axiom gives the reason for those two common human habits: *fama crescit eundo* [that glory increases the further it travels], and *minuit praesentia famam* [that it is diminished by the presence of the

---

* This is the revised version of The *New Science* of 1730, which was in press when Vico died in January 1744. For its relation to the *First* and *Second New Science*, see p. 12 above.

[1] Sections II, III and IV represent Vico's final attempt to explain the theoretical basis of his Science. Vico's adoption of the geometrical method for setting out the *Elements* of Section II is probably modelled upon Descartes' *The Principles of Philosophy* and Spinoza's *Ethic*. This suggests that Vico's rejection of the *a priori* character of rationalist philosophy did not commit him to thinking that philosophy should not be pursued in a formally rigorous manner. For the importance which he attached to the geometric method, see *N.S.*[3] 349 and the Appendix below pp. 269–70. For discussions of this point see the references given in n. 6, p. 163 below. Although set out quite differently, most of the principles asserted in Sections II, III and IV are discussed in The *First New Science*, often at much greater length.

[2] In the Chronological Table, Vico provides a highly schematised account of the chronology of some of the main events of ancient history known to him. The events appropriate to each of the seven nations considered are set out as though part of an individual national history, but there is a single chronological scale common to all. Only the events of Greek and Roman history are set out in any detail. The importance of the Table, however, lies in the fact that the dates ascribed to the various events depend upon the interpretation of the events themselves, which, although this is not made clear in the Table, requires that the sequence of events in any one nation's history be seen as embodying the stages of the 'ideal eternal history', and therefore presuppose everything which is required to establish the latter. This is the point of Vico's claim that the *Elements* will 'give form' to the materials of the Chronological Table.

thing itself]. For, over a journey as long as from the very origin of the world, this has been the continuous fount of all the glorified beliefs hitherto entertained about the most distant antiquities of which we are ignorant. This is a consequence of that property of the human mind to which Tacitus drew attention in the *Life of Agricola* in his aphorism, *omne ignotum pro magnifico est* [the unknown is always glorified].

II

122. It is a further property of the human mind that when men are absolutely incapable of forming an [appropriate] idea of things which are distant and unknown, they judge them by those which are present and known.

123. This axiom reveals the inexhaustible fount of all the mistakes perpetrated by entire nations, and by all the learned, concerning the origins of humanity. For the latter, which must by nature have been humble, uncouth and highly obscure, have been judged by [the standards of] those enlightened, cultured and glorious times in which the nations first became aware of them and scholars began to reason about them.

124. In this category should be located the two species of vanity mentioned earlier: that of nations and that of scholars.

III

125. On the vanity of nations we noted [earlier] Diodorus Siculus' invaluable remark: that every nation, be it Greek or barbarian, had had such a vanity, that is, of having been the first to have discovered the amenities of human life and of having preserved its memories of these things since the origin of the world.

126. This axiom sweeps away instantly the empty pride with which the Chaldeans, Scythians, Egyptians and Chinese each claimed to have been first in founding the humanity of the ancient world. Flavius Josephus the Jew, however, cleanses his nation [of this vanity] by his generous confession, noted earlier, that the Hebrews had lived concealed from all gentiles; and sacred history testifies that the world is almost young, in comparison with the great age which the Chaldeans, Scythians, Egyptians and, even today, the Chinese believe it to have. This is an important proof of the truth of sacred history.

IV

127. To this vanity of nations we add here the vanity of scholars, who want whatever they themselves know to be as old as the world.

128. This axiom sweeps away all the beliefs of scholars about the incomparable wisdom of the ancients; it establishes as fraudulent the oracles of Zoroaster the Chaldean and of Anacharsis the Scythian, which have not survived, the *Poimander* of Hermes Trismegistus, the *Orphics* (or verses of Orpheus), and the *Golden Verse* of Pythagoras, as all the shrewdest critics are agreed; and it censures, [on grounds] of impropriety, all the mystical meanings which scholars have given to the Egyptian hieroglyphics and the philosophical allegories given to the Greek fables.

V

129. To benefit mankind, philosophy must raise and support fallen and weak man, not distort his nature nor abandon him in his corruption.[3]

130. This axiom excludes from the school of this Science the Stoics, who demand the mortification of the senses, and the Epicureans, who make them their rule. Both of them, moreover, deny [the existence of] providence, the former allowing themselves to be dragged along by fate, the latter abandoning themselves to chance and holding that the human soul dies with the body: both should be called 'monastic or solitary philosophers'. But it admits [to our school] the political philosophers, and above all the Platonists,[4] who concur with all legislators on these three principal points: that divine providence must exist, that human passions should be moderated and human virtues made from them, and that human souls must be immortal. Accordingly, this axiom will provide the three principles of this Science.

VI

131. Philosophy considers man as he ought to be, and thus can profit only the very few who wish to live in the Republic of Plato and not wallow in the filth of Romulus.

VII

132. Legislation considers man as he is, in order to create of him good practices in human society: as, from violence, avarice and ambition, which are the three vices prevalent throughout the whole of mankind, it creates the army, commerce and the court, and thus the strength, wealth

[3] *Cf. N.S.* [1] 398.
[4] The neoplatonists. Vico distinguishes them from Plato, who, he held, did not understand the importance of marriage (see *N.S.* [1] 269).

and wisdom of states; and from these three great vices, which would certainly destroy the human species on earth, it creates civil happiness.

133. This axiom proves that divine providence exists and that it is a divine legislative mind which, from the passions of men concerned only for their own personal advantage, in pursuit of which they would live as wild beasts in solitude, has created the civil orders through which they may live in a human society.

VIII

134. Things neither settle down nor persist out of their natural state.

135. Since, from what is remembered of the world, mankind has lived and lives in a fitting manner in society, this axiom alone resolves the great dispute, in which the best philosophers and theologians are still opposed to Carneades the sceptic and Epicurus (and to which not even Grotius has put a stop): whether law exists by nature or whether human nature is sociable, which mean the same thing.⁵

136. This same axiom, taken in conjunction with the seventh and its corollary, proves that man has the free will, however weak, to make virtues of his passions; but that God helps him naturally, through divine providence, and supernaturally, through divine grace.

IX

137. Men who do not know the truth (*il vero*) of things endeavour to cling to the certain (*il certo*) in order that, since they are unable to satisfy their intellect with knowledge (*scienza*), their will may at least rest upon consciousness (*coscienza*).

X

138. Philosophy contemplates reason, whence comes knowledge of the true (*il vero*); philology observes the authority of human will, whence comes consciousness of the certain (*il certo*).

139. The second part of this axiom defines as philologists all grammarians, historians and critics, engaged in cognition of the languages and affairs of peoples, both internal, such as their customs and laws, and external, such as their wars, peaces, alliances, journeys and commerce.

140. This same axiom proves that the philosophers, who failed to ascertain their reasoning with the authority of the philologists, fell half-

⁵*Cf. N.S.*³ 309.

way short [in their task] as did the philologists, who failed to verify their authority with the reasoning of the philosophers. Had they not done this, they would have been more helpful to their states and have anticipated us in meditating this Science.[6]

XI

141. Human will, by its nature most uncertain, is made certain and determined by the common sense of men concerning human necessities and utilities, the two sources of the natural law of the gentes.[7]

XII

142. Common sense is a judgement lacking all reflection, felt in common by a whole order, a whole people, a whole nation or the whole of mankind.[8]

143. This axiom, together with the following definition, will produce a new critical art for those authors of nations amongst whom well over a thousand years must have elapsed in order that the writers with whom criticism has hitherto been occupied should arise.[9]

XIII

144. Uniform ideas born among whole peoples ignorant of one another must have a common basis of truth.[10]

145. This axiom is a great principle, which establishes that the common sense of mankind is the criterion taught to the nations by divine providence to define the certain in respect of the natural law of the gentes, which the nations ascertain by understanding the substantial unities of such law in which, with various modifications, all [nations]

---

[6] The task of the new science is, therefore, to bring philosophical and empirical studies into a reciprocal relationship which will issue in knowledge of the world which man has made. For Vico's complaints about the philologists, and philosophers, see *N.S.*[1] 12–24. For various interpretations of how he conceived this reciprocal relationship, see Berlin, *op. cit.,* Croce, *op. cit.,* Max H. Fisch's 'Vico and Pragmatism' in *Giambattista Vico: An International Symposium,* W. H. Walsh's 'The logical status of Vico's ideal eternal history', in *Giambattista Vico's Science of Humanity,* D. P. Verene's 'Vico's science of imaginative universals and the philosophy of symbolic forms' in the same volume, and his 'Vico's philosophy of imagination' in *Social Research,* 43(3), autumn 1976, E. McMullin's 'Vico's theory of science', and my 'Human nature and the concept of a human science', in the same journal, and my *Vico: A Study of the 'New Science'.*

[7] The 'human will' referred to here is human will at a public level, as embodied in institutionalised states of affairs. At the private level man's will is not determined (*cf. N.S.*[3] 136). *Cf.* also *N.S.*[1] 47.

[8] *Cf. N.S.*[1] 26–7.   [9] *Cf. N.S.*[1] 91–3.   [10] *Cf. N.S.*[1] 94.

concur. Whence comes the mental dictionary for giving origins to all the various articulated languages,[11] and with this [dictionary] the ideal eternal history is conceived, which provides the histories in time of all nations.[12] The axioms proper to this dictionary and this history will be set out below.[13]

146. This same axiom subverts all the ideas entertained so far about the natural law of the gentes, which was believed to have emerged in [some] one first nation from which the others received it. The Egyptians and Greeks, with their vain boast of having disseminated humanity throughout the world, were a very bad example of this and it must certainly have been the cause of [the false belief in] the passing of the Law of the Twelve Tables from Greece to Rome. But, were this the mode [of origin proper to the natural law of the gentes], it would be a civil law communicated to [these] other peoples by human provision and not a law which divine providence had already ordered naturally, with human customs themselves, in all nations. It will be one of the continuous tasks undertaken in these books to demonstrate that the natural law of the gentes was born independently in nations, without their knowing anything of one another, and that later, as a result of wars, embassies, alliances and commerce, it was realised that it was common to the whole of mankind.

XIV

147. The nature of things is nothing but their birth in certain times and by certain modes (*guise*), such that, provided they are thus, then thus and not otherwise are things born.[14]

XV

148. The inseparable properties of subjects must be produced by the modification or mode (*guisa*) by which things are born; hence they can verify for us that the nature or birth of these things was thus and not otherwise.

XVI

149. Vulgar traditions must have had a public basis of truth, whence they were born and maintained by whole peoples over long stretches of time.

[11]Cf. N.S.[1] 387, but also N.S.[1] 381–6.   [12]Cf. N.S.[1] 90.
[13]See N.S.[3] 161–2, 236–45, 294, 392–3.   [14]See p. 88, n. 14, above.

150. This will be another great task of this Science: to discover their basis of truth which, with the passing of the years and the changing of languages and customs, has reached us cloaked in falsehood.

XVII

151. Expressions of the vulgar must be witnesses of the utmost importance concerning the ancient customs which were practised by the peoples at the time when the languages were formed.

XVIII

152. Where an ancient nation has maintained its autonomy until it has reached its fruition, its language must be a great witness of the customs of the world's first times.

153. This axiom assures us that the philological proofs of the natural law of the gentes – a law in which the Romans were undoubtedly more learned than any other people in the world – drawn from the Latin languages must be of the utmost importance. For the same reason, scholars of the German language, which retains this same property as the ancient Roman language, will be able to supply similar proofs.

XIX

154. If the Law of the Twelve Tables constituted customs of the peoples of Latium, which had begun to be observed in Latium as far back as the age of Saturn, and which, while they were constantly changing elsewhere, were preserved in bronze by the Romans and guarded religiously by Roman jurisprudence, it is an important witness to the ancient natural law of the gentes of Latium.

155. We showed this to be true in fact, a good many years ago, in our *Principles of universal law;* it will be seen with greater illumination in these books.

XX

156. If the Homeric poems are civil histories of ancient Greek customs, they will be two great treasuries of the natural law of the gentes of Greece.

157. This axiom is here assumed: it will later be shown in fact.

XXI

158. The Greek philosophers quickened the natural course which their nation was due to take, by arising while [a state of] crude barbarity still obtained and then passing immediately to a state of the utmost refinement in which, at the same time, their fabulous histories, both divine and heroic, were wholly preserved. But the Romans, whose customs developed at a steady pace, completely lost their history of the gods (so that what the Egyptians called the 'age of the gods' is referred to by Varro as the Romans' 'dark age'), but preserved, in their vulgar language, their heroic history, stretching from Romulus to the Publilian and Petelian laws, and this will be found to be a continuous historical mythology of the heroic age of Greece.

159. This [account of the] nature of human, civil things is confirmed for us by the French nation where, although it was in the middle of the barbarism of the twelfth century, the famous school of Paris opened, at which Peter Lombard, the celebrated master of the [Four Books of] Sentences, began to teach Scholastic theology of the utmost sublety. Here also, like a Homeric poem, the story of Turpin, Bishop of Paris, endured, [a story] full of those fables of the French heroes, known as paladins, which later filled so many romances and poems. And, as a result of this premature passage from barbarism to these most subtle sciences, French remained a language of such refinement that, of all living languages, it seems to have reinstated in our times the elegance typical of the Greeks and, like Greek, to be superior to any other language for reasoning in the sciences. Also, like Greek, it retains many diphthongs, which are characteristic of a barbarous and still inflexible language, in which it is difficult to combine consonants with vowels. In confirmation of what we have asserted of these two languages, let us add here an observation that can still be made in connection with the young: that is, that, at the age when memory is strong, imagination vivid and ingenuity lively – [an age at] which they can fruitfully pursue the study of languages and of linear geometry without, in the process, overcoming that severity of mind, contracted from the body, which may be called the barbarism of the intellect – should they, in this still raw state, pass on to the over-refined studies of metaphysical criticism and algebra, they become most narrow in their manner of thinking for the whole of their lives and render themselves unfit for any great work.

160. But after longer meditation upon this work, we discovered a further cause of this effect, one which is perhaps more appropriate: that Romulus founded Rome amid other older cities of Latium, and did so by opening there an asylum, which Livy defines generally as *vetus consilium*

condentium urbes [the ancient plan of the founders of cities], because, since violent incidents still took place, he naturally ordered Rome in accordance with the same plan which had underlain the foundation of the earliest cities in the world. And since Roman customs were developing from these very same origins during times in which the vulgar languages of Latium had [already] made much progress, [this is how] it must have come about that, where the Greeks had expressed their civil things in heroic language, the Romans expressed theirs in the language of the vulgar – whence ancient Roman history will be found to be a continuous mythology of the heroic history of the Greeks. And this must be the reason why the Romans were the heroes of the world: that Rome laid her hands upon the other cities of Latium, then upon Italy, and finally upon the [whole] world, because heroism waxed young in her at a time when, in the other peoples of Latium, from whom, after she had conquered them, came all her greatness, it must already have begun to wane.

XXII

161. It is necessary that there be in the nature of human things a mental language common to all nations, which uniformly signifies the substance of things practicable in human social life and expresses it with as many different modifications as there are different possible aspects of things. We experience the truth of this in proverbs, which are maxims of vulgar wisdom, perceived as identical in substance by all nations, ancient and modern, [but] expressed under as many different aspects as there are nations.

162. This language is proper to this Science and if scholars of languages attend to the light [which it casts upon things] they will be able to form a mental vocabulary common to all the different articulate languages, living and dead. A particular example of this was offered in the first edition of the *New Science*, [in a passage] in which we proved that in a large number of languages, living and dead, the earliest family fathers were given names in accordance with the various properties they had in the state of the families and of the first states, when the nations first formed their languages.[15] We shall make as much use of this vocabulary in our reasonings here as our meagre learning permits.

163. Of the foregoing propositions, numbers I to IV provide bases for refutations of everything hitherto believed concerning the origins of humanity, refutations which rest upon the improbability, absurdity, inconsistency and impossibility of these beliefs. The next propositions,

[15] *N.S.*[1] 387–9.

from numbers V to XV, which provide the bases of the true, will serve to meditate this world of nations in its eternal idea, through that property of every science, pointed out by Aristotle, *scientia debet esse de universalibus et aeternis* [science must be of the universal and eternal]. The final propositions, from XV[I] to XXII, which provide the bases of the certain, will be used to see in fact this world of nations which we have meditated in idea, in accordance with the best ascertained method of philosophising of Francis Bacon, Lord Verulam, but transferred from [an enquiry into] natural things, upon which he worked [in] his book *Cogitata [et] visa,* to [an enquiry into] human civil things.

164. The propositions advanced so far are general and provide a foundation for this Science as a whole; those which follow are particular and provide it with detailed foundations for the different subjects with which it is concerned.

XXIII

165. Sacred history is older than any of the most ancient profane histories which have reached us, because it recounts so clearly, and for a long period of more than eight hundred years, the state of nature under the patriarchs, i.e., the state of the families, upon which, as the political philosophers all agree, the peoples and cities later arose. Of this state profane history either says nothing or it says little and in a most confused way.

166. This axiom proves the truth of sacred history, as against [the results of] the vanity of nations, of which Diodorus Siculus earlier told us, for the Hebrews have preserved their memories with so much clarity since the origin of the world.

XXIV

167. The Hebrew religion was founded by the true God by the prohibition of [the practice of] divination, on which the gentile nations all arose.

168. This axiom gives one of the principal reasons why the whole world of ancient nations divided itself into Hebrews and gentiles.

XXV

169. The Flood is proved neither by the philological proofs of Martin Schoock, which are altogether too insubstantial, nor by the astrological proofs of Cardinal Pierre d'Ailly, followed by Pico della Mirandola,

which are too uncertain, indeed false, since they fall back upon the Alphonsine Tables, which were refuted by the Hebrews and now by the Christians who, with their repudiation of the calculations of Eusebius and Bede, today accept those of Philo the Jew. The Flood is proved, rather, by physical histories recorded in the fables,[16] as will be seen in the axioms which follow.

XXVI

170. The bodies of the giants were huge in nature, like those clumsy, extremely wild beings whom travellers tell of finding at the foot of America, in the land known as *de los patacones* [Patagonia]. Setting aside those reasons, vain, incoherent or false, brought forward for this by the philosophers and collected and followed by Chassanion in his *De gigantibus,* we turn to the causes, part physical and part moral, noted by Julius Caesar and Cornelius Tacitus in their descriptions of the huge size of the ancient Germans, and upon reflection [we see that these causes] arose from the ferine upbringing of the children.[17]

XXVII

171. Greek history, which is the source of all that we possess concerning all other ancient gentile histories with the exception of Rome, begins with the Flood and the giants.

172. These two axioms reveal earliest mankind divided into two species: one, the gentiles, [composed] of giants, the other, the Jews, [composed] of men of correct size – a difference which cannot have arisen other than from the gentiles' ferine, and the Jews' human, upbringing. The origin of the Jews was therefore different from that of all the gentiles.

XXVIII

173. Two great fragments of Egyptian antiquity have nevertheless come down to us, as we noted earlier. One is [the tradition] that the Egyptians divided the whole of the world's past prior to them into three ages: those of the gods, of the heroes and of men. The other is [the tradition] that, through all these three ages, three languages had been spoken, corresponding in their order to the said three ages. These were the hieroglyphic or sacred language, the symbolic language or [the language

[16] Cf. N.S.[1] 100–3 and N.S.[3] 192–5. [17] Cf. N.S.[1] 101.

working] by means of resemblances, which is the heroic language, and the alphabetic or vulgar language of men, [working] by means of conventional signs for communicating the common needs of their life.

XXIX

174. In his two poems there are five places, which will be quoted below, in which Homer refers to a language older than his own, unquestionably heroic, language and calls it 'the language of the gods'.[18]

XXX

175. Varro had the diligence to collect thirty thousand names of gods (for such a number the Greeks truly had), these names relating to an equal number of natural, moral, economic or, lastly, civil, needs of life in the earliest times.

176. These three axioms establish that the world of peoples began everywhere with religion, [a proposition] which will be the first of the three principles of this Science.[19]

XXXI

177. Where peoples have grown wild through arms, so that human laws no longer obtain among them, religion provides the only effective means of subduing them.

178. This axiom establishes that in the lawless state divine providence began the direction of the wild and violent towards humanity and the establishment of nations, by arousing in them a confused idea of god which, because of their ignorance, they attributed to that to which it did not correspond. Thus, terrified of this imagined divinity, they began to put themselves in some order.

179. Thomas Hobbes was unable to observe such an origin of things among his 'wild and violent ones', for in his search for his origins he strayed into Epicurus' 'chance'. Whence, with an outcome as unhappy as the effort was heroic, he believed that he had augmented Greek philosophy with an important aspect in which it had certainly been deficient (as George Pasch points out in his *De eruditis huius saeculi inventis*): that of considering man within the whole society of mankind. But Hobbes would not otherwise have thought of this had the Christian religion, which commands not only justice but charity towards the whole of man-

[18]N.S.[3] 437.   [19]N.S.[3] 333; *cf.* N.S.[1] 397.

kind, not given him his motive. Whence begins the refutation of Polybius' false aphorism: that, were there philosophers on earth, religions would be unnecessary; since, if the world contained no states, and states cannot arise without religions, it would contain no philosophers.

XXXII

180. Wherever men are ignorant of the natural causes of things and are unable to explain them even by means of similar things, they ascribe their own nature to them, as, for example, [when] the vulgar say that the magnet loves iron.[20]
181. This axiom falls under the first: that whenever, because of its indeterminate nature, the human mind sinks into ignorance, it makes itself the measure of the universe in respect of everything that it does not know.[21]

XXXIII

182. The physics of the ignorant is a vulgar metaphysics, in which they ascribe to the will of God the causes of things of which they are ignorant, without considering the means of which the divine will makes use.

XXXIV

183. Tacitus' remark, *mobiles ad supersititionem perculsae semel mentes* [once minds are dispirited they are easily moved to superstition], points to a true property of human nature: that once men are gripped by a fearful superstition, they relate everything that they imagine, see, or even do, to it.

XXXV

184. Wonder is the daughter of ignorance, increasing according to the greatness of the admired effect.

XXXVI

185. The power of the imagination is proportionate to the weakness of the capacity to reason.

[20]Cf. N.S.[1] 111.   [21]N.S.[3] 120.

XXXVII

186. The most sublime work of poetry is that of giving sense and emotion to insentient things. Children have the property of holding inanimate things in their hands and, as they play, talking to them as though they were living people.

187. This philologico-philosophical axiom proves that in the infancy of the world men were by nature sublime poets.

XXXVIII

188. In a golden passage, in which he is discussing the origins of idolatry, Lactantius Firmianus states: *Rudes initio homines deos appellarunt sive ob miraculum virtutis (hoc vere putabant rudes adhuc et simplices); sive, ut fieri solet, in admirationem praesentis potentiae; sive ob beneficia, quibus erant ad humanitatem compositi* [In the beginning the ignorant called [things] gods either because of the miracle of their power (for thus did men who were still ignorant and simple truly believe), or, as is usually the case, in admiration of their actual power, or because of the benefits through which they had been brought to a condition of humanity].

XXXIX

189. When wonder first makes an opening in our mind, curiosity, that inherent property of man, daughter of ignorance but mother of knowledge, produces this habit: that wherever [man] observes some extraordinary effect in nature, such as a comet, parhelion or midday star, he immediately wonders what this thing might mean or signify.

XL

190. When witches are full of fearful superstitions they are also of the utmost wildness and cruelty, so that, if it is necessary for the solemnisation of their witchcraft, they will kill without pity and tear to pieces innocent and tender babes.

191. The above propositions, from numbers XXVIII to XXXVIII, disclose the principles of divine poetry or poetic theology; from number XXXI they provide us with the origins of idolatry; from number XXXIX with the origins of divination; and lastly number XL provides, through bloody religions, the origins of the sacrifices which, with offerings and human victims, arose amongst these first cruel and wildest of men. These victims,

as we learn from Plautus, continued to be known in vulgar Latin as *Saturni hostiae* [Saturn's sacrifices]; they were [also] the sacrifices to Moloch made by the Phoenicians, who passed infants consecrated to that false divinity through the heart of a fire; and some of these consecrations survived in the Law of the Twelve Tables. These things give us the correct sense both of the aphorism, *Primos in orbe deos fecit timor* [Fear produced the first gods in the world], i.e., that false religions arose not by deception by others but by [man's] own credulity, and of Agamemnon's unhappy offering and sacrifice of his pious daughter, Iphigenia, upon which Lucretius commented impiously: *Tantum relligio potuit suadere malorum* [So great were the evils religion could induce]. In so doing they direct [us] to providence's counsel, for this was all necessary to tame the children of the cyclopes and reduce them to a human nature of the likes of Aristides, Socrates, Laelius and Scipio Africanus.

XLI

192. We postulate, and it is a fair postulate, that for many centuries, sodden with humidity from the Flood, the earth ejected neither dry exhalations nor burning matter into the air, to generate thunderbolts.[22]

XLII

193. Jove strikes by thunderbolt and lays low the giants, and every gentile nation had a Jove.

194. This axiom contains the physical history which the fables have preserved for us: that the Flood covered the whole earth.[23]

195. The same axiom, with the foregoing postulate, should establish that, over a very long course of years, the impious races of the three sons of Noah must have entered a ferine state, scattering and dispersing themselves, in their ferine wandering, throughout the great forest of the earth, and that, with their ferine upbringing, giants must have arisen and existed among them at the time when the sky first hurled its thunderbolts after the Flood.

XLIII

196. Every gentile nation had its Hercules, who was the son of Jove. Varro, the most erudite scholar of ancient times, reached forty in his count of them.

[22]*Cf. N.S.*[1] 104.   [23]*Cf. N.S.*[1] 105.

197. This axiom gives the beginnings of the heroism of the first peoples, born of the false belief that the heroes were of divine birth.

198. The last two axioms, which give us first so many Joves and then so many Hercules among the gentile nations, demonstrate that nations can neither be founded without religion nor expand without strength, since in their early days they lived enclosed in forests and knew nothing of one another, by means of the axiom that 'uniform ideas, born among peoples unknown [to one another], must have a common basis of truth'.[24] In addition they provide us with this further great principle: that the first fables must have contained civil truths and must therefore have been histories of the first peoples.

XLIV

199. The first wise men of the Greek world were the theological poets, who were undoubtedly born before the heroes, since Jove was the father of Hercules.

200. The last three axioms establish that, since each had its Jove and its Hercules, all the gentile nations were poetic at the start and that divine poetry was born first among them, followed by heroic poetry.

XLV

201. Men are naturally led to preserve the memory of the laws and orders which hold them within their societies.

XLVI

202. All barbaric histories have fabulous origins.

203. All these axioms, from XLII onwards, give us the start of our historical mythology.

XLVII

204. The human mind is naturally led to find pleasure in the uniform.

205. This axiom is confirmed, in connection with the fables, by the custom of the vulgar who, when dealing with men who are famous in some or other way, placed in this or that situation, make suitable fables which fit what is common to them in their state. The fables are, [therefore,] ideal truths (*verità d'idea*), conforming to the merits of those of

[24]N.S.[3] 144.

whom the vulgar create them, and are false in fact only to the degree that they fail to give credit to those [individuals] who are worthy of it. So that, if one reflects carefully upon it, poetic truth is a [form of] metaphysical truth, in comparison with which [any] physical truth which fails to conform must be taken to be false. Whence arises this important consideration in poetic reasoning: that the true war leader, for example, is the Godfrey created by Torquato Tasso, and all leaders who do not conform to him in every way are not true war leaders.

XLVIII

206. It is the nature of children that they use the ideas and names of the [particular] men, women and things they have known first, to apprehend and name all [other] men, women and things which have some resemblance or relationship with them.[25]

XLIX

207. In a golden passage in his *De mysteriis aegyptiorum,* mentioned earlier, Iamblichus states that the Egyptians ascribed to Hermes Trismegistus all discoveries useful or necessary to human life.

208. With the support of the preceding axiom, this statement will turn back upon this divine philosopher [Iamblichus] all the meanings of sublime natural theology which he has himself given to the mysteries of the Egyptians.

209. The last three axioms provide us with the origin of the poetic characters which constitute the essence of the fables. The first axiom establishes the natural inclination of the vulgar to imagine fables and to do so with propriety. The second establishes that since the earliest men, the children of mankind, were incapable of forming intelligible genera of things, they had a natural need to imagine poetic characters, i.e., imaginative genera or universals, to be able to reduce, as to certain models or even ideal images, all particular resembling aspects [of things] to their own genera;[26] [and] because of this resemblance, the ancient fables were unable to be imagined other than with propriety. Precisely thus did the Egyptians when they reduced all their discoveries of mankind's utilities and necessities, which are the particular effects of civil wisdom, to the genus 'civil sage', which they imagined as Hermes Trismegistus, for they were unable to abstract the intelligible genus 'civil sage', much less the form of that civil wisdom in which they were themselves expert. Thus far

---

[25]Cf. *N.S.*[1] 262; *N.S.*[3] 412. [26]See pp. 18–19 above.

were the Egyptians, at the [very] time when they were enriching the world with discoveries of things necessary or useful to mankind, from being philosophers and coming to an understanding of universals or intelligible genera!

210. This last axiom, taken together with the preceding ones, is the principle of the true poetic allegories, in which the fables were given the univocal, and not analogical, meanings of various particulars comprehended under their poetic genera. Hence they were called *diversiloquia*, i.e., expressions comprehending in a general concept various aspects of men, events or things.[27]

L

211. Since memory is most vigorous in children, imagination, which is nothing but enlarged or compounded memory, is vivid in the extreme.

212. This axiom constitutes the principle of the perspicuity of the poetic images which the first childlike world must have formed.

LI

213. Where men lack the nature [required] for a certain ability they can succeed by a sustained study of the [appropriate] art, but in poetry it is quite impossible for one who lacks the nature [in question] to succeed by such study.

214. This axiom proves that since poetry founded gentile humanity, from which alone all the arts must have risen, the first poets were poets by nature.

LII

215. Children have a great capacity for imitation, as evidenced by the fact that we see them entertain themselves in the main by imitating whatever they are capable of apprehending.

216. This axiom establishes that in its childhood the world consisted of poetic nations, since poetry is nothing but imitation.

217. The axiom provides us, moreover, with the following principle: that all arts to do with the necessary, the useful, the comfortable and even, to a great extent, with human pleasure, were discovered in the poetic centuries before the coming of the philosophers, for arts are nothing but imitations of nature and, in a certain sense, real poems.

[27] See N.S.[3] 403.

LIII

218. First men [have a] sense [of things] without [conscious] consideration, then they consider [them] with a perturbed and agitated spirit, finally they reflect [upon them] with a pure mind.[28]

219. This axiom constitutes the principle of poetic judgements, which are formed by a sense of passion and feeling, in contrast to philosophical judgements, which are formed by reflection involving reasoning, whence the latter draw nearer the true the more they ascend to the universal, while the former become more certain the more they are appropriate to particulars.

LIV

220. Men naturally interpret anything doubtful or obscure which pertains to them in accordance with their own natures and with the passions and customs to which these have given rise.[29]

221. This axiom is a great canon of our mythology, showing that the fables which arose amongst the first savage and primitive men were wholly severe, conforming to the foundation of nations emerging from a ferocious and bestial liberty, [and that] then, with the passing of many years and changes of custom, they were altered, obscured and made inappropriate in dissolute and corrupt times even earlier than Homer. For religion mattered to the Greeks and, not wishing that the gods be opposed to their prayers as they were to their customs, they ascribed the latter to the gods and gave lewd, indecent and the most obscene senses to their fables.

LV

222. In a golden passage Eusebius, whose particular example of the wisdom of the Egyptians [will be] extended to apply to all gentile nations,

---

[28] The sequence of three modes of mind which is stated here underlies the sequence of three ages which is built into the ideal eternal history. In view of the presence of imagination at the very start of the account offered, the sequence is probably best thought of as sensory–imaginative, deliberative and self-conscious rather than the more usual sense, imagination and reason. For the first mode Vico uses the verb *sentire*, which has a wide range of meanings, including 'to sense', 'to feel' or 'to perceive'. At *N.S.*[1] 26–7, however, he describes the first stage as involving a 'certain human sense without consideration' and, again, as a 'certain human sense or instinct.' It is also that in virtue of which men do things, including coming together in their bestial state. This suggests that it is the mode of social cognition from which issue the judgements of common sense which determine human (social) will in the first human age. For this reason I have preferred 'having a sense of things' to 'sensing', or even 'feeling', which can have non-cognitive connotations.

[29] *Cf. N.S.*[3] 120.

says: *Primam aegyptiorum theologiam mere historiam fuisse fabulis interpolatam; quarum quum postea puderet posteros sensim coeperunt mysticos iis significatus affingere* [The first theology of the Egyptians was merely history dressed up in fables, for which, when they later became ashamed of them, their descendants gradually began to invent mystical meanings]. Thus did Manetho, or Manethus, the Egyptian high priest, when he translated the whole of Egyptian history into a sublime natural theology, as we mentioned earlier.

223. These two axioms are two great proofs of our historical mythology constituting, at one and the same time, two great whirlwinds with which to reduce to confusion any belief in the incomparable wisdom of the ancients, and two great foundations of the truth of the Christian religion, which, in its sacred history, contains no tales of which one should be ashamed.

LVI

224. The first authors among the orientals, Egyptians, Greeks and Latins and, in the recurrence of barbarism, the first writers in the new European languages, were poets.

LVII

225. The dumb express themselves through actions or objects which bear some natural relationship with the ideas they wish to signify.[30]

226. This axiom is the principle of the hieroglyphics in which all nations spoke during their first barbarism.

227. This same axiom is also the principle of that natural speech which Plato, in the *Cratylus*, followed by Iamblichus, in his *De mysteriis aegyptiorum*, conjectured was once spoken on earth. They were supported in this view by the Stoics and by Origen in his *Contra Celso*, but because they reached it by conjecture they were opposed by Aristotle, in his *On interpretation*, and by Galen, in his *De decretis Hippocratis et Platonis*. The controversy is discussed by Publius Nigidius in Aulus Gellius. The poetic idiom, involving images, likenesses, comparisons and natural properties, must have been subsequent to this natural speech.

LVIII

228. By singing, the dumb utter formless sounds and those with a stammer quicken their pronunciation of the language.

---

[30] A 'natural' as distinct from conventional relationship.

LIX

229. Men express deep emotion by breaking into song, as is shown by those in extremities of grief or joy.

230. Granted these two axioms, [it follows] that, having entered the ferine condition of dumb beasts, in which, being dull of wit, they were stirred only under the stimulus of the most violent of passions, the first authors of the gentile nations must have formed their first languages by singing.

LX

231. Language must have begun with monosyllabic words, just as, amid the present wealth of articulate words into which they are now born, children begin with such words, even though the fibres of the organ necessary to articulate speech are extremely supple in them.

LXI

232. The oldest verse of all is heroic and the slowest is spondaic: it will be found later that when it first arose heroic verse was spondaic.

LXII

233. Iambic verse most closely resembles prose and the iamb is a 'rapid foot', as it has been defined by Horace.

234. These last two axioms give rise to the conjecture that ideas and languages must have kept in step as they gathered pace.

235. All these axioms, from XLVII onwards, together with those propounded above as the principles of all the rest, complete the whole of poetic theory under [all] its headings, i.e., fable, custom and its propriety, judgement, idiom and its perspicuity, allegory, song and,mfinally, verse. In addition, the last seven axioms convince us that among all nations speech in verse arose before speech in prose.

LXIII

236. The human mind is inclined naturally to see itself through the senses outwardly in the body and with great difficulty to understand itself by means of reflection.

237. This axiom provides the universal principle of etymology in all languages, in which words are transferred from bodies and bodily properties to signify the things of mind and spirit.

LXIV

238. The order of ideas must proceed according to the order of things.[31]

LXV

239. Thus did the order of human things proceed: first there were forests, then isolated dwellings, whence villages, next cities, and finally academies.

240. This axiom is a great principle of etymology, for the histories of words of native languages should be narrated in accordance with this series of human things, as we can see in the Latin language, in which nearly its whole body of words is of rural and agricultural origin. By way of example [we may take] *lex*, which must first have meant 'a collection of acorns' from which, we believe, came *ilex*, as if it were *illex*, the holm-oak (just as *aquilex* is certainly the collector of waters), because the holm-oak produces the acorn round which the pigs collect. Subsequently, *lex* was 'a collection of vegetables', from which the latter were called *legumina*. Soon after, at a time when the vulgar letters in which laws were written had not yet been invented, *lex*, by a necessity of civil nature, must have meant 'a collection of citizens', or the public parliament, in which the presence of the people constituted the law which solemnised wills made *calatis comitiis* [by the gathered *comitia*]. Finally, the collecting of letters and making a sort of bunch of them in each word was called *legere* [reading].

LXVI

241. Men first have a sense of the necessary, then attend to the useful, next consider the comfortable, later take delight in pleasure, thence dissipate themselves in luxury and finally go mad, abusing their substance.

[31]*Cf. N.S.*[1] 90, where the converse claim is made. It is often implied that axiom LXIV is related in some way to Proposition VII of Book II of Spinoza's *Ethic*, which reads, *Ordo et connexio idearum idem est ac ordo et connexio rerum* [the order and connection of ideas is the same as the order and connection of things], (P. Rossi (ed.), *La Scienza Nuova* (Milan, 1963) p. 32, and F. Nicolini, *Commento Storico alla Seconda Scienza Nuova* (Naples, 1978) p. 94). Rossi adds, 'But here the order of things is the course of human history.' It is difficult, nevertheless, to see any connection between the two propositions since Spinoza specifically goes on to say that when a mode, in his sense, is considered under the attribute of thought, its whole explanation must be sought in that attribute, while when it is considered under the attribute of extension, its whole explanation must be sought in that attribute. Vico, on the other hand, seems to be suggesting that the order of the development of ideas (and, at *N.S.*[3] 240, of languages) must be related to that of things or ways of life.

LXVII

242. The nature of peoples is first crude, then severe, thence benign, next delicate and finally dissolute.

LXVIII

243. The first to arise in mankind are the huge and clumsy, such as Polyphemus; then the magnanimous and proud, such as Achilles; next the valiant and just, such as Aristides and Scipio Africanus; nearer to us come [those] impressive figures, with great shows of virtue accompanying great vices, who win a reputation for true glory among the vulgar, such as Alexander and Caesar; later still the sad, reflective type, such as Tiberius; and finally the violent, dissolute and brazen, such as Caligula, Nero and Domitian.

244. This axiom establishes that the first type was necessary in order to subject man to man in the state of the families and to dispose him to obedience to the laws in the state of the cities that was to come; that the second type, who naturally did not give way to his equals, was necessary in order to establish the aristocratic form of state on the basis of the families; that the third was necessary in order to open the way to popular liberty; that the fourth was necessary for the introduction of monarchies; that the fifth was necessary to consolidate them; and the sixth to overthrow them.

245. This and the antecedent axioms provide a part of the principles of the ideal eternal history, traversed in time by all nations, in their birth, growth, perfection, decline and fall.[32]

LXIX

246. Governments must correspond to the nature of the men governed.[33]

247. This axiom establishes that the public school of princes is, by the nature of human, civil things, the morality of the peoples.

LXX

248. Let the following, which is not contradictory in nature and will later be found true in fact, be granted: that first a few of the most powerful withdrew from the nefarious state of a world without law; that they founded families, with and for whom they brought the land under cultivation; and that, much later, many others also withdrew from the world

[32]Cf. N.S.[1] 90 and n. 41, p. 127 above.   [33]Cf. N.S.[1] 92.

without law, to take refuge on the cultivated lands belonging to these fathers.

LXXI

249. Native customs, and that of natural liberty above all, do not all change at once, but by degrees and over a long time.

LXXII

250. Assuming that all nations originated in the cult of some divinity, in the state of the families the fathers must have been the sages in the divinity of auspices, the priests who made sacrifices to procure them, that is, to understand them properly, and the kings who brought divine laws to their families.

LXXIII

251. There is a vulgar tradition that the first to govern in the world were kings.

LXXIV

252. There is another vulgar tradition that the most worthy by nature were created the first kings.

LXXV

253. There is a further vulgar tradition that the first kings were sages, whence Plato entertained the vain desire for those earliest times in which philosophers reigned or kings philosophised.

254. These axioms establish that in the persons of the first fathers wisdom, priesthood and sovereignty were united and that sovereignty and priesthood were dependencies of wisdom – not, however, the recondite wisdom of philosophers but the vulgar wisdom of legislators. In all nations, therefore, the priests later wore crowns.

LXXVI

255. There is a vulgar tradition that the first form of government in the world was the monarchic state.

LXXVII

256. But from axiom LXVII and its successors, in particular the corollary of LXIX, it follows that in the state of the families the fathers must have exercised monarchic rule, subject only to God, over the persons and acquisitions of their children and, to a greater degree, of the *famuli* who had fled to their lands, and that they were thus the first monarchs in the world, to whom we must understand sacred history to refer by the term 'patriarchs', i.e., 'princely fathers'. This monarchic right was reserved for them for the entire duration of the Roman Republic by the Law of the Twelve Tables: *Patrifamilias ius vitae et necis in liberos esto* [The family father shall have the right of life and death over his children], the consequence of which is, *Quicquid filius acquirit, patri acquirit* [What the son acquires, he acquires for the father].

LXXVIII

257. The families can only have been so named, preserving the propriety of their origin, after these *famuli* of the fathers in the then state of nature.

LXXIX

258. The existence of the first *socii,* who are properly partners with the aim of communicating utilities among themselves, can neither be imagined nor understood prior to those who had fled to the above-mentioned fathers to save their lives, and who, having been taken in for life, were obliged to sustain it by cultivating the fields of these fathers.

259. Such were the true *socii* of the heroes, *socii* who later became the plebeians of the heroic cities and, finally, the provincials of the ruling peoples.

LXXX

260. Men come naturally to the law of [feudal] benefices when they see that they can keep or retain in them a goodly and large share of useful things, these being the benefits to which they can aspire in civil life.

LXXXI

261. It is characteristic of the strong not to lose by indolence what they have acquired through strength but, through necessity or utility, to relinquish it little at a time and to the least extent possible.

262. From these two axioms flow the perennial springs of the fiefs called, with Roman elegance, *beneficia* [benefices].

LXXXII

263. Throughout all ancient nations we find clients and clienteles, which cannot be more fittingly understood than as vassals and fiefs nor, indeed, can scholars of feudal practice find more fitting Roman terms for expressing the latter clearly than *clientes* and *clientelae*.

264. The last three axioms, with the preceding twelve, starting with axiom LXX, reveal the origins of states, born of some great need (to be determined below) created for the fathers of the families by the *famuli*, as a result of which the states naturally, and of themselves, took on aristocratic form. For the fathers united into orders to resist the rebellious *famuli* and, thus united, they conceded the *famuli* a kind of rural fief to appease them and to reduce them to obedience. But the fathers [now] found their sovereign family powers (which can be understood only in accordance with the law of noble fiefs) subject to the sovereign civil power of their own ruling orders. The heads of these were called 'kings' and, as the most daring, they must have taken the lead during the revolts of the *famuli*. Were this [account of the] origin of cities (which will later be shown to be fact) to be offered [solely] as a hypothesis it would need of necessity to be accepted as true by dint of its naturalness and simplicity and because of the infinite number of civil effects which are governed by it, as by their proper cause. For in no other way whatsoever can one understand how civil power was formed from family powers and public patrimony from private patrimonies, nor how the material for states was found already prepared, [composed] of an order of a few who would command in them and the mass of plebeians who would obey: for these are the two parts which comprise the subject matter of politics. The birth of the civil states from families composed solely of children [of the fathers] will later be shown to have been impossible.

LXXXIII

265. This law relating to the fields establishes itself as the first agrarian law in the world, nor can one imagine or understand another which could be more restricted by nature.

266. This agrarian law distinguished the three kinds of ownership which can exist in civil nature, pertaining to three types of person: bonitary ownership, pertaining to the plebeians; quiritary ownership, guarded by arms and therefore noble, pertaining to the fathers; and

eminent ownership, pertaining to the order which constitutes the Seigniory, or sovereign power, in the aristocratic states.

LXXXIV

267. In a golden passage in his *Politics,* Aristotle lists, in his classification of states, the heroic kingdoms, in which kings administered the law at home, directed wars abroad, and were the heads of religion.

268. This axiom applies in precisely the same way both to the heroic kingdom of Theseus, as can be seen from the *Life* of him which Plutarch wrote, and to that of Romulus, [as we can see] by supplementing Greek with Roman history, [in the episode] where Tullus Hostilius administers the law in the indictment of Horatius. Moreover, the Roman kings were sovereign in sacred things also, being named *reges sacrorum* [kings of the sacred rites]. Hence, when the kings were hounded from Rome, for the certainty of the divine ceremonies they created a head of the *fetiales* or heralds, known as *rex sacrorum* [king of the sacred rites].

LXXXV

269. In another golden passage in the same work, Aristotle relates that the ancient states had no laws for the punishment of private offences and the correction of private wrongs. Such, he asserts, is the custom of barbaric peoples, since peoples are barbaric in their early days because they have not yet been domesticated by means of laws.

270. This axiom establishes the necessity for duels and reprisals in barbaric times, for in such times there are no judicial laws.

LXXXVI

271. In yet another golden passage in this work, Aristotle asserts that in the ancient states the nobles took an oath of eternal enmity against the plebs.

272. This axiom explains the proud, avaricious and cruel habits of the nobles over the plebeians, as can be clearly read in ancient Roman history. For within the [period] hitherto imagined [as one of] popular liberty, for a long time they drove the plebeians to serve them at their own expense in war, drowned them in a sea of usury and, when the poor wretches were unable to discharge [their debt], incarcerated them for life in their private prisons, in order that it be repaid in work and labour, and there, in tyrannical manner, lashed them with switches across their naked shoulders, like the vilest of slaves.

LXXXVII

273. Aristocratic states are most reluctant to engage in wars, in order not to train the mass of plebeians in the military arts.

274. This axiom is the principle of the justice of Roman arms until the Carthaginian wars.

LXXXVIII

275. Aristocratic states confine wealth to the order of nobles because it contributes to the power of that order.

276. This axiom is the principle of the clemency shown by the Romans in victory, in which they stripped the defeated only of their weapons but, under the law of suitable tribute, left them with bonitary ownership of all else. This is the reason why the fathers remained resistant to the agrarian policies of the Gracchi, for they did not want to enrich the plebs.

LXXXIX

277. Honour is the noblest stimulus to military valour.

XC

278. Peoples will behave heroically in war if, in peace, they engage among themselves in contests for honours, in which some aim to retain the honours and others to show themselves worthy of achieving them.

279. This axiom is a principle of Roman heroism in the period from the eviction of the tyrants until the Carthaginian wars, during which time the nobles naturally devoted themselves to the safety of their country, through which they held all civil honours safe within their order, while the plebeians undertook most remarkable exploits to prove themselves worthy of the honours of the nobles.

XCI

280. The contests for equality [brought about] by means of the law, which are fought by the orders in the cities, are the most potent means of making states greater.

281. This is another principle of Roman heroism, which was supported by three public virtues: the magnanimity of the plebs in wishing to have civil rights communicated to them through the laws of the fathers; the strength of the fathers in preserving these laws within their

own orders; and the wisdom with which the jurists interpreted them and gradually extended their utility to new cases requiring judgement. These are the three proper reasons why Roman jurisprudence became famous in the world.

282. All these axioms, from LXXXIV on, exhibit ancient Roman history in its just aspect as, in part, do the three which follow.

XCII

283. The weak desire laws; the powerful decline to accept them; the ambitious, seeking a following for themselves, promote them; princes, to bring equality between the powerful and the weak, protect them.

284. The first and second parts of this axiom are the torch of the heroic contests in the aristocratic states, in which the nobles want all laws to be [kept] secret within their order, so that they should depend upon their will, and they administer them by royal hand. These are the three reasons offered by the jurist, Pomponius, where he states that the Roman plebs desire the Law of the Twelve Tables, whose onerous nature he intimates in the expression, *ius latens, incertum et manus regia* [a secret uncertain law and royal hand]. It is the reason also why the fathers were unwilling to allow the plebs the Tables, claiming that *mores patrios servandos, leges ferri non oportere* [the customs of the fathers should be kept and laws ought not to be made public]. These expressions are reported by Dionysius of Halicarnassus who, because he wrote about Roman things with knowledge of the data gathered by Varro, himself acclaimed as 'the most erudite of Romans', was in general better informed than, and on this matter, diametrically opposed to, Livy, who claims that the nobles, to put it his way, *desideria plebis non aspernari* [did not reject the wishes of the plebs]. Hence, taking into account this and other greater contradictions noted in our *Principles of universal law,* since the first authors who wrote of this fable some five hundred years later were in such disagreement with each other, it would be better to believe neither of them. So much the more, indeed, since, in those self-same times, it was believed neither by Varro himself, in whose great work, *Rerum divinarum et humanarum,* origins indigenous to Latium are given to all Roman things, divine and human; nor by Cicero, who allows the orator, Marcus Crassus, in the presence of Quintus Mucius Scaevola, the foremost jurist of the day, to claim that the wisdom of the decemvirs went far beyond [either] that of Draco and Solon, who gave the laws to the Athenians, or that of Lycurgus, who gave them to the Spartans: which is to say that the Law of the Twelve Tables came to Rome neither from Athens nor from Sparta. And here, we believe, we reach the truth: that, having arisen from

that vanity whereby scholars ascribe the most erudite of origins to the knowledge which they themselves profess, there was widespread acceptance of the above fable, as is shown by Crassus' words, *Fremant omnes: dicam quod sentio* [Though they may complain, I shall say what I think], and that the sole reason why Cicero had Quintus Mucius present only on the first day was to ensure that nobody could object to an orator's discoursing on the history of Roman law, since knowledge of the latter lay within the province of the jurists, the two professions being separate at that time. Hence, were Crassus to have said anything false on the matter Mucius would certainly have reprimanded him, just as, according to Pomponius, he reprimanded Servius Sulpicius, who intervenes in the same discussion, with the words, *turpe esse patricio viro ius, in quo versaretur, ignorare* [it is unworthy that a partrician be ignorant of the law in which he is involved].

285. But Polybius exceeds Cicero and Varro in offering an invincible argument for disbelieving both Dionysius and Livy, and it is beyond argument that he knew more about politics than the pair of them and lived two hundred years closer to the decemvirs than they did. From Chapter IV onwards of his sixth Book (following Jacob Gronov's edition), he applies himself, on a sound basis, to contemplating the most famous free states of his time, and he notes that the Roman constitution differed from those of Athens and Sparta, but more so in the case of Athens than in that of Sparta, whereas those who assimilate Attic law with Roman law want Athens rather than Sparta as the source of the laws for ordering the popular liberty previously established by Brutus. But Polybius, on the contrary, notes resemblances between the constitutions of Rome and Carthage, and nobody has ever dreamed that Carthaginian liberty was ordered by Greek laws; and so true is this, [i.e., that Carthaginian liberty was not ordered by Greek laws] that in Carthage there was a law which expressly forbade the Carthaginians knowledge of Greek letters. Yet, though he be one of the most learned of those who have written about states, Polybius failed to engage in this reflection, so natural and obvious, and to investigate the reason for the disparity: that the Roman and Athenian states should be different, yet ordered by the same laws, the Roman and Carthaginian states similar, yet ordered by different laws. Whence, to absolve him from such wanton negligence, it is necessary to conclude that in Polybius' time the fable that Greek laws had come from Athens to Rome, for the ordering of free popular government there, had not yet arisen in Rome.

286. The third part of this same axiom reveals the way in which in popular states the ambitious can raise themselves to monarchy, by gratifying that natural desire of the plebs whereby, having no understanding

of universals, they want a law for every particular [case]. Hence, after Sulla, the leader of the nobles, had vanquished Marius, the leader of the plebs, when he reorganised the popular state with an aristocratic government he found a remedy for the multitude of laws through the *quaestiones perpetuae*.

287. The last part of this same axiom constitutes the hidden reason why, starting from Augustus, the Roman leaders created innumerable laws pertaining to private justice, and why, throughout Europe, sovereigns and powers accepted into their monarchies and free states the corpus of Roman civil law and that of canon law.

XCIII

288. Since in popular states the door to honours is open by law to the avaricious multitude which is in control, there exists no alternative in peacetime but to struggle for power by arms, and not by laws, and to use power to command laws, such as the agrarian laws of the Gracchi in Rome, for the increasing of wealth, thus giving rise, at one and the same time, to civil war at home and unjust wars abroad.

289. Because of its disparity [with Roman heroism] this axiom confirms the latter for the whole period prior to the Gracchi.

XCIV

290. Natural liberty is more ferocious the more that goods attach to [necessities of] the body itself, while civil servitude is anchored in goods of fortune not necessary to life.

291. The first part of this axiom offers another principle of the natural heroism of the first peoples; its second part is the natural principle of monarchies.

XCV

292. First, men wish to escape from subjection and they yearn for equality: thus the plebs in the aristocratic states which finally become popular states. Next, they strive to overcome their equals: thus the plebs in the popular states, corrupted into states of the powerful. Finally, they want the laws set beneath them: thus the anarchies or unbridled popular states, the worst of all tyrannies, in which there are as many tyrants as there are audacious and dissolute men in the cities. At this point the plebs, warned by their own sufferings, turn to the shelter of monarchies to find a remedy; and this is the natural royal law by which Tacitus

legitimises the Roman monarchy under Augustus, *qui cuncta, bellis civilibus fessa, nomine 'principis' sub imperium accepit,* [who, when all were wearied by civil wars, took them under his control in the name of 'prince'].

XCVI

293. When the first cities were established on the basis of the families, their natural lawless liberty made the nobles averse to restraints and burdens: thus the aristocratic states in which the nobles are the lords. Next, when the plebs were greatly increased in number and trained for war, the nobles were obliged to endure laws and burdens equally with their plebeians: thus the nobles in the popular states. Finally, to save the comfort of their life, they inclined naturally to submission under one man: thus the nobles under the monarchies.

294. These two axioms, with those from LXVI onwards, constitute the principles of the ideal eternal history mentioned above.[34]

XCVII

295. Let it be granted, as a postulate which does not offend against reason, that after the Flood men lived first in the mountains, that at some time later they descended to the plains, and that finally they had the confidence to venture to the shores of the sea.

XCVIII

296. Strabo mentions a golden passage from Plato, in which he states that after their particular Ogygian and Deucalionian floods men lived in caves in the mountains, and recognises in these men the cyclopes, whom he encounters again elsewhere as the first fathers of families in the world. Later they lived on the slopes of the mountains and he finds them in Dardanus, who built Pergamum, which then became the stronghold of Troy. Finally they lived on the plains and he discerns them in Ilus, by whom Troy was moved to the coastal plain and named Ilium.

XCIX

297. There is also an ancient tradition that Tyre was founded inland first and transferred to the shore of the Phoenician sea later; while it is

---

[34]*N.S.*[3] 145, 245.

[a matter of] certain history that from there it made the crossing to a nearby island, after which Alexander the Great reconnected it to the mainland.

298. The foregoing postulate and the two subsequent axioms show that inland nations were founded first and maritime nations later. They also provide a powerful argument demonstrating the antiquity of the Hebrew people, which was founded by Noah in Mesopotamia, the most inland area of the first habitable world, and was thus the oldest of all nations. This is [further] confirmed by the fact that the first monarchy was founded there, that of the Assyrians over the Chaldean people, who produced the first sages in the world, of whom Zoroaster was the foremost.

C

299. Men are induced to abandon their own lands, which are naturally dear to their natives, only for the ultimate necessities of life, and to quit them for a while only by greed for enrichment through trade or by anxiety to retain their gains.

300. This axiom is the principle of the transmigration of peoples, undertaken by the heroic maritime colonies, the barbarian invasions (of which only Wolfgang Latius wrote), the last known Roman colonies and the European colonies in the Indies.

301. This same axiom establishes that the lost races of the three sons of Noah must have gone astray like beasts, in order that [we may understand how], by fleeing from the wild animals (which must have abounded in the great forests of the earth), hunting women who were reluctant and unwilling (as they must have been in the extreme in such a wild state), and subsequently seeking pastures and water, they should be found dispersed through the whole world in those times when, after the Flood, the sky first roared with thunder: whence each gentile nation originated with its own Jove. For had they remained in [a state of] humanity, as did the people of God, they would, like the latter, have stayed in Asia which, given the vastness of that great part of the world and the dearth of men at that time, they would have had no necessary reason for abandoning, since it is not a natural custom that native lands be abandoned by caprice.

CI

302. The Phoenicians were the first navigators of the ancient world.

CII

303. Nations in their barbarism are impenetrable and must either be entered forcibly by war from outside or opened naturally for the benefits of commerce from within. Thus did Psammetichus open Egypt to the Greeks of Ionia and Caria who, after the Phoenicians, must have been famous for maritime trade, whence, because of their great riches, the temple of Samian Juno was founded in Ionia and the mausoleum of Artemisia built in Caria. These were two of the seven wonders of the world. Fame in maritime trade settled finally upon the people of Rhodes, who erected another of the above-mentioned [seven] wonders, the great Colossus of the Sun, in the entrance of their port. The Chinese have similarly opened their country to us Europeans for the benefits of trade.

304. These three axioms provide the principle of a further etymologicon, for words of certain foreign origin,[35] which is different from the etymologicon mentioned above for native words.[36] It can likewise give us the history of those nations which have been led by their colonies, one after another, into foreign lands. Thus Naples was first named with a Syriac word, Sirena, which shows that the Syrians were the first to lead a colony there, for reasons of trade. Later it was called Parthenope, which is a heroic Greek word, and finally, in vulgar Greek, Naples [Neapolis], these names proving that the Greeks later went there to open a trading community. Hence a language composed of a mixture of Phoenician and Greek must have developed there, of which it is said that it pleased the emperor Tiberius more than did pure Greek.[37] In exactly the same way a Syriac colony, called Siris, existed on the shores of Taranto, the inhabitants of which were called Sirites. The Greeks later named this colony Polieion, from which Minerva Polias, whose temple was there, took her name.

305. In addition this axiom provides principles of science for the thesis maintained by Giambullari: that the Tuscan language must be of Syriac origin. This language could have originated only among the most ancient Phoenicians, who were the first navigators of the ancient world, as we proposed in an axiom above.[38] For fame in this belonged later to the Greeks of Ionia and Caria and settled finally with the people of Rhodes.

CIII

306. Let the [following] necessary concession be granted: that some Greek colony had been brought to the shores of Latium, where, later,

---

[35]Cf. N.S.[1] 383–4.   [36]Cf. N.S.[1] 381–2; N.S.[3] 162, 240.
[37]Cf. N.S.[1] 386.   [38]N.S.[3] 302.

having been conquered and destroyed by the Romans, it lay buried in the shadows of antiquity.

307. If this is not granted, anyone who reflects upon and systematises the [facts of] antiquity, will be bewildered by Roman history when it places Hercules, Evander, the Arcadians and the Phrygians within Latium, and describes Servius Tullius as Greek, Tarquinius Priscus, the son of Demaratus, as Corinthian, and Aeneas as the founder of the Roman people. Tacitus certainly notes that Latin letters resemble ancient Greek letters, though at the time of Servius Tullius, according to Livy, the Romans were unable even to have heard of the famous name of Pythagoras, teaching [then] in his highly celebrated school at Crotona, while they began to make contact with the Greeks in Italy only upon the occasion of the war with Tarentum, which then brought about the war with Pyrrhus and the Greeks overseas.

CIV

308. Worthy of consideration is Dio Cassius' dictum that custom is like a king and law like a tyrant, these being understood as reasonable custom and law not animated by natural reason.

309. Through its consequences this axiom also settles the great dispute, 'whether law exists by nature or in the opinion of men', which is the same as that raised in the corollary of axiom VIII, 'whether human nature is sociable'.[39] For the natural law of the gentes was ordered by custom (said by Dio to command like a king by pleasure) and not by law (said by Dio to command like a tyrant by force), since it was born with those human customs which emerged from the common nature of nations (which is the proper subject of this Science) and it is this law which preserves human society; nor is there anything more natural (for there is nothing which gives more pleasure) than the celebration of natural custom. Hence human nature, from which such custom has emerged, is sociable.

310. This same axiom, with axiom VIII and its corollary, establishes that man is not unjust by nature in the absolute, but by fallen and weak nature. In consequence, it establishes the first principle of the Christian religion: Adam in his wholeness, the most perfect idea of whom must have been created by God. Hence it proves also the Catholic principles of grace: that it works in man, in whom there is a privation but not a negation of good works, so that man has an inefficacious capacity for good works, and grace is therefore efficacious; and that man cannot,

[39] N.S.³ 135.

therefore, exist without the principle of free will, which God assists naturally by His providence (as indicated above, in the second corollary of axiom VIII),[40] [a doctrine] in which the Christian religion concurs with all other religions. Grotius, Selden and Pufendorf ought, above all else, to have based their systems upon this[41] and [thus] to have concurred with the Roman jurists, who define the natural law of the gentes as a law ordered by divine providence.[42]

CV

311. The natural law of the gentes emerged with the customs of the nations, which conform with one another in [possessing] a human common sense, without reflection and without one nation following the example of another.[43]

312. This axiom, with the dictum of Dio mentioned above, establishes that because providence is queen of the affairs of men, she orders the natural law of the gentes.[44]

313. It establishes also the difference between the natural law of the Hebrews, the natural law of the gentes and the natural law of the philosophers. For the gentes received only ordinary aids from providence; the Hebrews received in addition extraordinary aids from the true God, as a consequence of which they divided the whole world of nations into Hebrews and gentiles; while the philosophers, who did not arise until some two thousand years after the founding of the gentes, represent the natural law more perfectly in their reasoning than do the gentes in their customs. But because they omitted to observe all three of these distinctions, the three systems of Grotius, Selden and Pufendorf must fail.

CVI

314. Doctrines must begin with the times in which their subject matters begin.

315. This axiom, placed here in connection with the particular subject matter of the natural law of the gentes, is applied universally in all the subjects with which we are concerned. Hence it ought properly to have been set down among the general axioms, but we have put it here because its truth and the importance of its application are revealed in this, more than in any other, particular subject matter.

[40]*N.S.*[3] 136.   [41]*Cf. N.S.*[1] 15–22.   [42]*Cf. N.S.*[1] 14; *N.S.*[3] 342.
[43]*Cf. N.S.*[1] 46–7; *N.S.*[3] 141–5.   [44]*Cf. N.S.*[1] 45.

CVII

316. The gentes began prior to the cities: these were those which the Latins called the greater gentes or ancient noble houses, such as those of the fathers of whom Romulus composed the senate and, with the senate, the city of Rome. In contrast, the new noble houses, founded after the cities, were called the lesser gentes: such, for example, were those of the fathers with whom, after the kings had been hounded out, Junius Brutus replenished the senate, when it was almost emptied by the departure of senators put to death by Tarquinius Superbus.

CVIII

317. The gods were divided as follows. [One class was composed of] those of the greater gentes, i.e., the gods consecrated by the families prior to the cities. Those of the Greeks and Latins (and, as we shall prove here, those of the first Assyrians or Chaldeans, Phoenicians and Egyptians as well) certainly numbered twelve, a number so famous among the Greeks that they referred to it by the single word δώδεκα [the twelve]. These gods of the greater gentes are collected together in a confused way in a Latin distich, which we mentioned in our *Principles of universal law*, but in Book II of the present work they will emerge, in accordance with a natural theogony, that is, a generation of gods created naturally in the minds of the Greeks,[45] in the following order: Jove, Juno; Diana, Apollo; Vulcan, Saturn, Vesta; Mars, Venus; Minerva, Mercury; Neptune. And [the other class was composed of] the gods of the lesser gentes, i.e., gods consecrated afterwards by the peoples, such as Romulus, who, upon his death, was named the god Quirinus by the Roman people.

318. Through [neglect of] these three axioms the three systems of Grotius, Selden and Pufendorf are [shown to be] deficient in respect of origins, for they begin with nations regarded in their relations within the society of the whole of mankind, whereas, as will be shown here, mankind began in all the first nations in the time of the families under the gods of the greater gentes.[46]

CIX

319. For men of limited ideas the law is [identical with] whatever is expressed in words.

---

[45] Cf. N.S.[1] 267–8; N.S.[3] 392.   [46] Cf. N.S.[1] 22.

CX

320. Ulpian offers this golden definition of equity: *probabilis quae-dam ratio, non omnibus hominibus naturaliter cognita* (as is natural equity), *sed paucis tantum, qui, prudentia, usu, doctrina praediti, didi-cerunt quae ad societatis humanae conservationem sunt necessaria* [a kind of probable reason, not known naturally to all men (as is natural equity), but to those few who, furnished with prudence, practice and learning, learn what things are necessary for the preservation of human society]. In good Italian this is called 'reason of state'.

CXI

321. The certain (*il certo*) in the laws is an obscurity of reason sup-ported solely by authority, when we find the laws inflexible when we practise them but are forced to do so [precisely] because they possess the certain. In good Latin *certum* [certain] means 'particularised' or, as the Schools say, 'individuated', and in this sense *certum* and *commune* [com-mon] were, in over-fastidious Latin, taken as contraries.

322. This axiom and the two definitions which follow it constitute the principle of strict law, of which civil equity is the rule. When confronted with the certain in civil equity, i.e., the determinate particularity of its words, barbarians, whose ideas are [of the] particular, are naturally pla-cated and they take this to be the law which is due them. Hence where, in such cases, Ulpian says, *lex dura est, sed scripta est* [the law is hard but thus is it written], in finer Latin and with greater legal nicety, we should say, *lex dura est, sed certa est,* [the law is hard but it is certain].

CXII

323. For intelligent men the law is whatever [the principle of] equal utility in cases dictates.

CXIII

324. The true (*il vero*) in the laws is a certain light and brilliance of natural reason which shines forth in them: hence jurists are in the habit of saying, *verum est* [it is true], for *aequum est* [it is right].

325. This definition and axiom CXI are particular propositions for proofs in the particular subject matter of the natural law of the gentes, deriving from the two general propositions, IX and X, which treat of the

true and the certain in general, for the establishment of conclusions in all subjects discussed here.[47]

CXIV

326. The natural equity of fully developed human reason is a practice of wisdom in matters of utility, since 'wisdom' in its fullness is nothing but the science of making that use of things which belongs to them by nature.

327. This axiom [CXII]and the two subsequent definitions constitute the principle of benign law, regulated by natural equity, which belongs naturally to civilised nations. This, as we shall show below, is the public school from which the philosophers have arisen.

328. These last six propositions establish that divine providence ordered the natural law of the gentes. For through the course of the many centuries in which the nations had to live incapable of [understanding] the true and natural equity (which was later clarified by the philosophers), she allowed them to hold fast to the certain and to civil equity, which scrupulously guards the words of orders and laws, and to be led by the words to observe the laws, even when they proved hard in their outcome, in order that the nations be preserved.

329. Their ignorance of these same six propositions caused all three princes of the doctrine of the natural law of the gentes to fall into error in establishing their systems. For they believed that natural equity, in its most complete conception, had been understood by the gentile nations from their very beginnings, without reflecting that some two thousand years were needed in order that philosophers should arise in them, and without granting that one people in particular was privileged by the assistance of the true God.[48]

[Section III] Principles

330. Now, in order to test whether the propositions so far enumerated as elements of this Science can give form to the materials laid out in the Chronological Table at the start, we beseech the reader that he reflect upon whatever has been written on the principles of any subject in the whole of gentile knowledge, divine and human, and that he compare it

[47]N.S.[3] 137–40.   [48]Cf. N.S.[1] 17.

with these propositions for incompatibility, be it with all, several or one, for it would be the same with one as with all, since each is compatible with all.[49] For certainly, in making this comparison, the reader will come to see that all such writings are pages of confused memory, fantasies of jumbled imagination, and that none of them are born of the understanding, which has been kept idle by the two vanities mentioned in the *Elements*. For the vanity of nations, that each was the first in the world, discourages us from seeking the principles of this Science among the philologists, while the vanity of scholars, who want all that they know to have been eminently understood since the origin of the world, makes us despair of finding them among the philosophers.[50] Hence, for this investigation, we must proceed as if there were no books in the world.

331. But in this dense night of darkness, which enshrouds earliest antiquity so distant from us, appears the eternal light, which never sets, of this truth which is beyond any possible doubt: that the civil world itself has certainly been made by men, and that its principles therefore can, because they must, be rediscovered within the modifications of our own human mind.[51] And this must give anyone who reflects upon it cause to marvel how the philosophers have all earnestly endeavoured to attain knowledge of the natural world which, since He made it, God alone knows, and have neglected to meditate upon this world of nations, or civil world, knowledge of which, since men had made it, they could attain. This bizarre result originated in that shortcoming of the human mind which we noted in the *Elements,* that, immersed and buried in the body, it is naturally inclined to have a sense of bodily things, but requires overmuch effort and work to understand itself, like the physical eye, which sees all objects external to itself, but needs a mirror to see itself.[52]

332. Now, since this world of nations has been made by men, let us see in what things men have continuously concurred and still concur, for such things can give us the universal and eternal principles, necessary to every science, upon which everything in nations arose and is preserved.

333. We observe that all nations, barbaric or human, though separately founded because of immense distances of time and space between them, preserve these three human customs: all have a religion, contract solemn marriages and bury their dead. And among the nations, no matter how savage and crude they be, no human actions are celebrated with more revered ceremonial and more sanctified solemnity than religion,

[49] For the claim, made here, that Vico is offering a systematic, coherent science, see also
N.S.[1] 44.
[50] *Cf. N.S.*[3] 125, 127.
[51] *Cf. N.S.*[1] 40 for the corresponding version of this famous passage.
[52] *N.S.*[3] 236.

marriage and burial. For, according to the axiom that 'uniform ideas born among peoples ignorant of one another must have a common basis of truth', it must have been dictated to all nations that humanity began in them all from these three things and that they must therefore be preserved with the utmost sanctity in order that the world should not again revert to its savage and wild ways. Hence we have adopted these three eternal and universal customs as the three first principles of this Science.[53]

334. Nor is our first principle to be impugned as false by those modern travellers who write that the peoples of Brazil or of the land of the Kaffirs or of other nations in the New World (or, as Antoine Arnauld believes, the inhabitants of the islands known as the Antilles) live in society with no knowledge of God. Persuaded, perhaps, by these, Bayle maintains in his *Treatise on Comets* that peoples can live in justice without the light of God,[54] thus exceeding what [even] Polybius dared assert in his widely acclaimed saying, that were philosophers to exist on earth, living in justice by dint of reason and not of the law, there would be no need of religion on earth.[55] [But] these are the tales of travellers seeking a sale for their books with their outrageous reports. Certainly Andreas Rüdiger, who wants his *Physics,* which he grandly entitles *Divine,* to be the sole mean between atheism and superstition, was gravely warned of such a belief that 'he states it with too much assurance', which is to say, with no little audacity, by the censors of the University of Geneva, and Geneva is a state which, being of the free popular type, must allow rather more freedom of writing [than must other states]. For all nations believe in a provident divinity, whence four, and only four, primary religions have been possible throughout all the times and places of this civil world: [first,] that of the Hebrews, from which came [the second,] that of the Christians, both of whom believe in the divinity of a single infinite, free mind; third, that of the gentiles, who believe in the divinity of several gods, each thought to be composed of a body and of free mind – so that when they wish to refer to the divinity who rules and preserves the world, they use the [plural] expression *deos immortales;* fourth and last, that of the Mohammedans, who believe in the divinity of a god who is an infinite mind in an infinite body, since they expect pleasures of the senses as their rewards in the after life.

335. No nation has believed in a god who is wholly body, nor in a god who is wholly a mind but who is not free. Hence neither the Epicureans, who admit only body and, with body, chance, nor the Stoics, who admit God as an infinite mind, subject to fate, in an infinite body (so that in this

---

[53]*Cf. N.S.*[1] 397–8.   [54]*Cf. N.S.*[1] 8 and no. 1, p. 81 above.   [55]*N.S.*[3] 179.

respect they are Spinozists), can reason about the state or the law, while Benedict Spinoza speaks of the state as if it were a society of traders. So Cicero was right when he said to Atticus that, since he was an Epicurean, there could be no reasoning with him about the law, unless Atticus were to concede the existence of divine providence. So much for the conformity of the Stoic and Epicurean sects with Roman jurisprudence, which lays down divine providence as its very first principle!

336. Next, the view that those sexual unions of free men and free women, which are certain in fact but lack the solemnity of marriage, contain no natural evil, is shown to be false by the human customs with which marriages are celebrated religiously by all nations on earth, thus establishing that, though it may be venial in degree, such sin is bestial. For, on their part, not being bound to each other by any necessary legal tie, such parents will proceed to cast their children aside and they, abandoned by both of their parents, who can part at any time, must lie exposed to be devoured by dogs; and if neither public nor private humanity is to look after them, they must grow up without anyone to teach them religion, language, or any other human custom. Hence, for their part, they will proceed to turn this world of nations, enriched and adorned by so many accomplished arts of humanity, into the great original forest in which, in nefarious, ferine wandering, the hideous beasts of Orpheus went astray, lying together in carnal bestiality, sons with mothers and fathers with daughters. This is the infamous *nefas* [sin or crime] of the lawless world which Socrates, adducing physical reasons of little relevance, hoped to prove was forbidden by nature; but it is by human nature that it is forbidden, since such acts of intercourse are naturally abhorred in all nations, nor have any practised them except in their ultimate corruption, as amongst the Persians.

337. Finally, [to understand] how great a principle of humanity burial is, imagine a ferine state in which human corpses lie unburied on the ground to become the lure of crows and dogs. For this bestial custom must certainly go hand in hand with that of leaving the fields uncultivated and the cities uninhabited, so that men would become like swine, eating acorns which have grown in the decayed remains of their dead relatives. Whence with great truth were burials defined for us in that sublime expression, *foedera generis humani* [treaties of mankind], and described by Tacitus, [though] with less eloquence, as *humanitatis commercia* [the commerce of humanity]. All gentile nations have, moreover, certainly concurred in the view that the souls [of the unburied] remain restlessly on earth wandering around their unburied bodies and, hence, that they do not die with their bodies but are immortal. And we are persuaded that such a concurrence of belief existed among the ancient

barbarians by [the examples of] the peoples of Guinea, as Hugo van Lin-
schooten attests, of those of Peru and Mexico, as Acosta attests in his *De
indicis,* and of those of Virginia, New England and the kingdom of Siam,
as attested by Thomas Harriot, Richard Whitbourne and Joost Schouten
respectively. Hence Seneca's conclusion: *Quum de immortalitate loqui-
mur, non leve momentum apud nos habet consensus hominum aut
timentium inferos aut colentium: hac persuasione publica utor.* [When
we talk of immortality the general agreement of men who either fear or
worship the gods of the underworld is of no little importance to us; I
make use of this public belief]

[Section IV] Method

338. For the complete establishment of the principles adopted in this
Science, it remains to us in this first book to reason out the method that
it must use. For since, as proposed in the *Elements,* it must commence
where its subject matter started,[56] we must reclaim it, through the philologists, from the stones of Deucalion and Pyrrha, the rocks of Amphion,
the men born of the furrows of Cadmus or from Virgil's hard oak; and,
through the philosophers, from the frogs of Epicurus, the cicadas of
Hobbes, the simpletons of Grotius, and those [destitutes] whom Pufendorf
throws into the world, bereft of the care and assistance of God, as clumsy
and wild as the giants called *los patacones* who are said to be found
near the Straits of Magellan, that is, from Homer's cyclopes, in whom
Plato recognises the first fathers in the state of the families[57] – [for] such
is the science of the origins of humanity which the philologists and philosophers have given us! But it is necessary for us to commence our reasoning concerning these origins at the point where these [beings] began
to think humanly and there was no means whereby their horrifying ferocity could be tamed and their unrestricted animal liberty curbed other
than the terrifying thought of some divinity, fear of which, as we noted
in the *Elements,* is the only effective means of restoring to duty a liberty
run wild.[58] Whence, to discover the mode of the first human thought
born into the gentile world, we met with severe difficulties, which cost us
a good twenty years of research, [requiring us] to descend from our own
civilised, human natures to those wild and horrifying natures, which it is
absolutely denied us to imagine and which only with great difficulty are
we allowed to understand.

[56]*N.S.*[3] 314.   [57]*N.S.*[3] 296.   [58]*N.S.*[3] 177.

339. So we must begin with some notion of God of which men, no matter how wild, fierce and horrifying they be, are not devoid. Such notion we show to be this: that when man has fallen into despair of all nature's help, he desires something superior to save him. But a thing superior to nature is God and this is the light which God has shone upon all men.[59] This is confirmed by this common human custom: that, as they grow old, and feel the lack of their natural forces, libertines naturally become religious.

340. But these first men, who were later the leaders of the gentile nations, must have thought under the powerful stimulus of the most violent passions, which is the thinking of beasts. Hence we must turn to a vulgar metaphysic (which was referred to in the *Elements*[60] and which the theology of the poets will be shown to be)[61] and from that derive the terrifying thought of some divinity which imposed form and order upon the bestial passions of these lost men, rendering their passions human. From this thought must have been born the conatus, which is proper to the human will, to restrain the movements communicated to the mind by the body, in order to quieten them entirely, which is [the way] of the wise man, or at least to change their direction towards better uses, which is [that] of civil man. This restriction of the movements of the body is certainly an effect of the freedom of the human will, and thus of free will, which is the home and abode of all the virtues, including that of justice, and when will is informed by justice it is subject to all that is just and to all the laws which are dictated by the just. For to ascribe conatus to bodies is as much as to ascribe to them the freedom to regulate their movements, for [without conatus] they are by nature necessary agents and the things which are called 'powers' 'forces' and 'conatus' in mechanics are [nothing but] the insensible movements of bodies themselves, which are either drawn towards their centre of gravity, as ancient mechanics claims, or move away from their centres of motion, as modern mechanics claims.

341. But because their nature is corrupt men are tyrannised by self-love, whence they pursue first and foremost only what is useful for themselves; so that, desiring all that is useful for themselves and nothing for their fellows, they are unable to bring their passions under conatus in order to direct them towards justice. Whence we establish: that in the bestial state man desires only his own well-being; having taken wife and fathered children, he desires his well-being together with that of the families; having come to civil life, he desires his well-being together with that of the cities; when the powers of the cities are extended over several

[59]*Cf. N.S.*[1] 8.   [60]*N.S.*[3] 182.   [61]*N.S.*[3] 374ff.

peoples, he desires his well-being together with that of the nations; when the nations are united by wars, peace, alliances and commerce, he desires his well-being together with that of the whole of mankind; [but] in all these circumstances man desires, first and foremost, what is useful to himself.[62] Therefore by divine providence alone is he constrained to remain within these orders to celebrate in justice [the practices of] the family society, civil society and, finally, human society; for though man is unable to achieve all that he desires, he may at least expect to achieve all those utilities which he needs, and this is called 'just'. Hence that which regulates the whole of human justice is divine justice, which is administered by divine providence for the preservation of human society.

342. In one of its principal aspects this Science must therefore be a rational civil theology of divine providence, such as we seem to have lacked thus far.[63] For the philosophers have either been completely ignorant of it, such, for example, as the Stoics and Epicureans, of whom the latter believed that a blind play of atoms agitates the affairs of men, and the former that they are dragged along by a chain of causes and effects which is deaf [to the dictates of providence]; or they have considered it solely through the order of natural things, whence they have called the metaphysics in which this attribute of God is contemplated 'natural theology', and have confirmed it by the physical order observed in the motion of bodies such as spheres and elements, and in the final cause observed in the various lesser natural things. But they ought to have applied their reasoning to the economy of civil things, accepting the full propriety with which providence is called 'divinity', from *divinare*, [that is] to divine or understand either what is hidden from men, which is the future, or what is hidden within them, which is consciousness; and of these the former appropriately occupies the first and principal place in the subject of jurisprudence, that which deals with things divine, upon which depends the other part which completes it, that which deals with things human. Hence this Science must be a demonstration, as it were, of the historical fact of providence, since it must be a history of the orders which, without human discernment or decision and often contrary to the intentions of men, providence has given to this great city of mankind:[64] for though this world has been created in time and particularity (*particolare*), the orders which providence has put there are universal and eternal.[65]

343. Whence, in contemplating this infinite and eternal providence, our Science discovers certain divine proofs by which it is confirmed and

---

[62]See pp. 14–15 above.   [63]*Cf. N.S.*³ 385.
[64]*Cf. N.S.*¹ 45; *N.S.*³ 1108.   [65]*Cf. N.S.*¹ 48–56.

demonstrated. For with omnipotence as minister, divine providence must express its orders through ways as easy as our natural human customs; and with infinite wisdom to advise it, what it arranges must be wholly [permeated by] order; and since its end is its own boundless goodness, what it orders must be directed towards a good ever superior to that which men have themselves proposed.[66]

344. Thus, given the deplorable obscurity of the origins of nations and the countless variety of their customs, no more sublime proofs can be desired than these which, based upon a divine thesis which encompasses everything human, confer [upon these origins and customs] naturalness, order and an end, which is the preservation of mankind. These proofs will become luminous and distinct when we reflect on the ease with which things are born and on the occasions upon which, often in the most distant of places and at times wholly contrary to men's intentions, of themselves they transform and adapt to one another; such proofs omnipotence supplies. [Next, let us] connect things and look at their order and at how, in the times and places proper to them, the things which ought now to be born are now born, while the birth of others is delayed until their own times and places, [circumstances] which, in Horace's view, constitute the whole beauty of order; such are the proofs which eternal wisdom sets out before us. And finally, consider if we are capable of understanding whether, upon these occasions, places and times, other divine benefits could have been born by which, in [the face of] such and such needs or ills of men, human society could be better led to the good and to [its own] preservation; such are the proofs which the eternal goodness of God will afford.

345. Whence the proper and continuous proof forged here will be by connecting [things] and reflecting whether our human mind, in the series of possibilities which we are allowed to understand, and to the extent that is allowed us, can think of more, less or different causes than these [which we have proposed,] from which arise the effects of this civil world. In so doing the reader will, in his mortal body, experience the divine pleasure of contemplating in its divine idea this world of nations in the whole extent of its places, times and variety. And he should find that he has proved to the Epicureans that their chance cannot in reality wander around dementedly and find a solution on all sides, and to the Stoics that their eternal chain of causes, with which they would shackle the world, itself hangs upon the omnipotent, wise and benign will of God, the Best and Greatest.[67]

346. These sublime natural theological proofs will be confirmed by the

---

[66]Cf. *N.S.*[1] 45; *N.S.*[3] 1108.   [67]Cf. *N.S.*[1] 12; *N.S.*[3] 130, 1108.

following kinds of logical proofs: that in [our] reasonings concerning the origins of the things of the gentile world, both divine and human, we reach those starting points beyond which it is foolish curiosity to seek others earlier, which is the characteristic proper to origins;[68] that [with respect to each thing] we explain the particular mode of its birth or, as it is called, 'nature', which is the most characteristic feature of science; and, finally, we confirm the theological proofs by the eternal properties which [things] retain, which cannot have arisen other than from such births, in such times and places and through such modes, that is, from these natures, as was proposed in two *Elements* above.[69]

347. In seeking to discover these natures of human things this Science proceeds by means of a strict analysis of human thoughts concerning the human necessities or utilities of sociable life, which are the two continuing sources of the natural law of the gentes, as we observed in the *Elements*. Hence, in this other principal aspect, this Science is a history of the human ideas through which it seems that the metaphysics of the human mind must proceed; and in accordance with the axiom that 'sciences must begin with the times in which their subject matter begins' this queen of sciences must begin with the times in which the first men began to think humanly and not with those in which philosophers began to reflect upon human ideas (as is the case in an erudite and learned little book lately published under the title *Historia de ideis,* which goes up to the most recent controversies between Leibniz and Newton, the two prime geniuses of our age).

348. In order to determine the times and places for a history of this sort, [to establish,] that is, when and where these human thoughts were born, and thus to ascertain it with its own, so to speak, metaphysical chronology and geography, this Science exercises a critical art, [which is] also metaphysical, with regard to the authors of those same nations, among whom well over a thousand years must have passed before the inception of the writers with whom philological criticism has hitherto been concerned was possible. And the criterion which it employs, in accordance with a foregoing *Element,*[70] is that taught by divine providence and common to all nations, that is, the common sense of mankind, determined by the necessary propriety of those same human things, which constitutes the whole beauty of this civil world. Whence this kind of proof is sovereign in this Science: that the things of the nations had, have, and will have to proceed in accordance with the reasonings of this Science, granted the orders of divine providence, even were infinite worlds periodically to be born in eternity, which is certainly false in fact.

[68]*Cf. N.S.*[1] 390.   [69]*N.S.*[3] 147–8.   [70]*N.S.*[3] 145; *cf. N.S.*[1] 46–7.

349. Hence this Science comes at the same time to describe an ideal eternal history, traversed in time by the histories of all nations, in their birth, growth, perfection, decline and fall.[71] Indeed, we venture to affirm that since this world has certainly been made by men (which is our first indubitable principle laid down above),[72] and since its mode must therefore be rediscovered within the modifications of our own human mind,[73] whoever meditates this Science narrates this ideal eternal history to himself inasmuch as he makes it for himself by demonstrating that 'it had, has and will have [to be thus]'; for when it happens that he who makes the things also narrates them, then history cannot be more certain.[74] Thus this Science proceeds exactly like geometry, which, as it contemplates the world of dimensions or constructs it from its elements, makes that world for itself, but the reality of our Science is as much greater [than that of geometry] as is that of the orders which pertain to the affairs of men than that of points, lines, planes and shapes.[75] And this is itself an argument that such proofs are divine in kind and that they ought to give rise to a divine pleasure in the reader, since in God knowing and making are the same thing.[76]

350. Moreover, according to the definitions of the true and the certain proposed above,[77] men were for long incapable of [grasping] the true, and of reason, which is the source of that inner justice which satisfies the intellect. This is the justice which was practised by the Hebrews who, enlightened by the true God, were prohibited by his divine laws even from entertaining thoughts which were less than just, something which

---

[71] *Cf. N.S.*[1] 90; *N.S.*[3] 145, 245, 294, 393.   [72] *N.S.*[3] 331.

[73] *Cf. N.S.*[1] 40; *N.S.*[3] 331, 1108.

[74] The above passage is important for the link it intimates between the mode rediscovered within the modifications of our own human mind and the 'ideal eternal history' the construction of which seems to presuppose knowledge of this.

[75] The theory of mathematics mentioned here is identical with that given in *On method in contemporary fields of study* (see above, p. 2), and *On the ancient wisdom of the Italians* (see above, pp. 13–14 and 61). The extension of this theory to cover human history has, however, only been made possible by Vico's discovery that there are some points of identity between the men who make history – the historical agents – and those who remake it – the historians (see above, pp. 25ff).

The analogy between historical and geometrical making has been much discussed. Some commentators treat it as a residual element of Cartesianism which is, like the attempt to set out the *Elements* in the geometrical mode, foreign to the rest of *The New Science*. This is, however, to forget that geometry provided the paradigmatic example of the *verum–factum* theory in Vico's earlier works. The theory of geometry which Vico there espoused was not, therefore, Cartesian, and in this case such a consideration can provide no support for claiming that the parallel between mathematical and historical making, however difficult to understand, should not be taken seriously. Vico makes a similar allusion to the parallel in the *Second New Science* of 1730 of which, in view of its importance, I have added a translation in the Appendix (see below, pp. 269–70).

[76] *Cf.* pp. 51–2ff. above.   [77] *N.S.*[3] 137–8.

has never been of concern to mortal legislators, for the Hebrews believed in a god composed wholly of mind who sees into the hearts of men, but the gentiles in gods composed of body and mind, who were unable to do this. It was later reasoned out by the philosophers, who emerged only after their nations had been founded for two thousand years, during which time men were governed by the certain which belongs to authority, that is, by the same criterion as our metaphysical criticism employs, the common sense of mankind (the definition of which is given above, in the *Elements*),[78] upon which the consciousness of all nations rests. Whence, as a result of this further important consideration, this Science comes to be a philosophy of authority, which is the source of the 'eternal justice' discussed by the moral theologians. This is the authority of which the three princes of the doctrine of the natural law of the gentes should have taken note, rather than that drawn from passages [in various works] of the writers, for, since it reigned among the nations well over a thousand years before they gave rise to writers, the latter could not have known of it. Hence Grotius, more scholarly and erudite than the other two, opposed the Roman jurists on almost every detail of this doctrine, but his blows fell upon empty air, for the Romans established their principles of justice upon the certain which belongs to the authority of mankind and not upon the authority of the learned.

351. The above are the philosophical proofs utilised by this Science and, hence, those which are absolutely necessary to attain it. The philological proofs, which must take last place, can all be reduced to the following kinds:

352. First, our mythologies, [which are] not forced and distorted but direct, simple and natural, are consistent with the things [here] meditated and will be seen to be civil histories of the first peoples, who are found everywhere naturally to have been poets.

353. Second, our explications of the heroic phrases, exhibiting them in the full truth of their sense and the full propriety of their expression, are also consistent with the things we have meditated.

354. Third, the etymologies of native languages, which give the histories of the things which words signify, beginning with the propriety [of their meanings] in their origins and tracing the natural progress of their transference [to other things] in accordance with the order of ideas (which, as laid down in the *Elements,* is the basis upon which the history of languages must proceed),[79] are [also] consistent with them.

355. Fourth, we develop that mental vocabulary of those human sociable things whose identity of substance is felt by all nations, though they

[78]N.S.[3] 142.   [79]N.S.[3] 236–40.

express them diversely in language because of their diverse modifications, which we projected in the axioms.[80]

356. Fifth, the true is sifted from the false in everything which, over the long course of the centuries, has been preserved for us by vulgar traditions which, having themselves been preserved for such a long period and by entire peoples, must, in accordance with an axiom set out above, have had a public basis of truth.[81]

357. Sixth, the great fragments of antiquity which have hitherto been useless to science because of their wretched, mutilated and displaced condition, afford us great illumination when they are cleansed, reassembled and restored to their proper places.

358. Seventh and last, by all these things, as by their necessary causes, are governed all the effects related by certain history.[82]

359. These philological proofs serve to allow us to see in fact the things pertaining to this world of nations which were meditated in idea, according to Verulam's method of philosophising, which is *cogitare videre* [think and see],[83] so that, by means of the philosophical proofs given first, the philological ones which succeed them come, at one and the same time, to have their authority confirmed by reason and to confirm reason with their authority.[84]

360. Let us terminate what we have in general proposed concerning the establishment of the principles of this Science [thus]: that, since its principles are [the ideas of] divine providence, the moderation of the passions through marriage and the immortality of the human soul through burial of the dead,[85] and since the criterion it utilises is that whatever is sensed as just by all or by the majority of men must be the rule of sociable life (and these principles and this criterion are consistent both with the vulgar wisdom of all the legislators and with the recondite wisdom of the philosophers of greatest esteem), these must constitute the limits of human reason.[86] And let anyone who would be drawn beyond them look to it that he be not drawn beyond all humanity.

---

[80]*N.S.*[3] 161.   [81]*N.S.*[3] 149.   [82]*Cf. N.S.*[3] 345.   [83]*Cf. N.S.*[3] 163.
[84]*Cf. N.S.*[3] 138–40.   [85]*Cf. N.S.*[3] 332–7.   [86]*Cf. N.S.*[3] 144–5, 341.

Book II
Poetic wisdom
[Section I]

[1] On poetic metaphysics, which gives the origins of poetry, idolatry, divination and sacrifices

374. The philosophers and philologists should all have begun to reason out the wisdom of the ancient gentiles from such first men, stupid, irrational and horrible beasts, that is, from the giants, [as] taken just now in their proper signification. In his *De ecclesia ante legem,* Father Boulduc says that the giants' names in the scriptures mean 'pious, venerable and illustrious men', which can be understood only in reference to the noble giants who, through divination, founded religion among the gentiles and provided the age of the giants with its name. And they ought to have begun from metaphysics, [understood] as that which seeks to take its proofs not from outside but from within the modifications of the very mind of him who meditates it, for, as we said above,[87] since this world of nations has certainly been made by men, it is within these modifications that they should have sought its principles. And human nature, insofar as it is like [that of] animals, carries with it this property: that the senses are the only means whereby it knows things.[88]

375. Hence poetic wisdom, the first wisdom of the gentile world, must have begun in a metaphysics which was not rational and abstract, like that of the learned today, but sensed and imagined, as that of these first men, devoid of reason and wholly composed of powerful senses and vigorous imaginations (as was shown in the *Elements*)[89] must have been. This metaphysics was their own poetry, a faculty which, since they were provided naturally with such senses and imaginations, was innate in them. [But] it was born [into the world] of that ignorance of causes which was the mother of their wonder about everything for which, as we noted in the *Elements*,[90] in their all-embracing ignorance, they felt great admiration. This poetry originated in them as a divine poetry because [it arose] at the time in which they imagined that the causes of the things which they were sensing and admiring were gods, as we saw with Lactantius in the *Elements*.[91] (And this is confirmed today by the Americans,

[87]N.S.[3] 331.   [88]Cf. N.S.[3] 218, 236.   [89]N.S.[3] 185.   [90]N.S.[3] 184.
[91]N.S.[3] 188.

who give the name 'god' to everything which exceeds their modest capacity [to reason], to whom we may add the ancient Germans who lived by the Sea of Ice, of whom Tacitus relates that they spoke of hearing the sun at night, as it crossed the sea from West to East, and claimed to see the gods. These roughest and simplest of nations enable us to understand much else about the authors of the gentile world who are the subject of our present reasonings.)[92] [But to return. The poetry of these authors originated as a divine poetry because it arose] at the same time, we say, as these first men conferred upon the things they admired the being of substances possessing ideas which pertained [in reality] to themselves,[93] which is characteristic of children whom, as noted in an axiom [above], we see holding inanimate things in their hands, and playing and talking to them as though they were living people.

376. In this mode the first men of the gentile nations, the children as it were, of nascent mankind, as we have already shown in the *Elements,* created things by means of their own ideas but by a creation which differs infinitely from that of God. For God, in his purest understanding, knows things and creates them in knowing them; [whereas,] because of their powerful ignorance, men created by dint of a highly corporeal imagination and, this being so, they created with a wonderful sublimity of such quality and magnitude that it perturbed to excess the very men who, by imagining things, created them, whence they were called 'poets' which, in Greek, means 'creators'. And these [indeed] are the three things which great poetry must do: invent sublime fables befitting the popular understanding; perturb to excess in order to attain the end which it has set itself; [and have, as its end,] to teach the vulgar to act virtuously, as the poets taught themselves to do.[94] An eternal property of this nature of human things has survived, to which Tacitus gave noble expression: that, when terrified, in vain do men *fingunt simul creduntque* [believe things as they invent them].

377. Such must have been the natures of the first authors of gentile humanity, a hundred years after the Flood in Mesopotamia and two hundred years after it in the rest of the world. For, as we indicated in a postulate,[95] such was the length of time needed to reduce the earth to that state in which, when it had dried from the humidities of the Flood, it discharged dry exhalations or igneous materials into the air to generate thunderbolts, whereupon the heavens were finally rent by terrifying

---

[92]Cf. *N.S.*[1] 42, where Vico suggests that we are not entitled to use such analogies. The position adopted in the *Third New Science* is more compatible with the notion that there is a determinate pattern of social and conceptual development through which, in certain circumstances, all nations will go, i.e., the concept of an ideal eternal history.
[93]*N.S.*[3] 180–1, 186–7.   [94]Cf. *N.S.*[1] 258.   [95]*N.S.*[3] 192.

flashes of lightning and claps of thunder, as must have occurred with the first impact of an impression of such violence in the air. Whence a few of the more powerful giants, who were scattered among the woods on the upper reaches of the mountains (just as the more powerful wild animals have their lairs there), terrified and dumbfounded by this great effect of unknown cause, looked upwards and became aware of the sky. And, as stated in the *Elements*,[96] in such a case the nature of the human mind leads it to attribute to the effect its own nature which, in this state, was wholly that of men of robust bodily strength, who gave expression to their very violent passions by howls and grunts; whence they imagined the sky to be a huge animate body who was trying to communicate something to them through the whistle of his bolts and the roar of his thunder and, under this aspect, they named him Jove, the first god of the so-called greater gentes; and thus they began to celebrate their natural curiosity, daughter of ignorance and mother of knowledge, which, through the opening she makes in the mind of man, gives birth to wonder, as has been defined above in the *Elements*.[97] This nature still obstinately endures in the vulgar, who, when they see a comet or parhelion or something else unusual in nature, particularly in the appearance of the sky, immediately give in to their curiosity and wonder anxiously about the meaning of the thing, as stated in an axiom. And when they admire the striking effects of the magnet upon iron, even in this age of minds which have been made shrewder and more erudite by philosophy, what they come out with is this: that the magnet possesses an occult sympathy with iron. In this way they turn the whole of nature into a vast animate body with passions and feelings, in accordance with our suggestions in the *Elements*.[98]

378. But since, even in the vulgar, the nature of our human minds has retreated very far from the senses, under the influence of abstractions which are as numerous as the abstract words with which languages are filled, and since they have, moreover, been sharpened by the art of writing, and spiritualised, as it were, by the use of numbers – for the vulgar can count and calculate – we are now naturally denied the capacity to form the vast image of this woman whom they call 'Sympathetic Nature'. For, though men utter the words by mouth, there is nothing in their minds, since their minds are in [the realm of] the false, which is nothing, nor have they retained the assistance of the imagination to enable them to form [such] a vast [but] false image. And, as this is now naturally denied us, so also are we naturally denied the capacity to enter into the vast imagination of those first men, whose minds were in no way

---

[96]*N.S.*[3] 180.   [97]*N.S.*[3] 189.   [98]*N.S.*[3] 177–89.

abstract, in no way sharpened and in no way spiritualised, being wholly immersed in the senses, moved by the passions and buried in their bodies: whence we noted above that we can now scarcely understand and are absolutely unable to imagine how the first men who founded gentile humanity thought.[99]

379. In this mode the first theological poets invented for themselves the first divine fable, the greatest of all they were later to invent, that of Jove, king and father of men and of gods, in the act, moreover, of hurling bolts of thunder and lightning – [a fable] so [suited to the] popular [understanding], and so perturbing and instructive,[100] that the very poets who invented Jove believed in him and, through terrifying religions which will be described later, feared, revered and worshipped him. And through that property of the human mind, noted by Tacitus and quoted in the *Elements*,[101] these men believed everything they saw, imagined, or even did, to be Jove; and to all the universe they could comprehend, and to every part of it, they gave the being of animate substance. This is the civil history of the saying, *Iovis omnia plena* [all things are full of Jove], which Plato later took as a reference to the aether which penetrates and fills everything. But for the theological poets, as we shall shortly see, Jove was no higher than the peaks of the mountains. Hence the first men, who spoke in signs, believed, in accordance with their nature, that thunder and lightning were Jove's signs (whence, later, from *nuo*, 'to make a sign', with an idea sublime enough to be worthy of expressing divine majesty, the divine will was called *numen*), that Jove gave his commands with signs, that such signs were real words and that nature was Jove's language. Throughout the entire universe the gentes believed that divination was the science of this language, which the Greeks called 'theology', meaning 'the science of the speech of the gods'. Thus to Jove came the dreaded kingdom of the thunderbolt, by reason of which he is king of men and of gods, together with two titles: 'the best', in the sense of strongest (as, conversely, *fortus* had the meaning among the first Latins which *bonus* had with the late Latins), and 'the greatest', from his vast body, insofar as he was the sky. From the first great benefit granted to mankind he received the title of *soter* or 'saviour', since he did not strike men down with his bolts of thunder and lightning (this being the first of the three principles taken for this Science);[102] while he was also called 'the stayer or stopper of things' because he put a stop to the ferine wanderings of the giants, as a result of which they later became the sovereigns of the gentes. The Latin philologists restricted [their interpretation of] this too much to the fact that, when invoked by

[99]*N.S.*[3] 338.   [100]*Cf. N.S.*[3] 376.   [101]*N.S.*[3] 183.   [102]*N.S.*[3] 333; *cf. N.S.*[1] 397.

Romulus, Jove stopped the Romans after they had been put to flight in their battle with the Sabines.

380. Hence every nation had a Jove (the vanity of the Egyptians causing them to claim, as we noted in the *Elements,* that their Jove Ammon was the oldest of all) and the many Joves, whose great number causes such astonishment among the philologists, are so many physical histories preserved for us by the fables, providing that demonstration of the universality of the Flood which we promised in the *Elements.*[103]

381. Thus, in consequence of our claims in the *Elements* concerning the origins of poetic characters,[104] [we conclude that] Jove was born naturally in poetry as a divine character or imaginative universal, to which all ancient gentile nations reduced everything connected with the auspices, whence these nations must have been poetic by nature. For they began their poetic wisdom with this poetic metaphysics in which God is contemplated in the attribute of his providence; and they were called 'theological poets', that is, sages who understand the language of the gods as conceived through Jove's auspices, and were appropriately designated 'divine', in the sense of 'diviners', from *divinari,* the proper meaning of which is to divine or to predict. The name 'muse' was given to their science, which Homer defined for us above as the science of good and evil, that is, the divination which God forbade to Adam, thereby dictating his true religion to him, as we again mentioned in the *Elements.*[105] The Greek poets were named *mystae,* after this mystical theology, a word which Homer knowledgeably translates as 'the interpreters of the gods', for they explained the divine mysteries of the auspices and oracles. Each gentile nation had one of its sybils in this science, and only twelve sybils have been recorded for us; [hence] sybils and oracles are the most ancient things of the gentile world.

382. Thus our reasonings agree with those of Eusebius, to which we referred in the *Elements,* concerning the origins of idolatry:[106] that the first people, simple and rough, invented the gods *ob terrorem praesentis potentiae* [from their fear of present power]. Thus it was fear which created the gods on earth, but, as we noted in the *Elements,* not fear which some men created in others, but fear which the same men created in themselves.[107] This origin of idolatry provides in addition a demonstration of that of divination, for they shared a single birth.[108] And these two origins are followed by that of the sacrifices which men made to 'procure' the auspices, that is, to understand them well.[109]

383. This generation of poetry is finally confirmed for us by this eter-

[103]*N.S.*[3] 169.   [104]*N.S.*[3] 209.   [105]*N.S.*[3] 167.   [106]*N.S.*[3] 188.   [107]*N.S.*[3] 191.
[108]*Cf. N.S.*[1] 9, 254–6.   [109]*N.S.*[3] 250.

nal property: that the subject matter proper to poetry is the credible impossibility,[110] for it is impossible that bodies should be minds but it was believed that the thundering sky was Jove. Hence poets engage for the most part in retelling the wonders brought about by witches through the casting of spells. All this must be founded on a hidden sense of God's omnipotence which the nations have, from which is born that other sense whereby all nations are brought naturally to pay infinite respect to divinity. And in this mode the poets founded religion among the gentiles.

384. The foregoing reasonings subvert everything which has been claimed about the origins of poetry, from Plato and Aristotle down to the likes of our own Patrizzi, Scaliger and Castelvetro, since we have discovered that it was a lack of human reason which gave birth to this poetry so sublime that, among the philosophies which came later, and the arts of poetry and criticism – and, indeed, as a result of these very things – nothing equal, let alone greater, arose. Whence the [position of] privilege by which Homer stands first among the sublime or heroic poets, no less by merit than by age. Our discovery of the origins of poetry dispels belief in the incomparable wisdom of the ancients, whose discovery has been coveted so much, from Plato down to Bacon of Verulam in his *Wisdom of the Ancients,* for this wisdom was the vulgar wisdom of the legislators who founded mankind and certainly not the recondite wisdom of great and rare philosophers. Hence, as we have begun to show in the case of Jove, all the mystical meanings of noblest philosophy with which scholars have adorned the Greek fables and Egyptian hieroglyphics will be shown to be as inappropriate as the historical meanings they must both naturally have contained will turn out to be natural.

[2] *Corollaries on the principal aspects of this Science*

I

385. It follows from the foregoing that divine providence, apprehended through such human sense as was available to these crude, wild and fierce men who, despairing of nature's assistance, desired something superior to nature to save them (which is the first principle of our earlier definition of the method of this Science),[111] allowed them to make the mistake of fearing the false divinity of Jove because he could strike them

[110]Cf. N.S.[1] 258.   [111]N.S.[3] 339; cf. N.S.[1] 8.

down by thunderbolt. And thus, by the glow of flashing lightning in the clouds of those first storms, they perceived this great truth: that divine providence watches over the safety of the whole of mankind. Hence, this Science comes to be a rational civil theology of providence,[112] beginning with the vulgar wisdom of legislators who founded nations by contemplating God through the attribute of [His] foresight, and fulfilling itself in the recondite wisdom of the philosophers who demonstrate Him rationally in their natural theology.

II

386. Whence begins also a philosophy of authority, another principal aspect of this Science,[113] taking the word 'authority' in its first meaning of 'property', the sense in which it is always used in the Law of the Twelve Tables. Consequently, in Roman civil law they continued to call those from whom we have right of property (*dominio*) 'authors' [*auctores*] (which most certainly comes from αὐτός, [that is,] *proprius* or *suus ipsius* [one's own]), for which many scholars write *autor* and *autoritas*, without the aspirate.

387. The first authority which arose was divine: [the authority] by which divinity appropriated to itself the few giants of whom we have spoken, literally by driving them underground to the bottom of the caves within the mountains and there concealing them. This is the coils of iron by which the giants, spread through the mountains, were held chained to the land wherever they found themselves, through their fear of the heavens and of Jove, when thunder and lightning first struck in the sky: hence Tityus and Prometheus, chained to a lofty crag, their hearts being devoured by an eagle, by the religion, that is, of Jove's auspices. Thus the Latins continued to use the heroic phrase *terrore defixi* for 'those struck still by fear', while artists portray Tityus and Prometheus bound hand and foot in the mountains by such coils. The latter formed the great chain which Dionysius Longinus admired as the height of sublimity in the whole of Homeric fable. This is the chain of which Jove, when he wants to prove that he is king of men and gods, asserts that if all men and all gods were to hold on at one end, he alone at the other would drag them along behind him. And if the Stoics want this chain to signify the eternal series of causes with which their fate encloses and binds the world, they should see that they are not themselves caught in a tangle by it, for the dragging of men and gods by such a chain itself hangs upon the will of Jove, whereas they want Jove himself to be subject to fate.[114]

[112]*Cf. N.S.*³ 342.   [113]*Cf. N.S.*³ 350.   [114]*Cf. N.S.*¹ 12; *N.S.*³ 130.

388. This divine authority was followed by human authority, in the full philosophical sense of a property of human nature which not even God can take from man without destroying him. This is the sense in which Terence spoke of *voluptates proprias deorum*, by which he meant that God's happiness is not dependent on that of others, and Horace of *propriam virtutis laurum*, that virtue cannot be deprived of its triumph by envy. It is the sense also of Caesar's *propriam victoriam*, which Denis Petau wrongly claimed not to be a Latin saying, since, with a positive excess of Latin elegance, it signifies a victory which the enemy could not take from his hands. This authority resides in the free use of the will, the intellect [on the other hand] being a passive capacity which is subservient to the truth; for this is the point of departure of everything human, at which man began to make use of that freedom of the human will to curb the motions of the body, either to still them completely or to change their direction for the better, which, as mentioned in the *Elements,* is the conatus proper to free agents.[115] Whence the giants abstained from their bestial habit of roaming through the great forest of the earth and grew accustomed to the quite contrary practice of staying put and remaining hidden, for long spells, within their caves.

389. This authority of human nature was followed by that of natural law, for, by occupying and for long remaining in the lands where by chance they found themselves during the period of the first thunderbolts, they became lords of those lands by that occupation and long possession which is the source of all ownership in the world. Hence these are those *pauci quos aequus amavit/Iupiter* [few beloved by Jupiter the just] whom the philosophers later transformed into those bequeathed by God with characters favourable for [the pursuit of] sciences and virtues. But the historical meaning of this expression is that in these depths and places of concealment they became the founders of the greater gentes, whose Jove is the first god, as noted in the *Elements.* As we shall show later, these gentes were the ancient noble houses of which, when they had ramified into many families, the first kingdoms and cities were composed. The following fine heroic phrases, deriving from them, survived among the Latins: *condere gentes, condere regna, condere urbes; fundare gentes, fundare regna, fundare urbes.*

390. This philosophy of authority comes after the rational civil theology of providence, because, by means of the former's theological proofs, it, with its philosophical ones, makes the philological proofs (of which we enumerated the three kinds in the section on *Method*)[116] clear and

[115]*N.S.*[3] 340.   [116]*N.S.*[3] 342–59.

distinct. Thus human will which, as we noted in the *Elements*, [117] by its nature is most uncertain, is reduced to certainty with regard to the things of the obscure distant past of nations, which is as much as to say that this philosophy of authority reduces philology to the form of a science. [118]

III

391. The third principal aspect [of our Science] is a history of human ideas, which, as we have just seen, began with divine ideas [which arose] through contemplating the sky with the physical eye. For in their science of augury the Romans used the word *contemplari* for their observation of those parts of the sky from which the auguries came or in which the auspices were to be seen, and these regions, which the augurs traced out with their crooks, were named *templa coeli* [temples of the sky], from which the Greeks must have derived their first θεωρήματα [*theōrēmata*] and μαθήματα [*mathēmata*], 'things, divine or sublime, worthy of contemplation', which ended as abstract metaphysical and mathematical things. This is the civil history of the expression, *a Iove principium musae* [from Jove, origin of the Muse], since, as we have just seen, the first Muse began with Jove's thunderbolts. This was the Muse Homer defined for us as 'knowledge of good and evil', whence philosophers later found it all too convenient to interpose here their maxim that 'the origins of wisdom must lie in piety'. The first Muse must therefore have been Urania, she who contemplates the sky in search of the auguries, and who, as we shall see, later came to represent astronomy. And since, as explained above, poetic metaphysics divided into all its subordinate poetic sciences, each with the same nature as its mother, so this history of ideas will provide us with the crude origins both of the practical sciences which obtain among the nations and of the speculative sciences, cultivated today, which are the concern of scholars.

IV

392. The fourth aspect [of our Science] is a philosophical [art of] criticism, [119] born of the foregoing history of ideas, which will apply the true in judgement upon (*giudicherà il vero sopra*) the authors of the nations themselves, amongst which more than a thousand years must have elapsed before the appearance of the writers who are the subject of philological criticism. Beginning thus with Jove, this philosophical criticism

[117]*N.S.*[3] 141.   [118]*Cf. N.S.*[3] 140.   [119]*Cf. N.S.*[1] 91–3; *N.S.*[3] 348.

will produce a natural theogony, or lineage of gods, born naturally in the minds of the authors of the gentile world, who were by nature theological poets; and the twelve gods of the greater gentes, whose ideas were created in their imaginations whenever certain human needs or utilities arose for them,[120] are defined in accordance with twelve specific epochs, to which the times in which the fables were born will be reduced. Hence this natural theogony will produce a rational chronology of poetic history, [occurring] at least nine hundred years before vulgar history, which came after the heroic age, began.

V

393. The fifth aspect [of our Science] is an ideal eternal history traversed in time by the histories of all nations; and wherever, in wild, fierce and savage times, the taming of men begins under the influence of religion, the nations begin, proceed and come to an end [in accordance] with the stages meditated in Book II,[121] which we shall encounter again in Book IV,[122] where we treat of the course traversed by the nations, and in Book V, which deals with the recourse of human things.

VI

394. The sixth [aspect of our Science] is a system of the natural law of the gentes, going back to the origins of the gentes where, in accordance with one of the axioms above,[123] the subject matter begins. Here also the doctrines of those three princes who treat of it, Hugo Grotius, John Selden and Samuel Pufendorf, should have begun, but all three erred in unison, by beginning their subject halfway through, with the most recent times of the civilised nations, and hence with the times of men enlightened by the fullest expression of natural reason, in which were born philosophers who ascended to the meditation of a perfect idea of justice.

395. [Let us consider] first Grotius, who, through his very love of the truth, leaves divine providence out of consideration, and claims that his system holds good even if all knowledge of God is discounted.[124] Hence the Roman jurists are quite immune from any of the criticisms which he levels against them on a large number of subjects, since, having posited divine providence as their principle in these matters, their reasonings were concerned with the natural law of the gentes and not that of the philosophers or of the moral theologians.

---

[120]*Cf. N.S.*[1] 267–8.   [121]*Cf. N.S.*[1] 90; *N.S.*[3] 349.   [122]*N.S.*[3] 915–46.
[123]*N.S.*[3] 314–15.   [124]*Cf. N.S.*[1] 16.

396. Next Selden, who accepts providence, but pays no attention whatsoever to the inhospitality of the first peoples or to the division which the people of God made of the whole world of nations of that time into Hebrews and gentiles.[125] Nor [does he attend to the fact] that since, during their captivity in Egypt, the Hebrews had lost sight of their natural law, God had to order it to them again through the law which he gave to Moses on Sinai; nor [to the fact] that in his law God forbids even thoughts which are less than just, [a matter] with which no mortal legislators ever concerned themselves; nor, moreover, to the bestial origins of all the gentile nations, the object of our earlier reasonings. And his claim, that the Hebrews afterwards taught the natural law to the gentiles, turns out to be impossible for him to prove, because of Josephus' magnanimous confession,[126] which is supported by the important reflection of Lactantius, mentioned above,[127] and by the enmity, also noted earlier, which the Hebrews have always displayed towards the gentiles, an enmity which, diffused as they are through all nations, they maintain to this day.

397. And finally Pufendorf, [who] commences [his treatment of] natural law with an Epicurean hypothesis, which has man cast into this world bereft of the care and assistance of God.[128] Notwithstanding the fact that, in the face of criticisms of these claims, he [tries to] justify them in a special treatise, he is quite unable, in the absence of providence as a first principle, even to begin to reason about law, as we heard[129] Cicero tell Atticus the Epicurean in the treatise in which he reasons about laws.

398. Whence we begin our own reasonings on law, which the Romans called *ius,* a contraction of the ancient *Ious,* at the first and oldest point of all times: the moment at which the idea of Jove was born in the minds of the founders of the gentes. A wondrous correspondence obtains here between the Latins and the Greeks, who, as Plato to our good fortune observes in the *Cratylus,* first called the law διᾶιον, meaning *discurrens* [running through] or *permanans* [penetrating],[130] and later, for ease of speech, must have pronounced it δίκαιον. The philosophical origin introduced here is, however, Plato's own, for in his erudite mythology Jove is taken to be the ether which penetrates and runs through everything, but the historical origin is from Jove himself, whom the Greeks definitely called Διός [Dios], following which the Latins used the expressions *sub dio* and *sub Jove* interchangeably to mean 'under the open sky'. Hence

---

[125]Cf. N.S.[1] 17.   [126]N.S.[3] 126.

[127]N.S.[3] 94, not here translated, in which Vico mentions Lactantius' denial that Pythagoras was a pupil of Isaiah.

[128]Cf. N.S.[1] 18.   [129]N.S.[3] 335.

[130]Reading *permanans* for *permanens,* 'persisting'.

let us commence our reasoning about law, which was divine by birth, with the propriety with which it was spoken of in divination or the science of Jove's auspices, these being the divine things by means of which the gentes regulated human things, which [two kinds of thing] together exhaust the suitable subject matter of jurisprudence. Thus we begin our reasonings on natural law from the idea of divine providence, with which the idea of law was also born; and in accordance with the mode which we meditated earlier, law began to be observed naturally by the founders of the properly named gentes, the most ancient kind of all, those who were called the greater gentes, whose Jove was the first god.

VII

399. The seventh and last of the principal aspects of this Science is that of the principles of universal history, which begins, at the first moment of everything human in the gentile world, with the first age of the world which the Egyptians said had preceded them, that of the gods, in which heaven begins to reign on earth and to create great benefits for men, as [indicated] in the *Elements;* and here begins the golden age of the Greeks, in which the gods had dealings on earth with men, as we have seen Jove commence to do. Starting from this first age of the world the Greek poets have faithfully told us in their fables of the Flood and of the existence of [beings who were] giants by nature, thus providing a true narration of the origins of profane universal history. But their successors were unable later to enter into the imaginations of the first founders of the gentile world, which had led them to believe that they were seeing gods, nor did these successors understand the proper meaning of the word *atterrare*, which was 'to drive underground'. Whence the giants who lived in hiding in the caves under the mountains were grossly distorted in the later traditions of the gentes, in which they were represented as having heaped Olympus, Pelion and Ossa upon one another in order to hound the gods out of the heavens, whereas, [in truth,] not only did the first impious giants not wage war against the gods, but they had no notion of them until Jove was hurling his bolts of thunder and lightning; while the sky, which was later to be raised to a disproportionate height in the much more developed minds of the Greeks, was for them, as we shall show below, the peak of the mountains. The above-mentioned fable [of the heaping of a number of mountains upon one another] must have been invented after Homer and [its presence] in the *Odyssey* foisted on him by others, for in his time it sufficed that Olympus alone should shake in order to bring about the fall of the gods, and in the *Iliad* Homer always describes the gods as living [solely] on the top of Mount Olympus. For

all these reasons profane universal history has hitherto lacked a [true] foundation, whence, lacking a rational chronology of poetic history, it has lacked also in continuity.

[Section II]

[1] *Poetic logic*

400. Now, since that which is metaphysics, by dint of contemplating things in all the categories of being, is also logic, by dint of considering them in all the categories of signification, and since we have just considered poetry as a poetic metaphysics, through which the poets imagined bodies for the most part to be divine substances, we now consider this same poetry as poetic logic, through which it signifies things.

401. 'Logic' derives from the word λόγος, which first and properly meant *favola* [fable] which became the Italian *favella* [language]. The Greeks also used the word μῦθος [mythos] for fable, whence the Latins derived *mutus* [mute]. Thus, in the mute era was born the mental language which, in a golden passage, Strabo says existed before vocal or articulated language: whence λόγος signifies both 'idea' and 'word'. And it was appropriate that divine providence should order it thus in such religious times, in view of the eternal property that it is of greater importance to religion that one should meditate it than that one should speak of it; hence, as we noted in the *Elements*, [131] the first language in the first mute age of the nations must have commenced with signs or actions or objects which were naturally related to their ideas, and for this reason λόγος or *verbum* also meant 'deed' to the Hebrews and 'thing' to the Greeks, as Thomas Gataker notes in his *De instrumenti stylo*. And we have, indeed, inherited the definition of μῦθος as *vera narratio* or 'true speech': that is, the 'natural speech' which first Plato and then Iamblichus claimed had once been spoken on earth. But, as we saw in the *Elements*, [132] since this claim was based on guesswork, not only did the effort which Plato expended in the *Cratylus* in search of this speech prove fruitless, but both Aristotle and Galen attacked him for it. For this first language, which was that of the theological poets, was not a language which accorded with the nature of things (as must have been the sacred language invented by Adam, to whom God granted divine onomathesia, or the application to things of names which accord with the nature of each),

---

[131] N.S.³ 225–7.   [132] N.S.³ 227.

but a language invented by the imagination, involving animate substances, mostly taken to be divine.

402. Thus, for example, they understood Jove, Cybele or Berecynthia, and Neptune, and, first by mute pointing, interpreted them as those substances of the sky, earth and sea which they imagined to be animate divinities, and therefore, in accordance with truths delivered by their senses, believed them to be gods. Through these three divinities, following our earlier claims about the poetic characters, they interpreted everything pertaining to the sky, the earth and the sea; and, in the same way, with the other divinities they symbolised the other kinds of things which pertain to each god, such as all flowers to Flora and all fruits to Pomona. This is something which we still do, though in a reverse direction, with regard to the things of spirit, as when we form ideas, for the most part of women, for the faculties of the human mind and for our passions, virtues, vices, sciences and arts, reducing to these ideas of women all the causes, properties and effects pertaining to each faculty; for when we wish to draw forth spiritual things from our understanding we require the assistance of the imagination to enable us to express them, and, like painters, to create human images for them. But since they were unable to make use of the understanding, the theological poets, by means of a more sublime but quite contrary activity, as we have just seen, gave sense and passion to [inanimate] bodies and to bodies as vast as the sky, the earth and the sea. Later, with the diminution of these vast fantasies and the strengthening of abstractions, the former were taken as miniature signs of the latter, while metonymy [then] cast an appearance of learning over our ignorance of these hitherto buried origins of human things: thus Jove became so small and light that he is carried in flight by an eagle; [similarly] Neptune rides over the sea in a frail chariot and Cybele is seated on a lion.

403. Hence the mythologies must have been the proper languages of the fables (as the word suggests); so that, since, as we have shown above, the fables were imaginative genera, the mythologies must have been allegories proper to them. The word 'allegory', as observed in the *Elements*,[133] was defined for us as *diversiloquium*, since, with an identity not of proportion but, in the language of the scholastics, of predicability, the allegories signify the different species or different individuals included within these genera. Whence they must have a univocal meaning, comprised of a quality common to their [various] species or individuals – as, in Achilles, an idea of valour common to all the strong, or, in Ulysses, an idea of prudence common to all the wise –so that such allegories must

[133]*N.S.*³ 210.

constitute etymologies of the poetic languages, providing them with origins wholly univocal, just as those of the vulgar languages are most often analogical. We have also inherited the definition of the word 'etymology', which has the same meaning as *veriloquium*, just as fable was defined for us as *vera narratio*.

[2]   Corollaries concerning tropes, monsters and poetic metamorphoses[134]

I

404. All the first tropes are corollaries of this poetic logic, and of these the most luminous, and hence the most necessary and frequent, is metaphor. This is ever most praised when it gives sense and passion to things which lack them, in accordance with the metaphysics reasoned out above,[135] in which the first poets gave to bodies the being of animate substances, with only as many capacities as they themselves possessed, that is those of sense and passion, thus creating the fables from them, so that every metaphor made in this way becomes a miniature fable. Whence we derive the following [principle of] criticism for the times in which metaphors were born in the [various] languages: that all metaphors which, by means of likenesses taken from bodies, come to signify the labours of abstract minds, must belong to times in which philosophies had begun to become more refined. This is shown by the following: that in all languages the words necessary to cultivated arts and recondite sciences have rural origins.

405. It is noteworthy that in all languages the greater part of expressions concerning inanimate things are created by metaphors drawn from the human body and its parts and from the human senses and passions. For example, 'head' for summit or beginning; '[in the] face[of]' and '[at the] back [of]' for in front and behind; 'mouth' for every [sort of] hole; 'lip' for the rim of a vase or anything [similar]; the 'teeth' of a plough, rake, saw or comb; a 'tongue' of sea; the 'gorges' and 'throats' of rivers and mountains; a 'neck' of land; the [two] 'arms' of a river; a 'hand[ful]' for a small number; 'flanks' and 'sides' for edges; 'heart' for the centre (which the Latins called *umbilicus*); 'foot' for [the end of] a country and

---

[134]H. V. White interprets this chapter as the foundation of the whole of Vico's theory of social and cultural development: see 'The tropics of history: the deep structure of the *New Science*', in *Giambattista Vico's Science of Humanity*.
[135]*N.S.*[3] 374–84.

the ends [of things in general]; 'sole' [also] for the base [of a ploughshare
or a shoe]; the 'flesh' of fruit; a 'vein' of water, stone or mineral; the
'blood' of the vine, for wine; the 'bowels' of the earth. [Similarly] the sky
and the sea 'smile', the wind 'whistles', the waves 'murmur', and objects
'groan' under a heavy weight. [Again] the peasants of Latium used the
expressions *sitire agros* [the fields are thirsty], *laborare fructus* [the
fruits labour] and *luxuriari segetes* [the grain swells], while for our
own peasants 'the plants are in love', 'the vines go mad' and 'the ash-
trees weep'. And there are innumerable others to be collected in all languages. All this follows from the axiom that 'when man is ignorant he
makes himself the measure of the universe', since, in the examples
brought forward, he has made of himself an entire universe. For, as
rational metaphysics teaches that *homo intelligendo fit omnia* [man
becomes everything through understanding], so this imaginative metaphysics shows that *homo non intelligendo fit omnia* [man becomes
everything through failing to understand]; and there is perhaps more
truth in the latter than in the former, for by understanding things man
unfolds his mind and comprehends things, but by failing to understand
he makes these things of himself and, in transforming himself into them,
he becomes the world.

II

406. By dint of this same logic, born of such a metaphysics, the first
poets must have named things in accordance with their most particular
and sensible ideas, these being the two sources of synecdoche and
metonymy respectively. For metonymy of the author for the product
arose because authors were more often given names than were their
products; that of subject for form and property arose because, as we
noted in the *Elements,* the first poets were unable to abstract forms and
qualities from their subjects; while many miniature fables are [examples
of] the metonymy of cause for effect, in which the causes were imagined
as women clad in the effects [of these causes], such as ugly Poverty, sad
Old Age and pallid Death.

III

407. Synecdoche next passed into metaphor by the raising of particulars to universals or by combining [some] parts with the other parts
which go to make up their wholes. Thus the word 'mortals' was first and
appropriately used only for men, as they must have perceived only themselves as mortal. 'Head' was used for 'man' or 'person', as is so frequent

in vulgar Latin, because in the dense woods only a man's head could be
seen from a distance, for 'man' itself is an abstract word which comprehends, as in a philosophical genus, the body and all bodily parts, the
mind and all mental faculties, the spirit and all its propensities. Thus it
was necessary that, with complete propriety, *tignum* [stick] and *culmen*
[stalk] should signify rafter and straw in the period when thatching was
practised, and that later, when the cities had blossomed, they should
stand for the whole material and adornment of the buildings of the cities.
Similarly, *tectum* [roof] stood for the whole house, because in those early
times coverings sufficed for houses. In the same way, *puppis* [poop] stood
for ship because, being high, it is the first part to be seen by land-dwellers,
and for the same reason, in the recurrence of barbarism they used 'sail'
for 'ship'. Thus also *mucro* [point] for sword, for the latter is an abstract
word, comprehending, as in a [single] genus, pommel, hilt, edge and
point, but it was the point which men felt and which caused their fear.
Similarly, the material for the whole with its form, as in 'iron' for 'sword'
for they were unable to abstract forms from matter. That little line combining synecdoche and metonymy, *tertia messis erat* [it was the third
harvest], was without doubt born of a necessity of nature, since well
over a thousand years had to elapse for the astronomical word 'year' to
arise among the nations; and in the Florentine countryside they still talk
of 'having harvested so many times' to indicate 'so many years'. Moreover, that cluster of two synecdoches and a metonymy, *Post aliquot,*
mea regna videns, mirabor, aristas [After several ears of wheat, shall I
marvel upon seeing my kingdoms?] implies an excessive awkwardness in
power of expression in those first rustic times, in which men used the
phrase 'so many ears of wheat', which are more specific [even] than har-
vests, for 'so many years'; and, [indeed,] because the expression was so
very awkward the grammarians have thought it over-contrived.

IV

408. Irony could certainly have begun only in the age of reflection, for
it is formed from falsehood by dint of a reflection which borrows a mask
of truth. Here a great principle of human things emerges, confirming the
origin of poetry which we have uncovered: that, since the first men of the
gentile world were as simple as children, who are truthful by nature, the
first fables could have represented nothing through falsehood, whence
they must necessarily have been, as they were defined earlier for us, true
narrations.[136]

[136]*N.S.*³ 401.

V

409. These reasons establish that all the tropes (for they all reduce to these four), which have hitherto been thought to be ingenious creations of the writers, were necessary modes of expression, possessed originally of complete native propriety, of all the first poetic nations; but that later, with the further unfolding of the human mind and the invention of words signifying abstract forms, whether they be genera which subsume their species or which relate parts to their wholes, these expressions of the first nations became metaphorical. Whence we begin to root out those two common errors of the grammarians: that the language of prose is proper and that of poetry improper; and that first a language of prose existed and later one of verse.

VI

410. Monsters and poetic metamorphoses arose by a necessity of this first human nature, demonstrated in the *Elements*,[137] by which men lacked the ability to abstract either forms or properties from their subjects; hence they had, with their logic, to compound [a number of] subjects, in order to compound their forms, or destroy one such subject, in order to separate its first form from a contrary form [later] introduced into it. This composition of ideas created the poetic monsters, rather in the way in which in Roman law, according to the observation of Antoine Favre in his *Iurisprudentiae papinianeae,* the children of whores are referred to as 'monsters' because they combine the nature of men with the bestial property of being born of roving or uncertain matings – such, we shall find, were the monsters (born of women who were honest but lacked the solemnity of marriage) of whom, in the Law of the Twelve Tables, it was decreed that they be thrown into the Tiber.

VII

411. Metamorphosis was created by the division of ideas. Among the diversity of heroic expressions which ancient jurisprudence has preserved for us we find that the Romans have bequeathed us *fundum fieri* [to become the ground of] for *autorem fieri* [to approve or support a law] for, as the inner regions of the earth support a farm or the soil and whatever is sowed, planted or built upon it, so the approver supports an act which without his support would come to naught, [and the approver does this] because, from the [form of a] self-moving agent, which he is, he extracts the contrary form of something stable.

[137]*N.S.*[3] 209.

[3] Corollaries concerning the language of poetic characters of the first nations

412. The poetic language which our poetic logic has enabled us to meditate pursued its course well into the historical period, rather as the great surging rivers spread widely into the seas but, through the force of their current, preserve the freshness of the waters which they carry out into them. Evidence for this lies in Iamblichus' claim, mentioned above in the *Elements*,[138] that the Egyptians ascribed to Hermes Trismegistus everything they discovered of use to human life; and we confirmed this with our axiom that 'with the ideas and names of the [particular] men, women and things they have seen first, children apprehend and name all subsequent men, women and things which have some resemblance or relationship with the first', this being the great natural source of the poetic characters in which the first peoples naturally thought and spoke.[139] But we made the point in the *Elements* that, had Iamblichus reflected upon this nature of human things and had he connected with it that custom of the ancient Egyptians to which he himself refers, he would certainly not have thrust the sublime mysteries of his own Platonic wisdom upon the mysteries of the vulgar wisdom of the Egyptians.[140]

413. Now, [supported] by [our axiom concerning] the nature of children and [our knowledge of] this custom of the ancient Egyptians,[141] we maintain that the poetic language, by dint of its poetic characters, can lead to many important discoveries relating to ancient times.

I

414. [For example, that] Solon must have been someone rich in vulgar wisdom, leader of the plebs in those early times when Athens was an aristocratic state. This [truth] is preserved in [that part of] Greek history where we are told that Athens was originally occupied by the optimates, which [is itself a proposition which] we shall demonstrate in these books [to be true] for all the heroic states. For the heroes, or nobles, believing that a certain nature of theirs was of divine origin, claimed the gods, and hence the auspices of the gods, as their own, when they confined the whole public and private law of the heroic cities within their own orders and conceded to the plebeians, who were held to be of bestial origin, and thus bereft both of gods and of the auspices, only the customs of natural liberty. (This is a great principle of things which will be reasoned out through almost the whole of this work.) And, [to return to Solon,] that

138 *N.S.*3 207.   139 *N.S.*3 206.   140 *N.S.*3 208.   141 *N.S.*3 207.

he urged the plebeians to reflect upon themselves and come to know that they were equal in human nature with the nobles, and that they ought therefore to be equal with them in law. Unless, of course, Solon was [none other than] the Athenian plebeians themselves, considered under this aspect [of their knowledge and desires].

415. For there must also have been such a Solon among the ancient Romans among whom, as ancient Roman history states quite plainly, during their heroic struggles with the nobles, the plebeians used to say of the fathers of whom Romulus had composed the Senate (and from whom the patricians were themselves descended), *non esse caelo demissos,* that is, that they lacked the divine origin of which they boasted and that Jove was equal for everyone. This is the civil history of the phrase, *Iupiter omnibus aequus* [Jove is equal for everyone], upon which the scholars later imposed their [own] thesis that minds are wholly equal and that their diversities arise from the diverse organisation of their bodies and diversities of civil education. By this reflection the Roman plebeians began to achieve equality of civil liberty with the patricians, until they completely changed [the form of] the Roman state from aristocratic to popular. We advanced this as a hypothesis in the 'Annotations to the Chronological Table', where we reasoned the Publilian Law in idea, and we shall show that this is what happend in fact, not only in the Roman state but in all the other ancient states; and [thus], both by reason and authority, we shall demonstrate that, starting from a reflection of the same sort as that of Solon, the plebs of the peoples universally changed their states from aristocratic to popular.

416. Hence Solon was made author of the famous phrase, *Nosce te ipsum* [Know thyself] which, because of the great civil utility it had brought to the Athenian people, was inscribed in all the public places of that city. But the scholars later took it as a great pronouncement on metaphysics and morality, as indeed it is, and Solon was hailed as a man rich in recondite wisdom, the foremost of the seven sages of Greece. In this way, with all the orders and laws which give form to a state starting in Athens from such a reflection, and because of this manner of thinking in poetic characters which was common to all the first peoples, the Athenians ascribed to Solon all their orders and laws, just as the Egyptians ascribed to Hermes Trismegistus everything they discovered useful to human civil life.

II

417. Similarly, to Romulus must have been attributed all laws concerning the orders.

III

418. To Numa, all laws concerning sacred things and divine ceremonies, of which in its most sumptuous times the Roman religion later made great show.

IV

419. To Tullus Hostilius, all laws and orders attaching to military discipline.

V

420. To Servius Tullius, the census, which is the basis of democratic states, and a large number of other laws to do with popular liberty, so that Tacitus acclaimed him as *praecipuus sanctor legum* [pre-eminent ordainer of laws]. For, as we shall show, the census of Servius Tullius was the basis of the aristocratic states, by means of which the plebeians won from the nobles bonitary ownership of the fields; this, in turn, was the reason why the tribunes of the plebs were later created for the defence of this part of their natural liberty; and the tribunes subsequently led them, step by step, to attain full civil liberty. Thus, because these occasions and movements originated in it, the census of Servius Tullius became the tax basis of the Roman popular state, as we reasoned by way of hypothesis in the Annotation to the Publilian Law, and as we shall later show to be true in fact.

VI

421. To Tarquinius Priscus, all the insignia and emblems with which, in its most brilliant times, the majesty of the Roman empire later glittered.

VII

422. Similarly, a large number of laws, which, as we show below, were passed in later times, must have been incorporated into the Twelve Tables. For, as was fully demonstrated in our *Principles of universal law,* since the law of quiritary ownership which the nobles communicated to the plebeians was the first law to be written on a public tablet, and since this provided the sole reason for the creation of the decemvirs, this aspect of popular liberty explains why all the laws which brought equality of

liberty and which were later inscribed on public tablets were attributed to the decemvirs. This may be demonstrated by reference to the matter of the Grecian luxury with which [Roman] funeral ceremonies were performed, for since the decemvirs would not have introduced this [custom] to the Romans by means of a prohibition, their prohibition must have come after the Romans had acquired it, and this could not have occurred until after the wars with the Tarentines and with Pyrrhus, when the Romans first became acquainted with the Greeks. Whence Cicero's observation that this law was accompanied in Latin by the same words with which it had been conceived in Athens.

VIII

423. Likewise Draco, the author of the laws written in blood in the period when, according to Greek history as described above, Athens was occupied by the optimates. As we shall see below, this was in the times of the heroic aristocracies when, again according to Greek history, the Heraclids had spread through the whole of Greece and even into Attica, as we proposed in the Chronological Table, finally halting in the Peloponnesus and settling their kingdom in Sparta which, we shall find, was certainly an aristocratic state. Draco must have been one of the Gorgon's serpents nailed to Perseus' shield which, as we shall show, stood for the rule of law and, with terrifying penalty, turned all who looked on it to stone; in sacred history, similarly, because they were exemplary punishments, such laws were called *leges sanguinis* [laws of blood], and it was with a shield of the same sort that Minerva, to whom the name Ἀθηνα [Athena] was given, armed herself, as we shall show more fully later; while among the Chinese, who still write in hieroglyphics, a dragon is the emblem of civil power. That this poetic manner of thought and expression should arise in these two nations so widely separated in time and place must be an unfailing source of wonder. [But, to return to Draco, the above account must be true of him] for he is not heard of again in the whole of Greek history.

IX

424. Our discovery of the [nature of] poetic characters offers the support for our claim that Aesop should be located well before the seven sages of Greece, which we promised in the 'Annotations to the Chronological Table' to give at this point, since the following history of ideas provides confirmation of that philological truth. The seven sages were admired for starting to furnish precepts of morality and of civil doctrine,

by means of maxims such as that of Solon their prince, the celebrated *Nosce te ipsum* [Know thyself] which, as we saw above, began as a precept of civil doctrine but was later transferred to metaphysical and moral doctrine. But Aesop had previously provided such instructions by means of analogies, through which the poets had still earlier expressed themselves. Now the order of human ideas proceeds by means of the observation of similarities, first for purposes of expression, then for those of proof, while things are proved by the adducing of examples where first one alone is sufficient but where ultimately induction involving a number of examples is necessary. Hence Socrates, the father of all philosophical schools, ushered in the dialectic of induction which Aristotle later brought to completion in the syllogism, which is invalid without a universal. But for those of limited understanding, the introduction of a single point of resemblance is enough to induce persuasion as, with a single fable of the sort which Aesop had invented, good Menenius Agrippa reduced the insurgent Roman plebs to obedience.

425. That Aesop was a poetic character of the *socii* or *famuli* of the heroes, is shown us, in a spirit of revelation, by well-mannered Phaedrus in the Prologue of one of his *Fables*:

> *Nunc fabularum cur sit inventum genus,*
> *brevi docebo. Servitus obnoxia,*
> *quia, quae volebat, non audebat dicere,*
> *affectus proprios in fabellas transtulit.*
> *Aesopi illius semitam feci viam.*

[Now I shall briefly explain why the genus 'fable' was invented. Servitude, liable to punishment and not daring to say what it wished, translated its sentiments into little fables. Of Aesop's path I made a road.]

The fable of the leonine society provides clear confirmation of this, for, as we noted in the *Elements*,[142] the plebeians were known as the *socii* of the heroic cities, partaking of the labours and dangers of war but not of the spoils and gains. Aesop was therefore called 'slave' because, as we shall show below, the plebeians were the heroes' *famuli*. Moreover, he was described as ugly because civil beauty was held to be born of the solemn marriages contracted by the heroes alone, as, again, we shall show below. In just the same way Thersites, who must have been the character for the plebeians who served the heroes in the Trojan war, was ugly and was thrashed by Ulysses who used Agamemnon's sceptre, just as the ancient Roman plebeians were lashed across their bare shoulders by the nobles with switches *regium in morem* [in royal fashion], as

---

[142]*N.S.*³ 259.

Sallust expresses it in St Augustine's *City of God,* until the Porcian Law drove the switch from Roman shoulders.

426. These directions, then, useful to free civil life, must have been sentiments, dictated by natural reason, nourished by the plebs of the heroic cities. Aesop was made a poetic character for this aspect of the plebeians, and later, when fables concerning moral philosophy were attributed to him, he was made the first moral philosopher, in the same way as Solon became the sage who established the free Athenian state with his laws. But because Aesop gave his directions through fables he was made to precede Solon, who gave his through maxims. These fables must first have been conceived in heroic verse, for there is a later tradition that they were conceived in iambic verse, and we shall show below that the Greek gentes spoke in iambic verse between speaking in heroic verse and in prose, which is the form in which, after they were finally written down, they have reached us.

427. Thus were the later products of recondite wisdom ascribed to the first authors of vulgar wisdom, and the likes of Zoroaster in the East, Trismegistus in Egypt, the Orphics in Greece and the Pythagoreans in Italy, [all of whom were] originally legislators, finally came to be thought of as philosophers, as is now the case with Confucius in China. For, as we shall show later, the Pythagoreans in Magna Graecia were certainly so called in the sense of nobles, being those who, after they had attempted to reduce their states from popular to aristocratic, had all been killed. And we demonstrated above that the *Golden Verse* of Pythagoras was a forgery, as were the *Oracles* of Zoroaster, the *Poimander* of Trismegistus and the *Orphics* or verses of Orpheus; nor did the ancients receive from Pythagoras any book on philosophy, Philolaus being the first Pythagorean to have written one, as Scheffer notes in his *De philosophia italica.*

[4] Corollaries concerning the origins of languages and letters, including therein the origins of hieroglyphics, laws, names, gentile insignia, medals and coins; and, hence, of the first language and literature of the natural law of the gentes

428. Now from the theology of the poets, i.e., from poetic metaphysics, via the poetic logic to which it gave birth, let us set out in search of the

origin of languages and letters, a subject in which the number of theories held matches the number of scholars who have investigated it. Thus in his *Grammatica*, Gerard Jan Voss asserts: *De literarum inventione multi multa congerunt, et fuse et confuse, ut ab iis incertus magis abeas quam veneras dudum* [Concerning the invention of letters, much has been compiled by many, copiously but confusedly, so that one departs from them with more uncertainty than when one came to them]; while in his *De [prima] origine scribendi*, Herman Hugo observes: *Nulla alia res est, in qua plures magisque pugnantes sententiae reperiantur atque haec tractatio de literarum et scriptionis origine. Quantae sententiarum pugnae! Quid credas? quid non credas?* [In no other matter is there to be found a greater number of opinions and more conflict than in the treatment of the origin of letters and writing. How great these battles of opinion! What is one to believe and disbelieve?]. Hence, because of the incomprehensibility of the mode, Bernard von Mallinckrodt, in his *De arte typographia*, followed by Ingewald Eling in his *De historia linguae graecae*, claims that they were of divine invention.

429. But this difficulty of the mode was created by the scholars because they all took the origin of letters to be a thing apart from that of languages, though the two were by nature connected, as, indeed, the scholars ought have been warned by the words 'grammar' and 'characters'. By the first, because grammar is defined as 'the art of speaking' and letters are γράμματα [grammata], so that grammar should have been defined as the art of writing, as it was by Aristotle, and as, in truth, it was at birth, since we shall here demonstrate that, being mute at first, the nations all spoke originally in writing. And by characters, in the sense of ideas, forms or models, of which those of the poets certainly preceded those of articulate sounds, since in Homer's time, as Josephus contends vigorously against the Greek grammarian Apion, they had not yet invented the 'vulgar' letters, as they are called. Furthermore, had these letters been the shapes of articulate sounds and not [, as they were,] arbitrary signs, they would, like the articulate sounds themselves, have been uniform in all nations. But, having abandoned all hope of learning the [proper] mode, the scholars have not discovered that the first nations thought in poetic characters, spoke in fables and wrote in hieroglyphics, which should have constituted the principles, which by their nature must be most certain, both of philosophy, whose concern is with human ideas, and of philology, whose concern is with human words.

430. As we must now embark on our reasonings on this matter, let us provide a short illustration of the many theories, uncertain, superficial, unseemly, vain and ludicrous, which have hitherto been advanced and which, being so plentiful and of such [absurd] character, must needs be

disregarded. Our illustration is drawn from the age of the recurrence of barbarism in which, because of the vanity of nations, Scandinavia was called *vagina gentium* and believed to have been the mother of all the other nations on earth, while, because of the vanity of scholars, Johannes and Olaus Magnus held the view that their Goths had preserved, since the beginning of the world, letters divinely invented by Adam: a dream which reduced the world of scholars to laughter. But this did not prevent Johannes van Gorp from following and surpassing them with the claim that his own Dutch language, which is not far removed from Saxon, came from the Earthly Paradise and was the mother of all other languages, a view which drew forth the derision of [many, including] Joseph Justus Scaliger, Johannes Camerarius, Christopher Becman, and Martin Schoock. Undeterred, this vanity puffed itself up further, erupting into the theory which Olof Rudbeck advanced in his *Atlantica:* that the Greek letters were descended from the runes and that the Phoenicians' letters were inverted runes, which were [first] altered by Cadmus so as to resemble Hebrew letters in order and sound, and finally straightened and rounded by the Greeks with their ruler and compass. Moreover, because the Scandinavian word for an inventor is 'Mercuovman', he wanted the Mercury who invented the Egyptians' letters for them to be a Goth. Such licence in belief about the origins of letters should warn the reader to receive our claims not only impartially, looking at what they bring by way of originality, but attentively, meditating upon them and taking them, as they need to be taken, as principles of all knowledge, human and divine, of the gentile world.

431. The philosophers and philologians ought all, we claim, to have begun their treatment of the origin of language and letters from the following principles: that the first men conceived the ideas of things through imaginative characters; that, being mute, these men expressed themselves by actions and objects which have natural relations to these ideas (such as, for example, are possessed by three shears of the scythe or three ears of wheat, through which they signify three years), and thus expressed themselves in a language of natural meaning, which, according to Plato and Iamblichus, was at one time spoken on earth. (This must have been the very ancient language of Atlantis in which, scholars believe, ideas were expressed by the nature of things, that is, by their natural properties.) But the scholars have treated these two things, [the origins of languages and letters,] in separation, whereas, as we have said, they are by nature connected, and this is why their research into the origins of letters has proved so difficult for them, raising difficulties equal to that of the origins of languages, to which they have paid little or no attention.

432. In commencing our argument, therefore, we lay down as our first

principle the following philological axiom: [143] that the Egyptians asserted
that in the whole previous duration of their world three languages had
been spoken, correspondent in number and order to three ages which
had elapsed in that world, the ages of the gods, of the heroes and of men;
and of these languages they said that the first had been hieroglyphic or
sacred or divine, the second had been symbolic or in signs or heroic coats-
of-arms, and the third had been alphabetic, in order that the needs of
daily life might be communicated among men distant from one another.
Two golden passages in Homer's *Iliad* are relevant to these three languages, making it clear that the Greeks were in agreement with the Egyptians about them. One is the passage in which Homer relates that Nestor
lived through three generations of men who spoke in different languages:
Nestor must thus have been a heroic character for the chronology established by the three languages which correspond to the Egyptians' three
ages, so that the expression 'to live for the years of Nestor' must have
meant the same as 'to live for the years of the world'. The other passage
[in the *Iliad*] is that in which Aeneas tells Achilles that men of a different
language began to live in Ilium, after Troy was transferred to the shores
of the sea and Pergamum became its citadel. [Finally] we link to our first
principle the tradition, which is also Egyptian, that their Thoth or Mercury invented both laws and letters.

433. In a group with the above truths we place those which follow.
Among the Greeks the words 'name' and 'character' were the same in
meaning, whence the Fathers of the Church did not discriminate between
them when they reasoned *de divinis characteribus* [about divine char-
acters] and *de divinis nominibus* [about divine names]. The words
nomen [name] and *definitio* [definition] are also the same in meaning,
whence in rhetoric the expression *quaestio nominis* [investigation of the
name] designates the search for a definition of the fact, [144] while in medicine the nomenclature of diseases is that which is connected with defining their nature. Among the Romans the word 'names' originally and
properly meant 'houses ramified into many families', and [the fact] that
the first Greeks also used [the word] 'names' in such a sense is shown by
the patronymics, meaning 'names of the fathers', which are so frequently
used by the poets, and most of all by Homer, the greatest of all. (In the
same way in Livy we find a tribune of the plebs defining the Roman
patricians as *qui possunt nomine ciere patrem,* that is, 'those who can
use their father's surname'.) These patronymics were subsequently lost in
the popular liberty [which extended] throughout all the rest of Greece,
but they were preserved in the aristocratic state of Sparta by the Hera-

[143] *N.S.*[3] 173.　[144]*Cf.* p. 55 above.

clids. In Roman law, again, *nomen* means right; among the Greeks the similar sounding νόμος [nomos] means law and from νόμος, as Aristotle noted, comes νόμισμα [nomisma], which means money; while the Latin *nummus* [money] comes from νόμος. Among the French, *loy* means law and *aloy* money, and during the recurrence of barbarism the word 'canon' was both ecclesiastical law and the payment made by the emphytenta to the lord of the land given him in fief. Such a uniformity of thought may perhaps explain why the Latins applied the name *ius* both to the law and to the sacrificial animal fat owed to Jove, who was originally called *Ious,* whence derive the genitives *Iovis* and *iuris,* which were mentioned earlier; and, similarly, among the Hebrews, of the three parts of which the peace offering was composed, the fat lay in the part owed to God, which was burned at the altar. The Latins used the word *praedia* [estates], which must have applied in rural areas before urban areas, because, as we shall show, the first cultivated lands were the first plunder (*prede*) on earth. Hence the first subjugation was of such lands, which were therefore called *manucaptae* in Roman law, from which those under obligation to the Treasury in real estate continued to be called *manceps,* and in Roman laws the expression *iura praediorum* remained in use for 'real' liabilities, that is, those which obtained in real estate. The lands known as *manucaptae* must originally both have been, and been called, *mancipia,* to which the Law of the Twelve Tables must certainly be understood to refer in the section entitled, *Qui nexum faciet mancipiumque,* that is, 'Whoever consigns a bond thereby consigns his estate', whence, with an understanding identical to that of the ancient Latins, the Italians called their estates *poderi* because they were acquired by force. We are further persuaded by the following: that in the recurrence of barbarism the expression *presas terrarum* designated the fields and their boundaries; that the Spanish call daring enterprises *prendas;* and that the Italians call family coats-of-arms *imprese,* talk of *termini* in the sense of 'words' (a use which it retained in Scholastic dialectic), and alternatively call family coats-of-arms *insegne,* from which the verb *insegnare* [to teach] comes. Similarly Homer, in whose time the 'vulgar' letters had not yet been invented, says that the letter against Bellerophon, which Proetus sent to Eureia, was written in σήματα [sēmata], that is, in signs.

434. To all of which let these last three unquestionable truths be added: first, that since, as we have shown, the early gentile nations were originally without speech, they must have expressed themselves by means of actions or bodies which bore natural relations to their ideas; second, that they must have ensured the limits of their farms and kept continuous testimony of their rights by means of signs; and third, that they all used coins. Taken together, these truths will here provide us with the origins

of languages and letters and, further on, with those of hieroglyphics, laws, names, family coats-of-arms, medals, coins, and of the language and writing in which the first natural law of the gentes was spoken and written.

435. To establish the principles of all this more firmly, it is necessary at this point to root out the false belief that the hieroglyphics were invented by philosophers in order to conceal within them the mysteries of their elevated, recondite wisdom, a belief which was held (also) by the Egyptians. For, as we proposed in an axiom above,[145] it was a common natural necessity of all the first nations that they should speak in hieroglyphics. We already have [the evidence of] the Egyptians in Africa, to whom, agreeing with [the account given by] Heliodorus in his *Aethiopica*, we may add the Ethiopians, who used the tools of all the manual arts as hieroglyphics. In the Orient the magic characters of the Chaldeans must also have been [used in] the same [way]. And we saw earlier in the case of northern Asia (having set aside, as a distortion, the [alleged] great age of the Scythians, which exceeded even that of the Egyptians, who vaunted themselves the oldest nation of all), that it was in quite late times that Idanthyrsus, the king of Scythia, replied to Darius the Great, who had declared war upon him, with five real words: a frog, a mouse, a bird, a ploughshare and a bow. The frog indicated that he was born of the land of Scythia, for frogs are born of [that] land in the summer rains, and thus that he was a son of that land. The mouse indicated that, like a mouse, he had made his home, that is, founded his nation, in the place where he was born. The bird indicated that he was in possession of the auspices, that is, as we shall shortly see, that he was subject to nobody other than God. The ploughshare indicated that he had brought those lands under cultivation and thus had tamed them and made them his by force. And, finally, the bow indicated that he had supreme command of the forces of Scythia, with the duty of defending her and the power to do so. If one sets this interpretation, so natural and necessary, alongside the absurd ones which, according to St Cyril, Darius' counsellors put upon the Scythian hieroglyphics, and if one takes the latter in conjunction with the remote, deceptive and distorted interpretations which the scholars have given of the Egyptian hieroglyphics, it will become evident in general that the proper and true use of the hieroglyphics employed by the first peoples has not hitherto been known. Nor have the Latins left us with a Roman history lacking such a tradition, [which is to be found] in the mute heroic reply which Tarquinius Superbus sent to his son at Gabii, by cutting off the heads of poppies with the rod he held in his hands in

[145]*N.S.*³ 226, 429.

the sight of the messenger. Some have believed that he acted thus through pride, whereas his need was for total trust. In his description of the customs of northern Europe, Tacitus notes that the ancient Germans lacked *literarum secreta* [the secrets of letters], that is, that they were unable to write their hieroglyphics, [a situation] which must have lasted until the times of Frederick the Swabian or, rather, those of Rudolf of Austria, when official documents began to be written in a vulgar German script. In northern France a hieroglyphic speech, called *rebus de Picardie,* existed, which, as in Germany, must have been a speech by means of things, that is, by means of the hieroglyphics of Idanthyrsus. In his *History of Scotland,* Hector Boyce records that even in furthest Thule, and in Scotland, its most remote region, people wrote in hieroglyphics in ancient times. In the West Indies, the Mexicans were found writing in hieroglyphics, and in his *Description of New India* Jan de Laet recounts that the hieroglyphics of the Indians consist of various animal heads, plants, flowers and fruits, and that their families are distinguished by their boundary posts, the latter performing precisely the same function as family coats-of-arms in our world. And in the East Indies the Chinese write in hieroglyphics to this very day.

436. Thus do we deflate that vanity of later scholars, that the other sages of the world had learned from the Egyptians how to conceal their recondite wisdom under hieroglyphics – a vanity so swollen as to exceed anything to which even the extremely pretentious Egyptians dared aspire.

437. Having set out these principles of poetic logic and disposed of the vanity of scholars, let us revert to the three languages of the Egyptians. As we noted in the *Elements,*[146] there are five places in Homer's two poems in which he agrees about [the existence of] the first, in which he mentions a language other than his own, which was certainly heroic, and calls it the 'language of the gods'. Three of these places are to be found in the *Iliad:* the first where he recounts that he whom the gods called Briareus was called Aegaeon by men; the second where he tells of a bird who was called χαλκίς [chalcis] by the gods and κύμινδις [cymindis] by men; and the third where he says that the river of Troy was called Xanthus by the gods but Scamander by men. In the *Odyssey* there are two [references]: one, that those whom the gods call πλαγκταὶ πέτραι [*Planctae Petrae*] are the Scylla and Charybdis of men; the other, in the passage where Mercury reveals to Ulysses a secret with which to counter Circe's magic arts, [a root] which the gods called μῶλυ [moly], knowledge of which is absolutely denied to men. Plato says many things in connection with these passages but all to no avail; so that Dio Chrysos-

146*N.S.*3 174.

tom was later to accuse Homer falsely of the pretence that he understood
the language of the gods, on the ground that such understanding is naturally denied to men. But our suspicion is that, in these places in Homer,
the word 'gods' ought perhaps to be understood to refer to the heroes.
For as we shall show below, the heroes adopted this name [in their ascen-
dency] over the plebeians of their cities, whom they called *uomini* [men],
in the same way as, when the age of barbarism returned, vassals were
referred to as *homines* [men], as Hotman notes with surprise, and the
great lords (as in the recurrence of barbarism) gloried in their possession
of wonderful secrets of medicine: thus these may be nothing more than
differences between noble and vulgar languages. However, there is no
doubt at all that Varro worked hard at this among the Latins, and that,
as we noted in the *Elements*, [147] he had the diligence to collect [the names
of] thirty thousand gods, which must have sufficed to provide a generous
divine vocabulary for the expression of all the human needs of the gentes
of Latium, which in those simple and meagre times must have been
extremely few, since they extended only to the necessities of life. The
Greeks also, as we observed in the *Elements*, [148] had thirty thousand
gods, for of their every stone, spring or stream, plant and crag, they made
a deity, among which were their dryads, hamadryads, oreads and
napeads, just as the American Indians make a god of everyong which
surpasses their slight understanding. The divine fables of the Latins and
Greeks must therefore have been the true first hieroglyphics, or sacred or
divine characters, [corresponding to those] of the Egyptians.

438. The second language, which corresponded to the age of the
heroes, was described by the Egyptians as a language spoken in symbols,
to which we should reduce the heroic coats-of-arms, which must have
been the mute likenesses which Homer calls σήματα [sēmata], the signs
in which the heroes wrote. The symbols must therefore have consisted in
the metaphors, images, likenesses and comparisons which, in articulate
language, were later to create the whole ornamentation of poetic speech.
For, on the strength of a resolute denial by Josephus the Jew that any
writer earlier than Homer has come down to us, [we may accept that]
the latter was undoubtedly the first author of the Greek language and,
since we have received all that has reached us concerning the gentile
world from the Greeks, that he was the first author of the whole of that
world. Among the Latins the earliest records of their language are the
fragments of the *Carmi saliari,* while the earliest writer of whom they
have given us some account is the poet Livius Andronicus. In the recurrence of barbarism in Europe, when various languages were reborn, the

[147]*N.S.*[3] 175.   [148]*Ibid.*

first language of the Spaniards was that called *el romance,* and therefore that of heroic poetry, for the *romanceros* were the heroic poets of the returned barbarian times. In France the first to write in vulgar French was Arnaut Daniel Pacca, the first of all the Provençal poets, a writer who flourished in the eleventh century. And finally the first writers in Italy were the Florentine and Sicilian composers of rhyme.

439. The alphabetic language of the Egyptians, a language necessary for expressing the needs of common daily life among people living at a distance from one another, must have been born among the vulgar [class] of a sovereign race in Egypt (which must have been that of Thebes, whose king, Ramses, as we indicated earlier, spread his authority over the whole of that great nation), for among the Egyptians this language corresponds to the age of 'men', the name given to the plebs of the heroic peoples, to distinguish them from the heroes, as we mentioned above.[149] It must, moreover, be conceived as having arisen by their free agreement, because of this eternal property: that vulgar speech and writing are the right of people. Hence, when the emperor Claudius invented three new letters of which the Latin language was in need, the Roman people was not willing to accept them, just as the Italians have not accepted those invented by Giorgio Trissino, the lack of which is felt in the Italian language.

440. These alphabetic or vulgar words of the Egyptians must have been written in letters which were also vulgar, while the resemblance which obtains between them and those of the Phoenicians forces us to believe that one of the nations must have received theirs from the other. Those who hold that the Egyptians were the first to discover everything necessary or useful for human society must claim, in consequence of their belief, that the Egyptians taught their letters to the Phoenicians. But Clement of Alexandria, who must have been better informed than any other author on Egyptian things, reports that Sanchuniathon or the Phoenician Sancuniates (who we have set in the Greek heroic age in the Chronological Table) had written his Phoenician history in vulgar letters, and suggests that he was therefore the first author of the gentile world to have written in such characters. This passage would force one to conclude that the Phoenicians, who were certainly the earliest merchant nation in the world, took their vulgar letters into Egypt when they entered that country for purposes of trade. But, setting arguments and conjectures aside, vulgar tradition assures us that these same Phoenicians fetched letters into Greece and it was on the basis of this that Cornelius Tacitus reflected that they brought in, as though invented by themselves, letters which were the inventions of others, by which he meant [to refer to] the Egyp-

[149] *N.S.*[3] 437.

tian hieroglyphics. But to allow this vulgar tradition some foundation of truth (such as we have shown to be necessary without exception for all such traditions),[150] we suggest that the Phoenicians took hieroglyphics belonging to another nation into Greece and that the only possible candidates here are the mathematical characters or geometrical figures which they had themselves received from the Chaldeans – for the latter were unarguably the earliest mathematicians, and, in particular, the earliest astronomers [in the world] of nations (hence their Zoroaster who, according to Bochart, was given this name because he was 'the observer of the stars', was the first sage of the gentile world) – and that they used them as shapes for [representing] numbers in the trading which, long before Homer, led them to ply the coasts of Greece. This is emphasised by Homer's poems themselves, and by the *Odyssey* in particular. For, as Josephus argues vigorously against the Greek grammarian Apion, in Homer's times the vulgar letters were yet to be discovered by the Greeks. But the latter, exercising ingenuity of the highest quality, in which they were certainly superior to all nations, later transformed these geometrical shapes into shapes for the various articulate sounds, forming the vulgar characters of letters of the utmost beauty from them. These were later taken over by the Latins, whose characters, as Tacitus himself observes, bore a resemblance to those of the earliest Greeks. Powerful confirmation of this is [provided by the fact] that the Greeks, for a long period, and the Latins, until their final times, used capital letters for the writing of their numbers. It must be these letters which Demaratus the Corinthian and Carmenta, the wife of Evander the Arcadian, taught to the Latins, as we shall explain later how, in ancient times, Greek colonies, both maritime and inland, were introduced into Latium.

441. Nor is there anything to be said for the view of those many scholars who, noting that the names of the vulgar letters of the Greeks and Jews are almost identical, hold that those of the Greeks must have come from those of the Jews. More reasonable, indeed, is the converse, that the Jews copied these names from the Greeks. For since everybody agrees both that after Alexander the Great conquered his eastern empire, which his captains divided upon his death, the Greek language spread through the whole of the East including Egypt, and that grammar was introduced relatively late among the Jews, it follows of necessity that Jewish literates used Greek names for their Jewish letters. Moreover, since by nature elements are of the greatest simplicity, the Greeks must at first have uttered the simplest sounds of letters which, from this point of view, must have been called 'elements'. The Latins continued naming them with the

[150]*N.S.*[3] 149.

same austerity, whence they retained forms of letters similar to those of the earliest Greeks. It is necessary to conclude from this that the naming of letters with compound sounds was a late introduction among the Greeks and that it was yet later that it was taken by the Greeks to the Jews in the East.

442. The above series of reasons disposes of the view of those who hold that Cecrops the Egyptian introduced the vulgar letters to the Greeks. The alternative of those who hold that Cadmus the Phoenician brought them from Egypt, on the ground that he founded in Greece a city with the name of Thebes [which was also the name of] the capital of the greatest of Egyptian dynasties, will be disproved below by the same series of reasons, taken in conjunction with our principles of *Poetic Geography,* through which we shall show that when the Greeks came to Egypt they named the capital of that country 'Thebes' because of a certain resemblance it had to their own native Thebes. Finally, our reasoning enables us to understand why certain shrewd critics, mentioned by the anonymous English author of the *Uncertainty of the Sciences,* [151] conclude from his excessive antiquity that Sancuniates never actually existed. Hence, in order not to exclude him from the world altogether, we believe that he must be located at some later time, certainly after Homer. Moreover, to retain the greater antiquity of the Phoenicians over the Greeks in the matter of the invention of the so-called 'vulgar' letters (allowing due measure, however, for the fact that the Greeks were more inventive than the Phoenicians), it is necessary to hold that Sancuniates existed somewhat before Herodotus, who was called the 'father of Greek history', which he wrote in vulgar language: for Sancuniates was called the 'historian of truth', that is, a writer of what Varro, in his division of times, calls the historical time, and in this time, according to the distinction which the Egyptians drew between three languages which corresponded to the three ages which had passed prior to them, people spoke in an alphabetic language which was written in vulgar characters.

443. Now, as the heroic or poetic language was founded by the heroes, so the vulgar languages were introduced by the vulgar who, we shall find, were the plebs of the heroic peoples, whose languages were properly called *vernaculae* [vernacular] by the Latins, [although] they could not have been introduced by those *vernae* whom the grammarians define as 'slaves bred at home, of slaves in war' for these naturally acquire the languages of the nation in which they are born. We shall show below that the first, properly named *vernae* were the *famuli* of the heroes in the state of the families, who later composed the larger part of the first plebs

---

[151] Thomas Baker. Vico had read a French translation of his *Reflections upon Learning,* published under the title *Traité de l'incertitude des sciences* (Paris, 1714).

in the heroic cities, and who prefigured the slaves whom the cities finally created by war. All this is confirmed by the two languages to which Homer alludes, that of the gods and that of men, which we have expounded above as heroic and vulgar language, of which we shall shortly give some further explanation.

444. The philologists have, however, accepted all too uncritically that in the vulgar languages signification was by convention, whereas, because of their natural origins, it must have been natural. This is easily observed in the case of vulgar Latin (which is more heroic than vulgar Greek and therefore as much more forceful as the latter is more refined) in which nearly all of its words have been formed by the substitution of [the] natures [of things] by either their natural properties or their sensible effects. And, in general, metaphor creates the major corpus of language in all nations. The grammarians, however, running up against a host of words which were productive of unclear and indistinct ideas of things, and being ignorant of those origins which must have made them clear and distinct at the start, tried to come to terms with their ignorance by establishing the maxim that articulate human words signified [things] by convention. And, as we saw above, they drew Aristotle, Galen and other philosophers into this [debate], and armed them against Plato and Iamblichus.

445. But we are left with the very difficult question how it is that there are as many diverse vulgar languages as there are nations. To resolve this difficulty the following great truth must now be established: that, as the difference in climates has certainly led to the various different natures of peoples, from which so many different customs have come, so from their different natures and customs are born languages equally different. For since this same difference in their natures has led them to consider the same utilities or necessities of human life under different aspects, thus engendering national customs which are in general different and at times conflicting, in this and in no other way have arisen as many different languages as there are different nations. Clear confirmation of this is provided by the proverbs [of different nations], which, as we noted in the *Elements*,[152] are maxims of human life which are the same in substance but expressed in accordance with as many different aspects as there are, and have been, nations. Hence the same heroic origins, condensed and preserved in the vulgar languages, are responsible for the fact which so amazes the Biblical critics, that, for the same things which are named in one way in sacred history, one finds different names in profane history. For in the one, men are, perhaps, [considered] by being looked at through

---

[152]N.S.[3] 161.

the aspect of power, and in the other, through that of their customs, their exploits or whatever. In the same way we still find that the cities of Hungary are given different names by the Hungarians, Greeks, Germans and Turks. And in German, which is a living heroic language, almost all names of foreign extraction are transformed into its own native names. We must suppose that the Latins and Greeks did the same [in the passages] where they consider so many barbarian things in their own elegant ways, which must be the cause of the obscurity one encounters in [their accounts of] ancient geography and of the natural history of fossils, plants and animals. Hence, in the first edition of this work we meditated upon an *Idea of a mental dictionary for giving meanings to all the different articulate languages,* [153] reducing them all to certain ideas which were one in substance but which, having been considered by peoples in accordance with various modifications [of mind], have been named by them with various different words, and this *Idea of a mental dictionary* is still employed in our reasonings in this Science. We gave a very full example of it in Book IV [of the first edition][154] where we showed that because, at the time when language must have been in [the process of] formation, the fathers of the families were observed under fifteen different aspects in the state of the families and of the first states, they were named with equally many different words by fifteen nations, ancient and modern — and, as we proposed in our axiom,[155] arguments concerning things of that time which are drawn from the native meanings of words are of the utmost importance. This passage is one of three in that book which prevent us from regretting its publication. Our *Dictionary* applies a different mode of reasoning to the subject with which Thomas Hayne deals in his works, *De linguarum cognatione, De linguis in genere* and *Variaraum linguarum harmonia.* From all this the following corollary is derived: that the richer languages are in these contracted heroic expressions the more beautiful they are, that they are more beautiful because they are more perspicuous and because they are more perspicuous they are more veracious and faithful; while, in contrast, the more they are laden with words whose origins are not perspicuous, the less do they give delight, because they are obscure and confused and hence the more liable to be deceptive and erroneous. The latter must hold for languages formed by an admixture of many barbarian languages, the history of whose origins and metaphors has not survived.

446. Now, to embark upon the very difficult [problem of the] mode of formation of all these three types of language and letters, it is necessary to establish the following principle: that since the gods, the heroes and

---

[153] Cf. *N.S.* [1] 387.   [154] Actually Book III; cf. *N.S.* [1] 383–9.   [155] *N.S.* [3] 152.

men all commenced in the same time (for they were nevertheless men who imagined the gods and believed their own heroic nature to be an admixture of that of the gods and that of men), so also did these three languages, the letters of each always being understood to be appropriate to it, but they did so with three extremely important differences. [For] the language of the gods was almost wholly mute and only very slightly articulate; that of the heroes was a language in which the mute and the articulate were mixed in equal degree, as, consequently, were expressions in the vulgar and the heroic characters in which the heroes wrote, which Homer calls σήματα [sēmata]; and that of men was a language almost wholly articulate and very slightly mute, since there is no vulgar language with a vocabulary so abundant that there are not more things than it has words. Whence it was necessary that heroic language should at first be extremely confused. This has been a great source of the obscurity of the fables, of which that of Cadmus affords a striking example. [For] he kills the great serpent, and sows its teeth in furrows from which armed men arise who, when he throws a huge rock among them, fight to the death, while Cadmus is himself finally changed into a serpent. But such was the ingenuity of this Cadmus who brought letters to the Greeks, who have bequeathed us this fable, that, as we shall explain below, the latter contains many centuries of poetic history.

447. It follows from this that at the time of the formation of the divine character of Jove, the first of all human thoughts in the gentile world, the formation of articulate language also began through onomatopoeia, by which we still see children happily expressing themselves. At first the Latins called this Jove *Ious,* from the roar of thunder, the Greeks called him Ζεύς [Zeus], from the hiss of lightning, and the orientals must have called him *Ur* from the sound of fire as it burns. *Ur,* from which came *Urim,* the power of fire, must also have been the origin of the Greek οὐρανός [ouranos], the sky, and of the Latin *uro,* to burn, while from the hiss of lightning must also have come the Latin *cel,* one of Ausonius' monosyllables, but pronounced with the Spanish 'ç' since this is required for Ausonius' own witticism about Venus in the following play on words: *Nata salo, suscepta solo, patre edita caelo* [born of the sea, received by the earth, raised by her father to the sky]. It must be noticed that among these origins, and with the same sublimity of invention as the fable of Jove which we considered above, are those of the equally sublime poetic way of talking through onomatopoeia. Dionysius Longinus certainly includes this among the sources of the sublime, pointing to [an example of] it in Homer in the sound σίζ [siz], which is given forth when Ulysses thrusts the burning stake into Polyphemus' eye.

448. The formation of human words continued with exclamations.

These are sounds articulated under the impetus of violent passions and they are monosyllabic in all languages. Hence the following is not beyond the bounds of probability: that, when the first thunderbolts had begun to arouse wonder in men, the first exclamation to be born should have been that for Jove, formed by the sound, *pa!;* when repeated, this then became *pape!,* the exclamation of wonder which gave birth next to Jove's title, 'father *(padre)* of men and of gods'; and from this all the gods were later called 'fathers' and all the goddesses 'mothers' *(madri),* from which there survived in Latin the words *Iupiter, Diespiter, Marspiter* and *Iuno genitrix.* The fables certainly tell us that Juno was sterile, and we observed earlier that very many other gods and goddesses in the heavens did not contract marriages among themselves – Venus [for example] being described as the concubine, and never as the wife, of Mars – yet all were nevertheless called 'fathers'. (In the *Notes* to our *Universal Law* we referred to some of Lucilius' verses which are relevant here.) These gods were named 'fathers' in the sense in which *patrare* must originally have signified the making or doing which is proper to God, as is supported by the account of the creation of the world given in the scriptures, where it is stated that on the seventh day God rested *ab opere quod patrarat* [from the work which he had done]. *Patrare* must then have become *impetrare,* which was pronounced rather like *impatrare,* and in the science of the auguries this became *impetrire,* which meant 'to receive a good augury', the origins of which the Latin grammarians have discussed to so little effect. This shows that the first interpretations, pronounced like *interpratatio,* were those of laws divinely ordered through the auspices.

449. Now, in the state of the families, the natural ambition which belongs to human pride led the strong to claim this divine title for themselves, calling themselves 'fathers'. (This may be the basis of truth in the vulgar tradition that the first strong men on earth had themselves venerated as gods.) But, because of that piety which is due to divinities, they then called the latter 'gods', and when, still later, the men of strength in the state of the cities bestowed the name 'gods' upon themselves, that same piety led them to refer to the divinities as 'immortal gods', as against the 'mortal gods', who were these men [themselves]. But in this one can see the crudeness of such giants, as travellers relate of those from *los patacones* [Patagonia]. An apt vestige of this has survived in the ancient Latin words *pipulum* and *pipare,* in the sense of wail and to bewail, which must have come from the exclamation of lament, *pi, pi;* and some maintain that in Plautus this sense of *pipulum* is the same as the word *obvagulatio* in the Twelve Tables which must come from *vagire,* which is properly children's weeping. It follows that the Greek

word παιάν [paian] which began as παί must have come from the exclamation of terror. Here the Greeks possess an invaluable ancient tradition
that, terrified by the great serpent called Python, they called upon
Apollo's help with the words ιὼ παιάν [io paian] which, in the weakness
inspired by their terror, they must first have uttered slowly three times,
to be followed, when they jubilantly acclaimed Apollo because he had
killed the serpent, by their uttering them rapidly the same number of
times, while dividing the ω [omega] into two o [omicrons] and the diph-
thong αι into two syllables. Thus heroic verse was naturally born spondaic at first and became dactylic later, and it remained an eternal property that it should cede pride of place to the dactyl everywhere except at
the end. Song, in the metre of heroic verse, was also born naturally
under the impetus of violent passions, as we still find that men burst into
song when they experience strong emotions, particularly those of sorrow
and happiness, as was noted in the *Elements*.[156] All this will shortly
prove of great use in our reasonings about the origins of song and verse.

450. The next advance was the formation of pronouns, for while
exclamations [serve to] express one's own feelings, which one does even
when alone, pronouns serve to communicate to others our ideas relating
either to things to which we are unable to attach a proper name or which
somebody else is unable to understand. And in all languages the greater
part of pronouns, indeed just about all, are monosyllables. The earliest,
or at least one of the earliest, of them must have been that which we have
inherited in a golden passage in Ennius, *Aspice hoc sublime cadens,
quem omnes invocant Iovem* [Behold this, resplendent on high, which
all call Jove], in which *hoc* [this] is used instead of *caelum* [the sky]. This
survived in the vulgar Latin phrase *Luciscit hoc iam* [Already it grows
light] which was used in place of *Albescit caelum* [The sky grows
light]. And from birth articles have possessed this eternal property: that
they precede the nouns to which they are attached.

451. Next in order of formation were the particles, the majority of
which are prepositions. The latter, which in most languages are also
monosyllabic, preserve in their name this eternal property: that they precede the nouns which require them and [those parts of] the verbs with
which they form compound words.

452. From time to time nouns were formed. In the first edition of this
work, in our chapter *The origins of the Latin language*,[157] we collected
a large number of words which originated in Latium, from the period of
Latin life in the forests, through that of the cultivation of the land, up to
that of the first civil life, all of which were formed as monosyllables with-

---

[156]*N.S.*[3] 229.   [157]*N.S.*[1] 368–73, not translated here.

out any trace of foreign influence, not even Greek, with the exception of the four words βοῦς, σῦς, μῦς and σήψ [bous, sus, mus, seps], the last of which means a ledge in Latin and a serpent in Greek. This is another of the three passages in that work with which we pronounce ourselves satisfied, for it can serve as an example to scholars of other languages of the need to investigate the origins of words for the greatest benefit to the republic of letters. Certainly in German, which is a mother language (for no foreign nation has ever intervened and taken command in Germany), all its roots are monosyllables. And that nouns were born before verbs is established for us by this eternal property: that a sentence makes no sense if it does not begin with a noun, expressed or understood, which governs it.

453. Finally, the authors of the languages formed verbs, as we see when children express nouns and particles but leave verbs to be understood. For nouns arouse ideas which leave firm traces, as do particles, which signify modifications of nouns; but verbs signify change, involving [reference to] the past and the future, which are measured from the indivisible [unit] of the present, which even philosophers have much difficulty in understanding. Our claim derives considerable support from the medical observation of a good man, who is still alive, who, after suffering a serious attack of apoplexy, could remember nouns but had completely forgotten verbs. [All verbs,] and even those which are the genera of all others, must have originated from imperatives. They include the following: *sum,* [I am, which is the indicative] of being, to which [genus] every essence, which is as to say everything metaphysical, reduces; *sto,* [I stand] and *eo,* [I move, which are the indicatives] of rest and movement, to which [genera] everything physical reduces; *do* [I give], *dico* [I say] and *facio,* [I make or I do, which are the indicatives of the genera] to which everything practicable [in human life], be it moral, domestic or, finally, civil, reduces. For in the state of the families, which was highly impoverished linguistically, only the fathers must have spoken, giving orders to their children and to the *famuli,* and the latter, who were subject to terrifying family powers, as we shall see below, must have executed their orders in silence and blind servility. Their imperatives are all monosyllabic, as they have remained in *es* [be], *sta* [stand], *i* [go], *da* [give], *dic* [say] and *fac* [make or do].

454. This genesis of languages is consistent both with the principles of universal nature, according to which the elements from which all things are composed, and into which they must resolve themselves, are indivisible, and the principles peculiar to human nature, in accordance with the axiom [158] that 'children, [though they are] born midst a wealth of

---

[158] *N.S.*³ 231.

language and [though their] organs for the articulation of words are of very supple fibre, commence with monosyllables'. How much more must this be judged to apply to those first men of the gentile world, whose organs of speech were highly inflexible and who had not yet heard a human word! In addition this genesis gives the order in which the parts of speech were born and therefore the natural causes of syntax.

455. All this seems more reasonable than the claims of Julius Caesar Scaliger and Francisco Sanchez concerning the Latin language. As if the peoples who invented languages should first have needed to attend the school of Aristotle, with whose principles these two have reasoned!

Book IV
Concerning the course [of human things] taken by the nations

[Introduction]

915. Book I saw the establishment of the principles of this Science, Book II the investigation and discovery within poetic wisdom of the origin of all things human and divine in the gentile world, and Book III the discovery that the Homeric poems were two great treasuries of the natural law of the gentes of Greece,[159] just as the Law of the Twelve Tables had already been seen to be a most important witness to the natural law of the gentes of Latium.[160] Now, in Book IV, using these sources of illumination, both philosophical and philological, and following the axioms concerning the ideal eternal history already laid down,[161] we proceed to [an account of] the course taken by the nations, as they develop with constant uniformity in their many various and different customs, in accordance with the division of three ages, those of the gods, the heroes and men, which the Egyptians said had passed in the world prior to them. For, in accordance with this [division], the nations will be seen to have been guided by a constant and uninterrupted order of causes and effects, ever operative within them, through three kinds of nature;[162] from these three natures came three kinds of custom,[163] from which, [in turn,] three kinds of natural law of the gentes were observed[164] and in consequence of which three kinds of civil states or governments were ordered.[165] For the communication of the foregoing three most important kinds of thing among men who had come to human society, three kinds of language[166] and of characters[167] were formed; and for their justification, three kinds of jurisprudence,[168] supported by three kinds of authority and as many kinds of reason[169] [embodied] in as many kinds of judgement, these kinds of jurisprudence being practised in the three sects of times which the nations profess in the whole course of the lives. These special triadic unities, with many others which follow from them and which will be enumerated in this book, fall under one general unity, that of the worship of a provident divinity, which is the unity of spirit which informs and

[159]Cf. N.S.³ 156.   [160]N.S.³ 154.
[161]N.S.³ 145, 241–5, 349, 393; cf. N.S.¹ 90 and n. 41, p. 127 above.
[162]N.S.³ 916–18.   [163]N.S.³ 919–21.   [164]N.S.³ 922–4.   [165]N.S.³ 925–7.
[166]N.S.³ 928–31.   [167]N.S.³ 932–6.   [168]N.S.³ 937–41.   [169]N.S.³ 942–6.

gives life to this world of nations. Since these things have been reasoned widely [through our work] we shall here display the order of their course.

[Section I] Three kinds of natures

916. The first nature was a poetic or creative or, as we may even call it, divine nature. For, since the imagination is most powerful in those in whom reason is weakest,[170] by weaving great illusions the first nature gave to bodies the being of substances animated by gods, and did so according to its own idea [of itself].[171] This was the nature of the theological poets, the most ancient sages in all the gentile nations, [of the times] when the gentile nations were founded upon the belief, possessed by each, in certain gods proper to each. It was, moreover, the wildest and most fearful of natures, but, through that same illusion of the imagination, they developed a terrifying fear of gods of their own invention. Whence endured these two eternal properties: that religion is the only potent means of controlling the wildness of peoples;[172] and that religions prosper when those who preside over them themselves possess an inner reverence for them.

917. The second nature was heroic, which the heroes themselves took to be of divine origin, for since they believed that the gods created everything, they took themselves, as those generated under Jove's auspices, to be his children; and being of the human species, they located in this heroism, and did so with justice, the natural nobility through which they were the princes of the human race. This natural nobility they vaunted over those who repaired to their asylums in order to save themselves from the perils of their infamous bestial communion in which, coming without gods, they were taken to be beasts, in accordance with the two natures we reasoned out above.

918. The third nature was human, an intelligent and therefore modest, benign and reasonable nature, which recognises conscience (*coscienza*), reason and duty as laws.[173]

[Section II] Three kinds of customs

919. The first customs were steeped in religion and piety, like those narrated of Deucalion and Pyrrha, which sprang up immediately after the flood.

[170]*N.S.*[3] 185.   [171]*N.S.*[3] 374ff.   [172]*N.S.*[3] 177–9, 338.   [173]*Cf. N.S.*[3] 323–7.

920. The second were choleric and punctilious, like those narrated by Achilles.

921. The third were dutiful, taught at the proper stage of civil duty.

[Section III] Three kinds of natural law

922. The first law was divine, for since men believed that the gods were everything or had made everything, they took themselves and everything connected therewith to be under the jurisdiction of the gods.[174]

923. The second law was heroic or a law of force, moderated, however, by religion, which alone can confine force within [the limits of] duty when there are no laws or when those which exist are incapable of restraining it. Hence providence arranged that the first peoples, who were ferocious by nature, should be persuaded of [the truth of] their religion, in order that they should naturally become resigned to force and that, being still incapable of reason, they should judge the law by fortune, whence they sought advice through the divination of the auspices. This law of force is the law of Achilles who located the whole of justice at the point of his spear.[175]

924. The third law is the human law which fully developed human reason dictates.[176]

[Section IV] Three kinds of governments

925. The first governments were the divine governments which the Greeks called 'theocratic', in which man believed that the gods commanded everything.[177] This was the age of the oracles, which are the most ancient things one reads of in history.[178]

926. The second governments were the heroic or aristocratic governments, which is as much as to say, governments of the 'optimates', in the sense of 'the strongest'. In Greek [they were] also the governments of the Heraclids, or men of the race of Hercules, in the sense of 'nobles', which were strewn throughout the whole of earliest Greece, of which the Spartan government later survived; and also the governments of 'Curetes' which, the Greeks noted, had spread into Saturnia or ancient Italy, Crete and Asia, and from which came the Romans' governments of the *Quir-*

---

[174]*N.S.*[3] 379.   [175]*N.S.*[3] 319–22.   [176]*N.S.*[3] 323–7.
[177]*N.S.*[3] 379; *N.S.*[1] 77.   [178]*N.S.*[3] 381.

ites, that is governments of armed priests in public assembly.[179] In these governments civil rights were wholly restricted to the ruling orders of the heroes themselves, because, as we mentioned above, the latter had the distinction of a nobler nature arising from their supposedly divine origin, while the plebs, as those of reputedly bestial origin, were allowed only the customary rights of life and natural liberty.

927. The third governments are the human governments in which, through that equality of intelligent nature which is the nature proper to man, all are equal in law. For either all are born free in their cities – the free popular cities, that is – in which the whole or the majority [of the people] constitute the just forces of the city, which thus makes them the lords of popular liberty; or [all are born free] in monarchies in which the monarchs make all their subjects equal in law and in which, by retaining in their hands alone the whole force of arms, the monarchs are themselves the only persons distinct in civil nature.[180]

[Section V] Three kinds of languages

928. Three kinds of languages.

929. The first of these was a divine mental language [operating] through mute religious acts or divine ceremonies,[181] whence in their civil law the Romans retained the *actus legitimi* [lawful acts] with which they celebrated all affairs to do with civil utility. This language is appropriate to religions because of the following eternal property: that it is of greater importance to them that they be revered than reasoned; and it was necessary in those first times since the gentiles were as yet unable to articulate speech.

930. The second was a language [operating] through heroic emblems, the speech of [military] arms, which, as we pointed out earlier, survived in military discipline.[182]

931. The third language is that of articulate speech which is used by all nations today.[183]

[Section VI] Three kinds of characters

932. Three kinds of characters.

933. The first characters were the divine characters, properly called

---

[179]*N.S.*[1] 76.   [180]*N.S.*[1] 77.   [181]*N.S.*[3] 401, 435.
[182]*N.S.*[3] 433.   [183]*N.S.*[3] 448ff.

'hieroglyphics', which, as we proved above, were employed by all nations in their origins.[184] These were certain imaginative universals dictated [to man] naturally by that property, innate to the human mind, of finding pleasure in what is uniform (as we proposed in an axiom above);[185] but since they were unable to create the uniform through genera [made] by abstraction, men did so through [ideal] images [made] by the imagination. All the particular species belonging to each genus were reduced to such poetic universals: everything, for example, to do with the auspices to Jove,[186] everything to do with marriage to Juno, and, similarly, other [collections of related] things to other imaginative universals.

934. The second characters were the heroic characters, which were also imaginative universals, to which all the different kinds of heroic things were reduced:[187] to Achilles, for example, all the deeds of mighty warriors, or to Ulysses all counsels of the wise. But, as the human mind later taught itself how to abstract forms and properties from their subjects, these imaginative genera gave way to intelligible genera, whence philosophers next arose; and later [still], the authors of the New Comedy, which appeared in the most human times of Greece, took these intelligible genera of human customs back from the philosophers and created [human] images of them in their comedies.

935. Finally came the vulgar characters whose development kept pace with that of the vulgar languages. And as the latter are genera, as it were, of the particulars in which the heroic languages had previously been spoken – in the way in which, as instanced earlier, 'I am angry' was created from the heroic expression 'the blood boils in my heart' – so, from the hundred and twenty thousand hieroglyphic characters still, for example, in use in China today, they made the few letters to which, as to genera, one can reduce the hundred and twenty thousand words of which the articulate vulgar language of the Chinese is composed. This invention is certainly a more than human work of mind, whence, as we noted above, Bernard von Mallinckrodt and Ingewald Eling believed that it was a divine invention.[188] It is easy, moreover, [to see how] this common sense of wonder led the nations to believe that such letters were revealed to them by learned divines, those of the Illyrians, for example, by St Jerome, those of the Slavs by St Cyril, and those of other nations by other divines, in the way noted and discussed by Angelo Rocca in his *Bibliotheca vaticana,* in which the authors of the 'vulgar' letters are portrayed together with their alphabets. The manifest falsity of such views is shown, however, if we ask the single question: why did these divines not teach the

[184]*N.S.*³ 435. [185]*N.S.*³ 204, 209. [186]*N.S.*³ 379.
[187]*N.S.*¹ 262; *N.S.*³ 412ff. [188]*N.S.*³ 428.

nations their own letters? We have already raised this difficulty in connection with Cadmus, who [supposedly] brought the Greeks their letters from the Phoenicians, though the Greeks later used letters very different in form from those of the Phoenicians.[189]

936. We asserted earlier that since such languages and letters were under the lordship of the vulgar [classes] of the peoples, both were called 'vulgar'. This lordship of language and letters must render the free peoples lords also of their laws, since the peoples give the laws those senses under which the powerful are drawn to observe them, [a thing] which, as we noted in the *Elements*,[190] they would not [of themselves] desire. It is naturally denied to monarchs to take this lordship from the people, yet, in consequence of this denial in the nature of human civil things, this lordship which is inseparable from the peoples constitutes in large measure the power of the monarchs, so that the latter can command their royal laws, which hold over the powerful, in accordance with senses which the people have given them. Such lordship of vulgar letters and languages makes it necessary that, in the order of civil nature, the free popular states should have preceded the monarchies.

[Section VII] Three kinds of jurisprudence

937. Three kinds of jurisprudence or wisdom.

938. The first jurisprudence was a divine wisdom called, as we saw above, 'mystic theology', which means the science of the divine language or [the science] of understanding the divine mysteries of divination. It was thus a science of the divinity of the auspices and [of] vulgar wisdom, its first sages being the theological poets, who were the first sages of the gentile world. These theological poets were called *mystae* after this mystic theology, a word which Horace knowledgeably renders 'interpreters of the gods'.[191] Hence to this first jurisprudence belonged the first and proper *interpretari* [interpreting], pronounced like *interpatrari*, that is, 'to enter the fathers', the first name given to the gods, as we noted above.[192] This is what Dante calls *indiarsi*, that is, to enter the mind of God (*Dio*). In such a jurisprudence, the just is decided solely by the solemnity of divine ceremonies, which explains why the Romans inherited so much superstition with their *actus legitimi* [lawful acts] and why the expressions *iustae nuptiae* and *iustum testamentum* for 'solemn' nuptials and testaments survived in their laws.

[189]*N.S.*[3] 440.   [190]*N.S.*[3] 283.   [191]*N.S.*[3] 381.   [192]*N.S.*[3] 448.

939. The second jurisprudence was the heroic jurisprudence, in which precautions were taken by means of certain proper words. This is the wisdom of Ulysses, whose talk in Homer is so guarded that he achieves the utility proposed to himself while preserving the propriety of his words. Hence the reputation of the ancient Roman jurists consisted entirely in their *cavere* [being on guard]; and their *de iure respondere* [replying in accordance with the law] was nothing other than their cautioning those who found it necessary to prove their rights in court to specify their exposition of the facts to the praetor in such way that they should fall under the formulae of action, to which the praetor would [then] be unable to deny them access. Similarly, in the recurrence of barbarism, the reputation of the doctors lay wholly in inventing clauses for safeguarding contracts and wills and in knowing how to formulate legal requests and articles: precisely the *cavere* and *de iure respondere* of the Roman jurists.

940. The third jurisprudence is the human jurisprudence which considers the truth of facts themselves and benignly shapes the justice of laws in accordance with whatever equity in cases requires.[193] This is the jurisprudence celebrated in free popular states and even more in monarchies, which are both human governments.

941. Thus divine and heroic jurisprudence held to the certain in the times of crude nations, but human jurisprudence considers the true in the times of enlightened nations. And all this in consequence of our definitions of the certain and the true and of the relevant axioms laid down in the *Elements*.[194]

[Section VIII] Three kinds of authority

942. There were three kinds of authority.[195] The first of these is that divine authority for which providence does not demand reason [in men]; the second is heroic authority, which resides entirely in the solemn formulae of the laws; and the third is human authority, which resides in esteeming people of experience, who are possessed of outstanding prudence in things practicable and sublime wisdom in things intelligible.

943. These three kinds of authority which jurisprudence adopts within the course traversed by the nations are a consequence of three kinds of senatorial authorities which develop within the same course.

944. The first of these [senatorial authorities] was that authority of

[193]*N.S.*[3] 327.　　[194]*N.S.*[3] 137, 321–2, 324–5.　　[195]*N.S.*[3] 350, 386–90.

ownership from which those from whom we hold rights of ownership retained the title *auctores* and which is itself always called *auctoritas* in the Law of the Twelve Tables.[196] This authority was rooted in the divine governments from the time of the state of the families, when divine authority must have belonged to the gods, since it was believed, in a correct sense, that everything belonged to the gods. Next, in the heroic aristocracies, when the senates constituted the governing body (as they still do in the heroic aristocracies of our own times), such authority belonged quite properly to these governing senates. Hence the heroic senates gave their approval to that which the people had already discussed or, as Livy says, *eius, quod populus iussisset, deinde patres fierent autores* [the senators later became the authors of that which the people had ordered]. This did not, however, come about in Romulus' interregnum, as history recounts, but in the aristocracy's less elevated times when, according to our earlier reasoning, citizenship had been communicated to the plebs. Under this procedure, as Livy again says, *saepe spectabat ad vim*, that is, revolt often threatened, so that if the people wished to achieve success by it, they needed, for example, to nominate consuls towards whom the senate might be favourably inclined, just as with the nominations of magistrates by the peoples under the monarchies.

945. From the law of Publilius Philo onwards, when the Roman people was declared free and absolute master of sovereignty, as we noted above, the authority of the senate was that of guardianship, rather like that approval given by guardians to the business undertaken by their wards, when the latter are lords of their own patrimonies, which is called *autoritas tutorum*. The senate lent this authority to the people in a legal formula drawn up in advance by the senate, in which, [again] rather like the authority which the guardian must lend to his ward, the senate would be present to the people, present in the great gatherings, present in the act of passing the law, if the people wanted it passed; otherwise the senate would 'antiquate' it and *probaret antiqua* [approve what already existed], which amounted to a declaration that the innovation was not required. All this was to ensure that in passing laws the people should not, as a result of unsound advice, do some public damage, and therefore that, in passing them, they should be regulated by the senate. Whence the formulae of the laws, which were brought by the senate to the people for the latter to pass, are knowledgeably defined by Cicero as *perscriptae autoritates*: not personal authorisations, like those of guardians who, by their presence, approve the acts of their wards, but authorisations

[196]*N.S.*[3] 386.

written out in full (for this is the meaning of *perscribere*), as distinct from the formulae for actions which were written *per notas* [in abbreviations], which the people did not understand. This is what the Publilian Law ordered: that from then on the authority of the senate, to speak with Livy, *valeret in incertum comitiorum eventum* [should be efficacious while the outcome of the public assembly was uncertain].

946. Finally, the state of popular liberty gave way to that of monarchy and the third kind of authority appeared, the authority of esteem or reputation for wisdom, and therefore that of advice, for which the jurists under the emperors were called *autores*. This must be the authority which belongs to senates under monarchs, who have full and absolute liberty to adopt or reject the advice of their senates.

Book V
Concerning the recourse of human things taken by the nations as they rise again

Conclusion of the work
On an eternal natural state, ordered by divine providence, containing the best of each kind [of thing]

1097. Let us then draw this work to a conclusion with Plato, creator of a fourth kind of state, whose supreme lords would be men of worth and honesty: this would be the true natural aristocracy. Providence would thus lead the nations from their origins to a state such as Plato conceived, by ordering that, when the first thunderbolts struck after the Flood, the strongest of those men of gigantic stature, who must have roamed the heights of the mountains as do the strongest of the wild beasts, should drive themselves into the depths of the mountain caves, subject themselves to a superior force which they imagined as Jove, and, amazed, proud and fierce in equal measure, humble themselves before a divinity.[197] Nor, in this order of things human, can one understand any other plan which divine providence [could have] adopted to bring men's bestial wandering in the great forest of the earth to a halt, in order to introduce among them the order of human civil things.[198]

1098. For here developed a world of what may be called monastic states or solitary sovereigns, under the rule of a Greatest and Best[199] whom they themselves both invented and worshipped as, through the flare of the thunderbolts, this true light of God shone upon them: that He rules over men; so that they then imagined that all human utilities administered to them, and all the aids provided for their human needs, were gods and, as such, they feared and venerated them. And so, [caught] between the powerful constraints of a fearful superstition and the stinging incitements of a bestial lust – which must both have been very violent in such men – and because they felt that the sky's countenance demanded reverence of them, and therefore prohibited their promiscuous ways, they must have held in conatus the bodily impulses of their lust. Thus they

[197]Cf. N.S.³ 377–9.   [198]Cf. N.S.³ 343–5.   [199]Cf. N.S.³ 379.

began to exercise their human liberty, for this is the liberty to restrain the impulses of desire and give them a different direction, and since it comes not from the body, from which desire originates, it must belong to the mind and therefore be proper to man.[200] And thus, under this liberty, did they change direction: by forcible seizure of women, who are naturally withdrawn and shy, whom they then dragged into their caves where, in order to mate with them, they enclosed them in continuous company for life. In this way, through these first human, that is, chaste and religious, matings, they initiated the marriages through which they bred certain children by certain women and became their certain fathers, thus founding families in which they ruled over their children and wives with cyclopean family powers proper to natures so wild and proud, in order that later, when the cities arose, men should be disposed to fear civil sovereignty. Thus providence ordered certain family states, monarchic in form, under fathers (or princes in that state) who were pre-eminent in sex, age and virtue; and these fathers, in what should be called the state 'of nature' (which was the same as the state of the families) must have formed the first natural orders. For they were the pious, chaste and strong, who had settled on their lands, and being no longer able to sustain life in flight – as they had formerly in their days of ferine roaming – they had to kill the wild animals which molested them, in order to protect themselves and their families, while, since they no longer migrated in search of food, they had to cultivate their land and sow it with grain, to support themselves and their families. And all this for the salvation of nascent mankind.

1099. At the end of a long period of time, driven by the force of the ills created by the infamous communion of things and of women in which, spread in great profusion throughout the plains and valleys, they had lived, [other] impious, unchaste, nefarious, feeble, lost and isolated men – for they feared no gods, lived in brazen and bestial venery, lying often with their mothers and daughters, and were hunted for their lives by their strong and powerful fellows in the brawls born of that infamous communion – fled to take shelter in the asylums of the fathers; and the fathers, taking them under their protection, began to enlarge their family kingdoms with *famuli* through these clienteles. In this way states developed on the basis of orders [of men who were] naturally superior in virtues which were certainly heroic. Such, for example, as that of piety: for they worshipped divinity, though, because of their comparative lack of [inner] light, it was divinity multiplied and divided into [a number of] gods, formed in accordance with their various fears (as is deduced and

[200]Cf. N.S.³ 340, and p. 44 above.

confirmed by Diodorus Siculus and, still more clearly, by both Eusebius in his *De praeparatione evangelica* and St Cyril of Alexandria in his *Against the Emperor Julian*). And for their piety they were graced with prudence, which led them to take advice through the auspices of the gods; with temperance, for each man lived in decency with a single woman taken, under the divine auspices, in perpetual company for life; with the strength to kill the wild animals and cultivate the lands; and with the magnanimity to help the weak and give aid to those in danger. Thus, by nature, were the Herculean states, in which the pious, wise, decent, strong and magnanimous subdued the proud and defended the weak, in which the excellence of civil government consists.

1100. But finally the fathers of the families, grown mighty through the religion and virtue of their ancestors, the labours of their clients and their own abuse of the laws of protection, came to rule their clients with harshness, and the natural order, which is that of justice, being thus forsaken, their clients rebelled against them. But since, in the absence of order, which is as much as to say in the absence of God, human society is unable to sustain itself for even a moment, providence naturally led the fathers of the families to unite with their clans in orders against the clients; and to pacify them they granted them, through the first agrarian law, bonitary ownership of the fields, while retaining to themselves the higher or sovereign family ownership: whence the first cities came into being, based upon reigning orders of nobles. And upon the passing of the natural order, which, conforming to the state of nature as it then was, had been an order through [superiority in] kind, sex, age and virtue, providence brought about the birth of the civil order simultaneously with that of these cities, beginning with that which was newest to [the foregoing state of] nature, an order on the basis of the nobility of the human species – for in such a state of things no other order could be understood than that [which arose out] of a human procreation with wives taken under divine auspices. Thus [providence brought it about that] by means of a heroism [of this sort] the nobles should rule over the plebeians, who did not contract marriages with such solemnities; and that, when the divine kingdoms in which the families had been governed by means of the divine auspices were ended and the heroes had to rule by means of the form of the heroic governments themselves, the principal support in such states should be religion within the custody of the heroic orders, through which the laws and all civil rights should belong solely to the heroes. But because such nobility had become a gift of fortune, providence brought it about that within these nobles there should arise an order [comprised] of the fathers of the families, as being naturally the most worthy in age, and, [further,] that of these family fathers the most powerful and spirited should emerge as kings, with a duty to take the lead over the others and hold them within their orders, in order to terrify the clients who had rebelled against them.

1101. But as, with the passing of the years and the further unfolding of the human mind, the plebs of the peoples finally saw this vanity of heroism for what it was, and understood themselves to share the same human nature as the nobles, they desired equal access to the civil orders of the cities. And since these peoples had eventually to become sovereign, providence permitted that, for a long period of time earlier, the plebs should compete against the nobility for piety and religion, in heroic contests over the duty of the nobles to communicate the auspices to the plebeians, in order to bring about the communication of all the public and private civil rights which were held to depend on them, and, thus, that a concern for piety and a love of religion should themselves lead the peoples to become sovereign in their cities. And because the Roman people surpassed all others in this, it was the master people in the world. In this mode, as the civil orders were increasingly interwoven into the natural order, were born the popular states; and there, since it was necessary to bring everything under [the rule of] lot or balance, in order that neither chance nor fate should reign, providence ordered that the census should be the measure of office. Hence the industrious and not the idle, the thrifty and not the prodigal, the prudent and not the frivolous, the magnanimous and not the niggardly – in short, the rich with some virtue or [at least] an appearance of virtue and not the poor with their many brazen vices – were judged best for government. In such states, where the whole people in common wills justice, the laws which are ordered are just because they are good for all, whence Aristotle's divine definition, 'will without passion', thus including the will of the hero who has control over his passions. And here philosophy arose, awakened by the very form of such states to create that of the hero, and interesting itself in the truth in order to do so. Providence ordered things thus so that, since virtuous actions no longer arose from a sense of religion, as had formerly been the case, philosophy should render the virtues intelligible in idea, by reflecting upon that idea, so that if men should [still] lack virtue, they would at least be ashamed of their vices: for only thus can providence confine people trained in evil ways within the bounds of duty. From the philosophies, moreover, eloquence was allowed to arise, in order that, by the same form of these popular states in which good laws are ordered, it should be filled with a love for justice, and that through these ideas of virtue it should inflame the people to command good laws.[201] We firmly

[201]*Cf.* pp. 44–5 above.

establish the flowering of such eloquence in Rome at the time of Scipio Africanus, in whose times civil wisdom and military valour, which together happily established Rome's domination of the world on the ruins of Carthage, must of necessity have brought in their wake an eloquence at once powerful and full of wisdom.

1102. But as the popular states relapsed into corruption, so also did the philosophies, which sank into scepticism as learned fools gave themselves over to vilification of the truth, whence, in turn, was born a false eloquence, equally prepared to support either of the opposed parties in a case. Thus the citizens became dissatisfied with orders based on wealth, and putting eloquence to bad use (as did the tribunes of the plebs in Rome) they sought to seize power through it; whence, whipping up civil wars in their states, as the tempestuous southerlies do the sea, they threw them into total disorder, causing them to fall from a perfect liberty into a perfect tyranny, the worst indeed of all, the anarchy or unbridled liberty of free peoples.

1103. When this great sickness besets cities, providence makes use of one of three great remedies, in accordance with the following order of human civil things.

1104. It arranges first that within the people itself there should be found one, like Augustus, who should spring up and establish himself as monarch, and that, since the orders and laws created through liberty have no capacity whatsoever to regulate and restrain it, he should take these orders and laws into his own hands by force of arms. Counterbalancing this, however, it arranges that the very form of the monarchic state should limit the will of the monarch, in respect of which his sovereignty is infinite, to the natural order whereby the people may be kept contented and satisfied with their religion and natural liberty. For in the absence of such universal satisfaction and contentedness in their peoples monarchic states are neither durable nor secure.

1105. Next, should providence fail to find such a remedy within [peoples], it goes in search of it outside [them]. And since peoples of such corruption are already enslaved by the nature of their unbridled passions – [enclosed, that is,] by luxury, indulgence, greed, envy, pride and pomp – and, as a result of the pleasures of their dissolute life, have relapsed into all the vices typical of the vilest of slaves, becoming liars, opportunists, slanderers, thieves and hypocrites, [providence arranges that] they be enslaved, by the natural law of the gentes which is born of the nature of nations, and that they become subject to better nations, which, when they have conquered them by force, preserve them in their reduced state as provinces. Here shine forth two great lights of the natural order: first, that whoever lacks the ability to govern himself should allow himself to be governed by others who have this ability; and second, that the world should always be governed by those who are by nature the best.

1106. But should the nations waste away in that ultimate civil malady in which they neither consent to a native monarch from within nor are conquered and preserved by better nations from without, then for this most extreme of diseases providence avails itself of the ultimate remedy. For such peoples have, like beasts, become accustomed to each individual thinking solely of his own particular utilities, and succumbed to that extreme of indulgence or, more accurately, of pride in which, [again] like wild animals, should they fall out over a mere trifle, they grow resentful and wild. Thus at the height of their fame and the peak of their numbers they live hideous and beastly lives in the deepest solitude of spirit and will, where scarcely two can agree, since each is bent on his own personal pleasure or whim. [And when such a state is come to pass, providence must apply this remedy]: that, with their ever continuing factions and reckless civil wars, these peoples must turn their cities into forests and the forests into human dens and in this mode, over long centuries of barbarism, rust will blunt the misbegotten sharpness of that malicious wit which has turned them into beasts made even more appalling by the barbarism of reflection than they had been in the first barbarism of the senses. For the latter was an open savagery, against which the rest could defend themselves by flight or by being on their guard, whereas the former is a vile savagery of flattery and embraces, which lays snares against the lives and fortunes of confidants and friends. Whence peoples of such reflective malice, stunned and confused by this final remedy to which providence has recourse, are no longer sensitive to comfort, indulgence, pleasure and pomp, but only to those utilities of life which are necessary; and since the number of men left at the end is small, while the necessities of life are abundant, men naturally become sociable and, through the return of the original simplicity of the first world of nations, religious, truthful and faithful. Thus does providence restore to them the piety, faith and trust, which constitute the natural foundations of justice and are graces and beauties of God's eternal order.

1107. From this simple but sound observation about the things belonging to the whole of mankind, even had we received nothing additional from the philosophers, historians, grammarians and jurists, one would certainly conclude that this great city of nations has been founded and governed by God. For Lycurgus, Solon, the decemvirs and so on, have been elevated to the heavens in eternal praise of their legislative wisdom, because of the hitherto prevalent belief that, by their good orders and laws, they were responsible for the founding of Sparta, Athens and Rome, the three most enlightened cities from which the finest and greatest of civil virtues ever shone forth. Yet these cities were of brief duration and limited extension taken in the context of the universe of nations, which is regulated and stabilised by laws and orders such that, through the very corruptions of the nations themselves, it adopts those forms of the state which alone can enable it everywhere to preserve itself and to endure in perpetuity. And must we not consider this the plan of a superhuman wisdom, regulating and leading [things] in a divine manner, not by the force of laws which caused Dio to assimilate them to a tyrant in the *Elements*,[202] but by utilising those very wisdoms of men whose practice is as free from force as is man's celebration of his own nature, whence, because they commenced through pleasure, they were likened by Dio to a king?

1108. For, though men have themselves made this world of nations – and this became the first indisputable principle of this Science, since we despaired of discovering a science among the philosophers and philologists[203] – it has without doubt been born of a mind often unlike, at times quite contrary to and ever superior to, the particular ends these men had set themselves, which narrow ends, made means to serve wider ends, it has always used to preserve the human race on this earth.[204] Thus men would indulge their bestial lust and forsake their children, but they create the purity of marriage, whence arise the families; the fathers would exercise their paternal powers over the clients without moderation, but they subject them to the civil powers, whence arise the cities; the reigning orders of nobles would abuse their seignorial freedom over the plebeians, but they fall under the servitude of laws which create popular liberty; the free peoples would break loose from the restraint of their laws, but they fall subject to the monarchs; the monarchs would weaken their subjects by all the vices of depravity which secure their allegiance to them, but they dispose them to tolerate slavery under stronger nations; the nations would dissolve themselves, but their survivors seek safety in solitude whence, phoenix-like, they are born anew. Yet that which did all this was mind, for men did it with intelligence; it was not fate, for they did it by choice; nor was it chance, for, to the end of time, by their ever acting thus, the same things are born.

1109. Thus Epicurus, who favours chance, is refuted by fact, as are his followers, Hobbes and Machiavelli; and so also is Zeno, and with him Spinoza, who favour fate.[205] On the other hand, fact pronounces in favour of the political philosophers, prince of whom is the divine Plato, who establishes that providence regulates [the world of] human

---

[202]*N.S.*[3] 308–9.   [203]*N.S.*[1] 15–24, 40; *N.S.*[3] 330–1.
[204]*Cf. N.S.*[1] 41; *N.S.*[3] 341.   [205]*Cf. N.S.*[1] 398; *N.S.*[3] 130.

things.[206] Hence Cicero was in the right when [he claimed that] he could not discuss the law with Atticus unless the latter were to abandon his Epicurean position and concede in advance that providence regulates [the world of] human things,[207] for providence, disregarded in Pufendorf's hypothesis, accepted [but misunderstood] by Selden and [consciously] set aside by Grotius,[208] was established by the Roman jurists as the first principle of the natural law of the gentes.[209] For in this work we have fully demonstrated that, through providence, the first governments in the world had religion as their whole form and that religion alone was the basis of the state of families; then, passing to the heroic or aristocratic civil governments, religion must have been their main stable basis; whence, advancing to the popular governments, religion itself served as the means whereby the peoples reached them; and stopping finally with the monarchic governments, religion must have been the shield of princes. Hence, when religion is lost among peoples, they are left with nothing for their life in society: no shield of defence, no means of advice, no basis of support, no form for any existence in the world at all.

1110. Hence let Bayle see whether nations can in fact exist on earth without any cognition whatsoever of God![210] And let Polybius see how much truth there may be in his claim that were the world to contain philosophers it would have no need of religions![211] For religions alone bring peoples to virtuous works through their emotions, which are efficacious in moving men to perform them, and the rational maxims of virtue of the philosophers serve only as a means by which good eloquence inflames the emotions towards performing the duties of virtue.[212] There remains, however, this essential difference between our Christian religion, which is true, and all the other religions of the different peoples, which are false: that in our religion divine grace causes virtuous action for the attainment of an infinite and eternal good, which cannot itself be an object of the emotions and on behalf of which the mind therefore moves the emotions to virtuous action; but in the false religions, on the contrary, in which the goods proposed are finite and ephemeral, both in this life and the next (in which they look forward to a happiness consisting in corporeal pleasures), the emotions must therefore drag the mind towards doing works of virtue.

1111. But, in the light of the order of civil things reasoned out in these books, providence also reveals itself clearly to us in these three emotions: first, the wonder [of the scholars]; second, the veneration which they have all hitherto entertained for the incomparable wisdom of the

---

[206] Rather. the neoplatonists. See n. 4, p. 161 above.   [207] N.S.³ 335.
[208] N.S.¹ 15–22; N.S.³ 395–7.   [209] Cf. N.S.¹ 41; N.S.³ 310, 335, 342.
[210] See n.1, p. 81 above.   [211] N.S.³ 179.   [212] Cf. pp. 44–5 above.

ancients; and third, the ardent desire by which they were inspired to seek and attain it. For these are in truth three lights of its divinity by which providence awakened in them the three most beautiful and just emotions mentioned above, which were later corrupted by the vanity of scholars and the vanity of nations, which we placed among our first axioms and have corrected throughout these books.[213] These three beautiful and just emotions are that scholars should admire, venerate, and desire to be united with, God's infinite wisdom.

1112. In short, from the whole reasoning of this work, it must finally be concluded that this Science brings inseparably with it the study of piety, and that if one be not pious one cannot be truly wise.

[213] N.S.[3] 125–8.

Appendix

[The Second New Science, 1730]
Giambattista Vico to the Reader

1131. Let us conclude finally with the following few words of advice to any young reader who may wish to profit from this Science.

1132. Firstly, its work is entirely metaphysical and abstract in conception. Hence it is necessary in reading it to divest yourself of everything corporeal and of everything to which this gives rise in pure mind and, therefore, for a while, to put the imagination to sleep and lull the memory. For if these faculties are aroused, the mind is unable to reduce itself to a state of pure understanding, unshaped by any particular form;[214] and, as a result, you would be quite unable to arouse in it the form of this Science and, for your sins, you would fail to understand it.

1133. Secondly, its reasoning is conducted in accordance with a strict geometric method, by means of which it passes from [each] truth to [its] immediate truth and thus produces its conclusions.[215] Whence it is necessary that you should have acquired the habit of reasoning geometrically and that you should neither open these books in any arbitrary place, in order to read them, nor dip into them here and there, but follow their teaching from start to finish. And you must consider whether its premises are true and well arranged but not be surprised if almost all of its conclusions are a source of wonder – something which often happens in geometry as, for example, in the case of two parallel lines which converge *ad infinitum* but never meet – for its conclusions are affected by the imagination but the premises hold fast to pure abstract reason.

1134. Thirdly, it presupposes a large and varied body of learning and scholarship, from which truths are drawn as being already known by you, which it employs as limits for the establishment of its propositions. For this reason, should you not be fully possessed of these, you will find that you lack the basis for accepting it in its final arrangement.

1135. Fourthly, in addition to these adornments, it requires of you a comprehensive mind, for there is nothing with which the reasonings of this Science is concerned which is not compatible with the innumerable other kinds of things with which it deals and, indeed, which does not

---

[214]Cf. p. 62 above.   [215]Cf. N.S.³ 349.

cohere with them, taken severally or in their totality, in which alone consists the whole beauty of a perfect science.[216] Whence, if you lack this or that antecedent aid, together with many others [which are necessary] for reading it, you will have the same experience as those who are hard of hearing, who, when they hear one or two of the more resonant notes on the harpsichord, do so with displeasure, because they fail to hear the others with which, under the touch of a master of the keyboard, they [combine to] make a sweet and agreeable harmony.

1136. Fifthly, it contains many discoveries about the things here reasoned, largely diverse from, and many of them quite contrary to, the beliefs hitherto entertained about them. Whence you will have need of much acuteness of mind if you are not to be dazzled by the large amount of new light which it everywhere diffuses.

1137. Sixthly, the ideas which it expresses are, in addition, wholly new of their kind. Whence I beseech you that you be prepared to familiarise yourself with them by reading the work at least three times.

1138. Seventhly, and finally, to enable you to experience the full strength of its proofs, which are weakened by their wide extension, little is here said and much is left for you to ponder. Therefore you need to meditate longer upon the things which it contains, combining them and seeing them in a wider context, in order that you may acquire the faculty for them.

[216]*Cf. N.S.*[3] 330.

Bibliography

The number of articles and sections of books which discuss Vico is now too large for it to be practicable to list them here. The following short bibliography is confined to major translations of Vico's works, bibliographies in English and major books in English written on Vico. The reader will find lists of the many articles on Vico in the bibliographies listed below and many articles themselves in the four anthologies edited by Dr Giorgio Tagliacozzo and others.

English translations

The Autobiography of Giambattista Vico, translated with introduction and notes, by T. G. Bergin and M. H. Fisch (Cornell University Press: Ithaca, 1944). Reprinted with corrections and supplementary notes, Great Seal Books, 1963; Cornell Paperbacks, 1975.

On the Study Methods of Our Time, translated with introduction, notes and bibliography, by E. Gianturco (Bobbs-Merrill: Indianapolis, 1965).

The New Science of Giambattista Vico, translation of the third edition, by T. G. Bergin and M. H. Fisch (Cornell University Press: Ithaca, 1948). Second revised edition, with Introduction by M. H. Fisch, 1968. Abridged version of the revised edition, Cornell Paperbacks, 1970.

Bibliographies in English

A Selective Bibliography of Vico Scholarship (1948–68), by E. Gianturco (*Forum Italicum Supplement:* Florence, 1968).

'Critical writings on Vico in English', by Molly Black Verene, in *Giambattista Vico's Science of Humanity,* edited by G. Tagliacozzo and D. P. Verene (The Johns Hopkins University Press: Baltimore, 1976).

Vico in English, by R. Crease (Humanities Press: New Jersey, 1978).

Books

Adams, H. P. *The Life and Writings of Giambattista Vico* (Allen and Unwin: London, 1935). Reprinted (Russell and Russell: New York, 1970).

Berlin, I. *Vico and Herder* (The Hogarth Press: London, 1976, reprinted 1980).

Caponigri, A. R. *Time and Idea. The Theory of History in Giambattista Vico* (University of Notre Dame Press: Notre Dame, 1968).

Croce, B. *The Philosophy of Giambattista Vico,* translated by R. G. Collingwood
(Howard Latimer: London, 1913). Reprinted (Russell and Russell: New York,
1964).

Flint, R. *Vico* (Blackwood: Edinburgh, 1884).

Manson, R. *The Theory of Knowledge of Giambattista Vico* (Archon Books:
Hamden, 1969).

Pompa, L. *Vico: A Study of the 'New Science'* (Cambridge University Press:
Cambridge, 1975).

Verene, D. P. *Vico's Science of Imagination* (Cornell University Press: Ithaca,
1981).

Anthologies of Articles.

Forum Italicum, vol. 11, no. 4, 1968.

Social Research, vol. 43 (3 and 4), 1976). Reprinted in *Vico and Contemporary
Thought,* edited by G. Tagliacozzo, M. Mooney and D. P. Verene (The
Humanities Press and MacMillan: Atlantic Highlands, 1979).

Giambattista Vico: An International Symposium, edited by G. Tagliacozzo and
H. V. White (The Johns Hopkins University Press: Baltimore, 1969).

Giambattista Vico's Science of Humanity, edited by G. Tagliacozzo and D. P.
Verene (The Johns Hopkins University Press: Baltimore, 1976).

Vico: Past and Present, edited by G. Tagliacozzo (The Humanities Press: Atlantic
Highlands, 1981).

Index

abstraction, 53, 222-3, 226
Academics, 43, 72
Accursius, 123
Achilles, 107-8, 114, 126, 155, 181, 222, 235, 252
Acosta, José de, 201
Adam, 86, 91, 98-9, 105, 110, 132, 134, 140, 144, 193, 213, 223
Aegaeon, 238
Aeneas, 148, 193, 235
Aesop, 230-2
Agamemnon, 173, 231
Alexander the Great, 98, 181, 191, 241
allegory: of fabulous history, 146; philosophical, 90, 145; poetic, 144-5, 176, 222
Amphion, 152, 201
Anacharsis, 161
analysis, 35, 53, 205
Ancus Marcius, 148-9
Andronicus, Livius, 239
antonomasia, 144, 148-53, 167, 175
Apion, 233, 241
Apollo, 107, 195, 247
Ariadne, 36
Aristides, 124, 173, 181
Aristotle, Aristotelianism, 1, 49, 54, 66, 73, 74, 81n, 98, 178, 185, 214, 221, 231, 233, 236, 243, 249, 262
Arnauld, Antoine, 39, 199
arts, 34-5
atheists, society of, 81-82, 147, 199, 266
Athena, 230
Atlas, 94, 97, 125
atomists, 1
Atticus, Titus Pomponius, 200, 219, 266
Augustine, St, 2, 67, 96, 232
Augustus, 189-90, 263
Ausonius, 245
auspices, see divination
authority, 134; philosophy of, 207, 215-17; three kinds of, 256-8

Bacon, Francis, 1, 33, 90, 168, 208, 214
Baker, Thomas, 242n

Bayle, Pierre, 1, 22, 81n, 147n, 199, 266
Becman, Christopher (Christian), 234
Bede, 169
Belaval, Y., 35n
Bellerophon, 236
Benevieni, Geronimo, 94
Berecynthia, 222
Bergin, T. G., 156n
Berlin, I., 6n, 11n, 13n, 27, 127n, 163n
Berosus, 96
Boccaccio, 1
Bochart, Samuel, 129, 131-2, 241
Bodin, Jean, 155
boria, see vanity
Boulduc, Jacques, 209
Boyce, Hector, 238
Boyle, Robert, 1
Briareus, 238
Brutus, Lucius Junius, 121, 195
Budé, Guillaume, 11
burial of the dead, 82, 118, 156, 198, 200-1
Burnet, Thomas, 130
Burtt, E. A., 40n

Cadmus, 201, 234, 242, 245, 255
Caesar, Gaius Julius, 131, 169, 181, 216
Cain, 99, 105, 131-2
Caligula, 181
Camerarius, Johannes (Philipp), 234
Candella, Francesco, 96
Cantelli, G., 10
Caraffa, Antonio, 10
Carmenta, 241
Carneades, 35n, 162
Cartesian, Cartesianism, 2, 28, 35n, 37n, 38n, 39n, 75; Vico's rejection of, 6-9; see also Descartes
Castelvetro, Lodovico, 140, 214
Castor, 150
cause, causes: as form involved in knowledge, 6, 26-9; of human affairs or civil world, 9, 13, 26-9, 92, 204; of the just, 100
Cecrops, 242